The Jacobin Republic
1792–1794

The Jacobin Republic
1792—1794

MARC BOULOISEAU

Translated by

JONATHAN MANDELBAUM

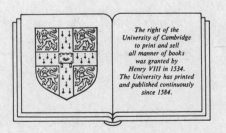

The right of the
University of Cambridge
to print and sell
all manner of books
was granted by
Henry VIII in 1534.
The University has printed
and published continuously
since 1584.

CAMBRIDGE UNIVERSITY PRESS

Cambridge

London   New York   New Rochelle   Melbourne   Sydney

EDITIONS DE LA MAISON DES SCIENCES DE
L'HOMME

Paris

Published by the Press Syndicate of the University of Cambridge
The Pitt Building, Trumpington Street, Cambridge CB2 1RP
32 East 57th Street, New York, NY 10022, USA
10 Stamford Road, Oakleigh, Melbourne 3166, Australia
and Editions de la Maison des Sciences de l'Homme
54 Boulevard Raspail, 75270 Paris Cedex 06

Originally published in French as *La République jacobine* (*1792–1794*)
by Editions du Seuil, Paris 1972
and © Editions du Seuil, 1972
First published in English by Editions de la Maison des Sciences de l'Homme and
Cambridge University Press 1983 as *The Jacobin Republic 1792–1794*
English translation © Maison des Sciences de l'Homme and
Cambridge University Press 1983

Reprinted 1987

Printed in Great Britain by the University Press, Cambridge

Library of Congress catalogue card number: 83–5293

British Library cataloguing in publication data

Bouloiseau, Marc
The Jacobin Republic 1792–1794.—(The French Revolution; 2)
1. France–History–Revolution, 1791–1794
I. Title   II. La République jacobine. *English*   III. Series
944.04'5   DC186

ISBN 0 521 24726 8 hard covers
ISBN 0 521 28918 1 paperback
ISBN 2 7351 0034 0 hard covers (France only)
ISBN 2 7351 0035 9 paperback (France only)

'Until now we have studied the history of Movements; we have not devoted enough attention to the history of Resistances... The resistance of ingrained mentalities is one of the major factors in the slower-moving currents of History.'

(Ernest Labrousse, *L'Histoire sociale: Sources et méthodes,*
Introduction, p. 5)

Contents

Chronology

1792

10 August	National Convention called
11 August	Universal suffrage introduced
14 August	Lafayette tries in vain to lead his army against Paris
17 August	Special tribunal set up to try the defenders of the Tuileries
22 August	Royalist riots in the Vendée, the Dauphiné and Brittany
23 August	Longwy taken by Prussians
2 September	Electoral assemblies meet; Verdun capitulates
2–6 September	Prison massacres in Paris and the provinces
4 September	Grain requisitioned for the army at fixed price
8–9 September	Workers' riot in Tours
20 September	Recording of births, marriages and deaths entrusted to civilian authorities; end of the Legislative Assembly; French victory at Valmy; the Convention elects its officers
21 September	Monarchy abolished; Year I of the Republic
24 September	Savoy freed by French troops
25 September	Republic declared 'one and indivisible'
29 September	French occupy Nice
8 October	Prussians retreat, evacuating Verdun
21 October	General Custine occupies Mainz, then Frankfurt
6 November	Dumoriez victorious at Jemappes; Belgium occupied
19 November	France offers 'fraternity and aid' to all peoples
20 November	King's secret papers discovered in iron chest at Tuileries
22 November	Peasant unrest in the Beauce against price controls on grain
27 November	Savoy annexed to France
2 December	New Paris Commune elected
8 December	Free trade of grain declared
11 December	King's trial opens
19 December	Saint-Just elected president of Jacobin club

1793

7 January	King's trial proceedings end
11 January	Royalist demonstration in Rouen
20 January	Le Peletier de Saint-Fargeau assassinated by a royalist
21 January	Louis XVI executed
23 January	Poland partitioned between Prussia and Russia
1 February	France declares war on Britain and Holland; First Coalition formed
14 February	Pache elected mayor of Paris
21 February	Decree on 'amalgamation' of volunteers and troops of the line
24 February	Levy of 300,000 men; provincial disturbances
25–27 February	Groceries looted in Paris; soap and sugar sold at 'controlled' prices
5 March	Royalist uprising in Lyons quashed
7 March	Convention declares war on king of Spain
10 March	Creation of special criminal Tribunal later called 'Revolutionary'
11 March	Outbreak of Vendée rebellion
18 March	Dumoriez defeated at Neerwinden; death penalty decreed for advocates of *loi agraire*
21 March	*Comités de surveillance* created
28 March	'Civil death' decreed against *émigrés*, who are banished for life from French territory
3–5 April	Dumoriez goes over to enemy; Philippe Egalité, Duc d'Orléans, arrested
6 April	Committee of Public Safety set up; Prussians lay siege to Mainz
11 April	*Assignat* made sole legal tender; sale of specie banned
17 April	Romme demands women's franchise
24 April	Marat, tried by decree of Convention, acquitted by Revolutionary Tribunal
26 April	Chappe inaugurates signalling network
29 April	Rising in Marseilles
4 May	Price controls on grain and flour
20 May	Forced loan of a thousand million francs to be levied on the rich
29 May	Insurrection in Lyons
31 May	Demonstrations outside the Convention against *girondin* representatives
2 June	Arrest of 27 *girondin* representatives and 2 *girondin* ministers

3 June	*Emigré* property put up for sale in small lots
7 June	Federalist rebellion in Bordeaux and the Calvados
8 June	British fleet blockades French coasts
10 June	Optional division of communal lands decreed
24 June	Constitution of the Year I voted
26–28 June	'Soap riots' in Paris
27 June	Paris stock exchange closed
29 June	*Enragés* violently attacked by Commune and Jacobins
10 July	Committee of Public Safety revamped; Danton removed
12 July	Royalist rebellion in Toulon
13 July	Marat assassinated by Charlotte Corday
17 July	All feudal dues abolished without compensation
18 July	*Vendéen* victory at Vihiers
23 July	French troops leave Mainz and are sent to the Vendée
26 July	Decree instituting death penalty against food hoarders
27 July	Robespierre joins Committee of Public Safety
28 July	Coalition forces take Valenciennes
8 August	Kellermann's army besieges Lyons
23 August	*Levée en masse* decreed
24 August	Grand Livre de la Dette Publique [national debt register] created
25 August	The Convention's troops occupy Marseilles
27 August	Royalists hand Toulon over to British
4–5 September	Popular riots in Paris; Terror 'the order of the day'; 'revolutionary army' set up in Paris
6–8 September	French victory at Honschoote
7 September	Property of enemy aliens in France confiscated
11 September	National price controls for grain
17 September	Law on suspects
18 September	Varlet arrested
21 September	Women obliged to wear tricolour cockade
29 September	*Maximum général* on commodities and wages
5 October	Revolutionary calendar adopted

Year II

VENDÉMIAIRE

18 (9 October)	Lyons capitulates
19 (10 October)	Government declared revolutionary for the duration of hostilities
25 (16 October)	French defeat Austrians at Wattignies; Marie Antoinette executed

BRUMAIRE

3 (24 October)	Trial of 21 *girondin* representatives
10 (31 October)	*Girondins* executed
11 (1 November)	*Tutoiement* [use of familiar second person singular] made compulsory, even in official correspondence
16 (6 November)	Municipalities allowed to renounce Catholic worship
20 (10 November)	Festival of Liberty and Reason at Notre-Dame in Paris
23 (13 November)	*Vendéens* defeated outside Granville
25 (15 November)	Lotteries abolished

FRIMAIRE

1 (21 November)	Robespierre attacks dechristianization and atheism
[14 (4 December)	Decree on revolutionary government]
16 (6 December)	Ban on 'revolutionary taxes' on the rich
22 (12 December)	Marceau crushes *Vendéens* at Le Mans
26 (16 December)	Hébert's friends Ronsin and Vincent arrested
29 (19 December)	Toulon recaptured; later renamed Port-de-la-Montagne

NIVÔSE

3 (23 December)	*Vendéens* defeated again at Savenay
6 (26 December)	Hoche wins battle of the Geisberg; relief of Strasburg and Landau

1794

23 (12 January)	Debate on Compagnie des Indes affair at Convention
27 (16 January)	Marseilles renamed Ville-sans-Nom
28 (17 January)	General Turreau's 'infernal columns' ravage the Vendée

PLUVIÔSE

9 (28 January)	Speech by Robespierre at Jacobin club denouncing 'British crimes'
13 (1 February)	Ten million francs allocated for poor relief
16 (4 February)	Slavery abolished in French colonies
22 (10 February)	Jacques Roux commits suicide in prison
24 (12 February)	Momoro denounces Jacobin moderatism at Cordelier club

VENTÔSE

3 (21 February)	Barère presents *maximum général* scales to Convention
8 (26 February)	After report by Saint-Just, Convention orders seizure of suspects' property
9 (27 February)	Stiffer sanctions against food hoarders
13 (3 March)	'Popular commissions' set up to 'sort out' suspects
16 (6 March)	Barère's report on elimination of pauperism
23 (13 March)	Hébert and his friends arrested

GERMINAL

4 (24 March)	*Hébertistes'* trial ends; leading *sans-culotte* militants executed
7 (27 March)	'Revolutionary army' disbanded
10 (30 March)	*Dantonistes* arrested
12 (1 April)	Committee of Public Safety sets up Police Bureau
13 (2 April)	Provisional Conseil Exécutif abolished; ministers replaced by commissions
13–16 (2–5 April)	*Dantonistes* tried and executed
21–24 (10–13 April)	'Luxembourg plot' trial; widows of Hébert and Desmoulins executed
25 (14 April)	Rousseau's ashes brought to Panthéon
26 (15 April)	Saint-Just's report on 'Police générale de la République'; nobles and foreigners forbidden to reside in Paris and fortified towns

FLORÉAL

11 (20 April)	Austrians take Landrecies
19 (8 May)	27 farmers-general executed, including Lavoisier
21 (10 May)	'Popular commission' set up at Orange
22 (11 May)	Grand Livre de la Bienfaisance Nationale [national welfare register] created
23 (12 May)	British democrats arrested in London

PRAIRIAL

3–4 (22–23 May)	Assassination attempts on Robespierre and Collot d'Herbois
7 (26 May)	Decree forbidding the taking of British and Hanoverian prisoners
10 (29 May)	After his victory at Dinant, Jourdan takes command of Sambre-et-Meuse army

13 (*1 June*)   Ecole de Mars founded to replace Ecole Militaire
14 (*2 June*)   Naval battle off Ouessant; *Vengeur* incident
16 (*4 June*)   Robespierre elected chairman of Convention
20 (*8 June*)   Festival of the Supreme Being
22 (*10 June*)   Revolutionary Tribunal reorganized
29 (*17 June*)   Trial of the 'Red Shirts'

MESSIDOR

3 (*21 June*)   Paoli offers Corsica to king of England
7 (*25 June*)   In Saint-Domingue, Toussaint L'Ouverture comes out
                     in favour of French Republic
8 (*26 June*)   French defeat Austrians at Fleurus
17 (*5 July*)   Paris Commune votes new wage controls
20 (*8 July*)   French enter Brussels
26 (*14 July*)   The representative Fouché expelled from Jacobin club

THERMIDOR

1 (*19 July*)   Pro-French insurrection in Geneva
4–5 (*22–23 July*)   Joint meetings of 'government Committees'; attempts
                     at reconciliation
8 (*26 July*)   Robespierre's last speeches at Convention and Jacobin
                     club
9 (*27 July*)   Convention orders arrest of Robespierre, his brother,
                     Couthon, Saint-Just and Le Bas, and declares them
                     outlaws
10–12 (*28–30 July*) 105 *robespierristes* executed in Paris

Introduction

In 1792, just as in 1789, the Revolution exploded. The shock, stronger this time, threatened to sweep everything away, including the sacrosanct notion of property. 'Watch out ahead!' went a popular song. The time-honoured institution of royalty was driven out from the Tuileries – the new Bastille. The defenders of the monarchy left the sinking ship and went into winter quarters in prison, in the provinces or in exile. From the 'dark depths' dear to Michelet there rose a people moved not by misery but by disappointment, a people that vehemently claimed its due and, to achieve victory, was willing to die. Another bourgeoisie, called forth by the insurrection, climbed up the rungs of the Republic; until 9 Thermidor, the ordinary Frenchman was on the stage. This was the Jacobin period; it lasted barely two years.

When seen 'from above', through debates in the Assembly and in political 'clubs', through decrees and official correspondence, the history of Jacobinism appears to follow a straight path, unaffected by any deviations or by the quirks of fate. The conventional history of the period is replete with political rivalry, factions and *journées*. It puts excessive emphasis on these factors, focuses too often on orators and leaders, and grants too much space to ideas, as if the written word were a sufficient mainspring for action, and as if the ignorant were better left ignored. Thanks to that history, some legends have retained their emotional sway, in particular the tales of 'blood-drinkers' and 'heroes in rags'.

Later, because of the social character of the Jacobin revolution, historians 'socialized' it by transferring onto that smouldering past a set of present-day problems that distort the perspective. Whereas the Marxists appropriated this dramatic period as their own, others subjected it to systematic belittlement and demystification. Does it deserve such honour and such ingratitude? An objective explanation, the only one we are aiming at, must concern itself with the forces unleashed by Jacobinism and with their interrelationships.

I

To set out these factors socio-economic analysis, focusing on the food crises (*crises de subsistances*) that punctuated the revolutionary movement, has produced charts and tables whose mathematical rigour pales in the face of biological imperatives. The application of electronics has made the economy reveal its cycles more readily, and society its structures and hierarchies. But the analysis has often gone astray in a pseudo-scientific gibberish that repels those who love the past.

Narrative had to be revived; man – who, by his massive and constraining presence, was the collective artisan of history – had to be put back in his environment. Is he not possessed of flesh and blood, of mind and heart? How can one overlook his behaviour, his attitudes, and their explicit or hidden motives? Georges Lefebvre, my mentor and friend, quietly invited us to follow this new approach. Soboul, Cobb, Rudé and a few others heeded his call. Their valiant efforts have revealed the abundance of primary sources and the usefulness of treating them methodically. Pierre Goubert has stressed the urgent need to listen to the Revolution thinking, to watch it live, in order to appreciate 'collective attitudes, the force of ancestral brutalities and grudges and the power of hopes thwarted for too long, and a whole unconscious – several, rather – repressed for centuries.'[1]

The First Republic, a continuous and ever-threatened creation, lends itself to this broader research. Are we prepared for it? Is there not a risk of over-interpreting recollections, giving too much credit to second-hand accounts, applying a Parisian pattern to the French countryside, and attributing 'terrorist' opinions to every patriot? Until there are enough local monographs comparing social, mental and economic aspects to allow us to 'nationalize' the issues of sociological analysis, any attempt at summary will be premature. I shall therefore confine myself to an interim report based on little-known research carried out by many hands spontaneously for over twenty years, whose results I have assembled without premeditation. Even as they stand, these results can encourage other attempts, guard against fallacies, and corroborate certain findings.

Semantic confusion is the first barrier to a comprehensive explanation. During these troubled years, the meaning of words changed. The 'people' differentiated itself from the 'mass' and the 'crowd', which

[1] P. Goubert, *L'Ancien Régime*, Paris, 1969, 'Collection U', vol. 1, chapter 11, p. 257. [Quoted from the English translation by Steve Cox, *The Ancien Régime: French Society 1600–1750*, New York, 1973. Trans.]

were quick to coalesce and fast to break up. At first identified with
the nation – the community of citizens – the 'people' shrank at the
same rate as the nation by casting out the elements that oppressed it.
As a catchword of the Jacobin ideology, it took on the same ambiguity
as the word 'homeland' (*patrie*). Contemporaries who were aware of
this tried to define the 'people'. At times the 'people' encompassed
'the immense class of the poor... which provides the homeland with
men and our borders with defenders, which feeds society by its labours,
uplifts it by its talents, adorns and honours it by its virtues'; at times
it was restricted to the 'toiling and indigent class'. The absence of
wealth and property conferred a presumption of civic virtue (*civisme*).
The patriot people was the worker people, and the homeland merged
with the Revolution.[2]

The terms describing political attitudes underwent a parallel change.
'Jacobin', 'patriot', 'revolutionary' and *sans-culotte*, all of which had
several meanings at first, became more precisely defined in the minds
of militants, while provincial *sociétés populaires* adopted all these tags
at once. They also called themselves *montagnards* in order to prove their
allegiance to the Convention, home of the 'Mountain' that inspired
their loyalty. This profusion of terms was in fact deplored. 'We have no
right wing, no left wing, no mountain, no valley, nor any of those
denominations that would be as ridiculous as they are insignificant were
they not dangerous,' declared the inhabitants of Aurillac in April 1793;
'Here, all patriots are united in defence of their liberty.' Actually, the
labels *girondin* and *hébertiste* caught on only after the *girondins* and the
hébertistes had been denounced at their trial; these terms were used
sparingly, as was *enragé*, to which *maratiste* was preferred.

On the other hand, during the Year II, the *montagnard* was still linked
to the Jacobin and the *sans-culotte*. Whereas the first referred more
specifically to members of the Convention, the 'true Jacobin' was also
a 'sincere *montagnard*' and, in the countryside, the 'good' and 'pure'
sans-culotte gradually established himself. This designation, derived
from the urban workers' custom of wearing their trousers buttoned
onto their coats, retained a popular and social connotation. After the
summer of 1793, the petty bourgeois Jacobin distinguished himself
from 'genuine *sans-culottes*, that is, men who have no other resources
to live on than their manual labour', nor 'any other property than the
wages for services rendered to their fellow citizens'. Thus the

[2] See A. Geffroy, 'Le Peuple selon Saint-Just', in *Actes du Colloque Saint-Just*, Paris, 1966,
p. 231.

Convention was *montagnard*, the people *sans-culotte* and the nation patriotic.

The collective mentality similarly confused patriotism with Jacobinism, thus bringing about, in practice, a fusion of the two concepts. The national consciousness, sharpened by the war and the aristocratic plot, momentarily – and ostensibly – obliterated social cleavages. The bourgeoisie, the town-dwelling *sans-culotterie* and the peasantry set aside their differences in a composite society that transcended their traditional behaviour. By attending his *section*, his club and his 'watch-committee' (*comité de surveillance*), the citizen got away from his family and professional environment to look after the higher interests of the homeland. He became a soldier, imposed duties on himself, and freely accepted the constraints they entailed. These constraints in turn influenced traditional behaviour and spread the notion of a natural order of things that did not involve the responsibility of those who carried out orders.

Henceforth, several attitudes towards the Revolution were possible: unconditional support, passive or active resistance, or indifference. Only the first was tolerable. Descriptions of attitudes became tantamount to verdicts: they condemned citizens or cleared them; they implied praise or scorn. Aristocrat, *feuillant*, federalist, fanatic, 'starver' (*affameur*) – these epithets were used as indictments. After September 1793, *muscadin* was added to the list. It applied to young men of means, to those declared unfit for military service, to the idle, to pleasure-seekers who wandered about town and haunted sleazy taverns. Finally, a distinction was drawn between true patriots and false patriots, who concealed themselves behind their exaggerated rhetoric.

For the revolutionary spirit was engendered by a unanimity of feelings, and national solidarity manifested itself through work. The *conventionnel* Simond recognized only three classes of citizens: 'those who clothe man by their handiwork, those who feed him by agriculture, and those who defend him by warfare'. Yet the artisans, peasants and soldiers who were all worthy elements of Jacobin society did not adopt a common outlook. Despite the 'supreme law' of public safety, each category persisted in its attitudes, which had been shaped before the Revolution by professional working conditions and the quest for food, regardless of subsequent changes in social environment. One should always remember to what extent mental structures are conservative, and to what extent man is a 'creature of habit'.

This limited and homogeneous group thus provides more solid grounds for analysis than the notion of an embryonic class. The bourgeoisie and the peasantry, under the cloak of a broad agreement, concealed too many antagonistic interests and internal conflicts. Consensus, when there was one, took the shape of slogans and hard-hitting catch-phrases, not a coherent programme of demands; it was sustained by a common aggressiveness against designated enemies. This tension, which culminated in civil and foreign war, sublimated patriotism and civic feeling, and so made it possible, to a great extent, to channel the blind interplay of social forces. However, their flow could not be halted. After 10 August 1792, the Revolution therefore continued on its logical course, which naturally had to make room for the aspirations of the *sans-culottes*.

At the same time, the Revolution locked Jacobinism into a dilemma: the choice between a republic and democracy. At first, for most patriots, one was unthinkable without the other; then it was noticed that the two terms were not synonymous. The Republic designated the State, its framework and its laws, while democracy stood for a social process. This semantic equivocation soon ceased, revealing two pathways towards equality: equal rights or equal enjoyment of property. The Republic made do with Jacobin ideology, while the democratic movement got out of hand, then stumbled. Despite its fundamental contradiction, the Republic remained just as the *montagnards* had wanted it, and its enemies blamed all their misfortunes on the *jacobinerie* ('Jacobin-making factory').

Could the Republic have been anything other than bourgeois? Only those who possessed either knowledge or the means of production, or both, were in a position to lead the Republic, to breathe an infectious energy into it, to achieve a compromise with the masses. The requirements of national defence and of the revolutionary struggle put immense powers in the hands of the *montagnard* bourgeoisie, which used these powers against its former supporters. But, although the men of 1793 were of the same generation as those of 1789, the four intervening years had made them wiser. Some did not hesitate to overcome their fears, while others were blinded by the fear of being overcome. This gradual hardening of attitudes inevitably led to Thermidor.

The fact is that patriotic fervour was tempered in civilian and military societies that made no distinction between service to the nation and service to the State, and fostered personal ambitions within conformist frameworks. The Year II, therefore, cannot be regarded as an 'unfortunate' and useless 'deviation'.³ The bourgeoisie and property-owners, after a brief moment of disarray, remained in control. Although they may have seemed to go astray in 'popular side-tracks', the authorities in fact followed the only course laid down by a mass consensus that allowed them to govern efficiently. It would be disregarding the facts to deny a tragic grandeur to the Jacobin Republic; just as it would be going against the evidence to underrate the spirit of sacrifice of those who put their trust in it. The Republic was, whatever one may say, and in spite of Germinal, 'the ascending phase of the struggle for liberty'.

* The number in bold type refers to the bibliography on pp. 234–47.
³ See François Furet and Denis Richet, *La Révolution française*, vol. 1 (**12**) and Claude Mazauric's critique of that work in 'Réflexions sur une nouvelle conception de la Révolution française', *Annales Historiques de la Révolution Française* [hereafter referred to as *AHRF*. Trans.], 1967. The reader should also consult F. Furet's reply to his critics in 'Le Catéchisme révolutionnaire', *Annales ESC*, March–April 1971 [available in English in F. Furet, *Interpreting the French Revolution*, trans. by Elborg Forster, Cambridge, 1981. Trans.].

1

Forces and attitudes

The fall of the French monarchy unleashed opposing forces that have never been studied jointly. They seem to follow parallel tracks that overlap only on occasion and by chance. Because of this highly artificial separation, it is difficult to appreciate the influence of the opposition on the stiffening of revolutionary attitudes. The revolutionary movement provoked resistances each of which blocked it in turn. Whenever the Revolution was threatened by a new peril, it expelled its untrustworthy elements. Every crisis was met by a collective reaction of self-defence that required greater precautions and severity. Thus the reaction, its ranks increased by scares and successive purges, grew with every aggravation of economic constraints and social protest. Time, which worked in its favour, provided new recruits who were a far cry from the aristocratic counter-revolution.

The counter-revolution has long been the object of excessive admiration or superficial attention. 'Left-wing' French historians have scoffed at it. In Mathiez's work, its role is marginal and confined to political explanations, particularly with regard to the 'foreign plot'. At a very late stage, Mathiez encouraged research on emigration and international finance. He was rightly wary of diplomatic documents, as, incidentally, was Georges Lefebvre. But Lefebvre took a different view, and stressed the social aspects of disaffection. He suggested adopting the attitude of the revolutionaries, who regarded all those who were not with them as being necessarily against them. Thus he was able to grasp the true dimensions of the problem, and he regretted the difficulty of obtaining proper statistics about it. The opening of the Coalition archives, investigations into private papers, and the cataloguing of the O^3 series at the Archives Nationales (Maison du Roi) gave him new hope. But researchers followed narrow paths, studying the networks and secret agents whose mysteries some investigators are still trying to solve.

On the other hand, British and American historians who were involved in the study of ideas produced solid analyses of theoreticians and doctrines. They nevertheless persisted in looking at anti-Jacobinism 'from the outside'. Finally, and more recently, some young sociologists, breaking with tradition, have bravely set about examining the structures of the passive and armed resistance of the Vendée, and the behaviour of its troops.

These are the directions increasingly being followed in historical research. One can already perceive the frailty of certain commitments to the Revolution and the existence of a stable mass of peasantry indifferent to any attempt at innovation, as we shall see in more detail later. Not only does there seem to be a huge gap between the attitudes of the Parisian militant and those of the peasant of the west, but geographical conditions and patronage relationships in each community fostered diametrically opposed political choices. As for the army, its popular recruitment encouraged the intermingling of opinions. It is no longer regarded, therefore, as a backward institution and a frozen society; it is now seen as a factor of social development and national unity.

Finally, the analysis of attitudes points to the continuity of the Terror. Punitive reaction, which was anarchic in 1792, then legalized in 1793, was part of the revolutionary movement and the counter-revolutionary outlook. It stemmed from identical motives and similar collective impulses. In both camps it manifested itself with the same violence: the individual was fighting for survival, the social group for its material and moral interests. The Parisian uprising can thus be explained by an intuition that led the people to forestall royalist schemes.

The Republic, born of the 10 August rising and timidly assigned the 'birthday' of 21 September 1792, was consecrated by Valmy. Although it prided itself on a popular victory over both foreign invaders and anti-Jacobinism, its legal status was almost fraudulent. The fallen monarchy served as its catalyst; the Republic was the monarchy's antithesis and hence ceased to be an abstraction. But it remained devoid of institutional and social content. While the people intended to make full use of their rights, the Rousseauian concept of national representation survived. The Paris Commune, an insurrectionary institution, set itself up against the discredited Assembly.[1] There was the danger that this

---

[1] The Commune, in the name of the people, had sent Huguenin to the Legislative Assembly as early as 11 August to serve notice of its dismissal.

could lead to a dual structure of power, creating anarchy and civil war, all the more so as this 'second revolution' did not meet with unanimous approval in the country.

In fact, property-owners were worried about the unrest that was spreading from Paris to the large towns and to rural France, which was thought to be indifferent and passive. Socially defined parties were preparing for a clash. One camp comprised those who wanted to end the Revolution with the gains of 1789. These were the law-abiding citizens, the *honnêtes gens*, pusillanimous by temperament and attached to the Constitutional order. They included both rich and poor, and their fear of adventure led them to prefer their present situation, however uninspiring, to an uncertain future. The other camp consisted of those who had higher hopes and dreamt of a better society, those who wanted to drag the Revolution out of its quagmire for their own sake but also for the sake of their children and all people – their fellow men.

THE DEMOCRATIC REVOLUTION

The Jacobin ideal partook of that wider world which had supported the uprising that had in turn confirmed Jacobinism's popular following. Opinion was split both on the issue of 10 August and on Jacobinism. These two issues were the dividing lines between supporters and opponents, and acquired their full significance in the coming conflicts between a democracy that was finding its way and a recalcitrant society encased in an obsolete framework. The aftermath of the August events was dominated by atavistic 'fears' and a collective mentality influenced by war and invasion. However brief, this period deserves examination. It foreshadows the 'prophetic Year II', in which all its traits expressed themselves to the extreme, spawning the same violence, the same resistance and, in some respects, the same audacity. The terrorist mentality and the revolutionary dictatorship asserted themselves by the Year I of the Republic, which was also the Year I of equality.

Insurrection, sovereignty, legality

'The State must be saved by whatever means, and nothing is unconstitutional except what can lead it to ruin.' Thus Robespierre, on 29 July 1792, settled in advance the question of legality in favour of the insurrection. Its legality was that of the Revolution and liberty. The rising was dictated by circumstances alone, not by the will of an individual or party. 'Must one keep referring to the penal code in order to assess the salutary precautions required by public safety in times of crisis brought about by the impotence of laws?' Robespierre was already distinguishing between regimes that were the product of 'wars and upheavals' and those suited to 'peace and concord'.

Most people defended their point of view by referring to the same principle: popular sovereignty, that is, 'the nation's rightful power to determine its own destiny'. The nation possesses 'all the rights that each man has to himself, and the general will governs society in the same way as individual will governs each single individual'. The nation was now vested with all the powers that the Constitution had separated; it was inalienable and non-transferable. Hence 'the people's delegates (*mandataires*) occupy the same position with respect to the sovereign as a private individual's proxies with respect to their principal, and the servant with respect to the head of a family'. The people could thus invoke this subservience to rise against their unfaithful officials, cast aside the old order and establish a new one, which, even if not yet codified, was no less formal. As its supreme recourse, the people confirmed the nation in its absolute prerogatives, which were vested in every fraction of the sovereign authority. So long as the nation remained in arms, its role was to guide the people's thoughts and actions. Everything emanated from the people and everything came back to the people.

This notion of revolutionary right, in its simplicity and rigour, contained a latent strength. It prompted Parisian *sectionnaires* and provincial *fédérés* to storm the Tuileries; it convinced the *sans-culottes* of their own existence and supremacy. From that moment on, they acquired self-awareness. Their concept of sovereignty moved them to exercise it without intermediaries, and justice represented one of its functions. Experience had made them vigilant. 'The sovereign must be at his post, leading his armies, going about his duties; he must be everywhere.' Given the deficiencies of the State, and 'in the absence of protective laws, [the sovereign people] must look after itself'. It set out to place ministers and civil servants – that is, its delegates – under permanent watch, and to dismiss those who infringed the 14 August oath to Liberty and Equality. In late August, a Versaillais, Frotié, went so far as to suggest appointing a tribune in each *département* to counter abuses by public officials and offset their influence. 'Think of your own interest, O humble class in the towns and in the countryside. The time has come for your happiness or slavery.'

The democratic revolution, led by the *section* militants, was triumphant in the despondent capital. The Duke of Brunswick had advanced beyond Longwy and reached Verdun. His progress was magnified by alarming rumours. Prussian scouts were said to have been spotted near the camp at Châlons. Some thought he would be at the outskirts of Paris by the following day, and the capital was hastily provided with makeshift fortifications. After the solemn proclamation of 11 July that the homeland was 'in danger', scores of patriots set out across the country. The obsession with treason kept the population in a permanent state of alert. France was succumbing to a feeling of unease and insecurity.

The bloody autumn of 1792

The succession of measures taken until the autumn was a consequence of these fears, and bore the signs of haste. Domiciliary visits, arrests of prime suspects, the internment of Louis XVI and his family in the Temple, the muzzling of the royalist press — all these actions met with the approval of the Commune and the *sections*. Other measures were wrested from the dying Legislative Assembly against its will: the creation of a special tribunal to judge the defenders of the Tuileries, the banishment of non-juror priests, and sanctions against *émigrés* and their relatives. An anarchic terror began to spread, punctuated by punitive reactions, private vendettas and summary executions.

In the provinces, notably in the Orne, massacres took place earlier than in the capital; then from 4 to 16 September there were outbreaks in Gisors, Marseilles, Lyons, Toulon, Versailles, Lorient and elsewhere. The same process, the same impetus, the same violence manifested themselves everywhere. But this violence was neither blind nor triggered off by watchwords, as has been claimed. Although those responsible for it were sometimes unaware of their victims' identity, public rumour had designated them. In this respect, the acts perpetrated in small towns are more significant than the bloodshed in Paris prisons, whose victims included a high proportion — three-quarters — of common-law prisoners. Popular fury vented itself on aristocrats and non-juror priests, on merchants and the wealthy, who were jealous of their authority and fortune. They had condemned themselves by their selfishness, lack of civic spirit and arrogance.

The 'terrorists' were neither bandits nor hotheads, but townspeople and country folk enrolled to serve their homeland and fight its enemies. Among the executioners, many were married and had families. At

Alençon, their wives went along and encouraged them to get rid of 'all those bloody aristocratic rogues'. 'Plain countrymen', just like the Parisians, were convinced of the need for this precaution. 'That gang would have taken up arms to slit our throats after the departure of our valiant youth.' Few thought of pillaging for personal gain. They destroyed to set an example, to spread the sight of a spectacular vengeance that would deter evil-doers. From Paris to Châlons, the volunteers' advance was marked by identical scenes, with the participation of local inhabitants. On 3 September in Reims and 4 September in Meaux, suspects were executed, municipal officers molested and local administrations purged.

Moreover, although the people, in arms for the defence of their rights, had taken the law into their own hands, they often demanded help from the authorities and the use of established legal procedure. Local officials and the national guard, by their lack of foresight, their cowardice or helplessness, bear a great burden of responsibility. The *district* of Neuville-aux-Bois (Loiret) sent the following account on 18 September:

Anarchy is rampant; there is no more authority. Official services are discredited and cannot enforce their writ...There is a state of frenzy that we can hardly describe to you. All we hear is threats to kill, break down houses and ransack them. There is talk of tearing down all the former châteaux...Finally all these people are saying that they want no more administration, no more courts, that the law is in their hands, and that they will enforce it.[2]

Revolutionary action was disorderly and incoherent. By threatening property, it also put the young Republic at risk.

The Paris Commune was enlarged to include 288 hitherto almost unknown members and set itself up as a dictatorial assembly. Robespierre, who was elected to it, contributed his experience and popularity. He was able to put enthusiasm to use and channel the Commune's zeal. Moreover, among the people's most faithful supporters, some, like Marat, questioned its political maturity. To guide itself in its struggle, it had to put its trust in reliable mentors, wholehearted and incorruptible patriots. Under the influence of the Jacobin leaders, there emerged the outlines of a democratic revolution whose solutions to the 'great social problem' appeared less frightening to property-owners.

[2] Quoted in G. Lefebvre, *Etudes orléanaises*, vol. 2 (21), p. 62.

It was up to the Republic to determine its own nature and the paths it had to follow. Its first concern was to protect the people from arbitrary rule and to reassert its authority. Only democracy would do, but it had to be tempered by arrangements tailored to the size of the population, which precluded direct democracy. Thus the political concept of the sovereign's role was modified. 'Guided by laws of his own making, he must do on his own whatever he can accomplish efficiently, and delegate whatever he cannot do by himself.' Where was the dividing line? Where did the people's responsibility end and that of its representatives begin? How was this compromise between the collective character of sovereignty and its partial alienation to be implemented?

Popular sovereignty was transferred in its entirety to its delegates through the constituent power. The National Convention, which met on the very evening of 10 August, was indeed exceptional in character. It was a new 'constituent assembly', invested with unlimited powers, and, in keeping with Sieyès's theory, it was the 'mind and arm of the nation'. Despite the institution of universal suffrage and public elections, the future of democracy would not lie in the hands of the mob. Democracy's fate depended on the handful of citizens who were now vested with authority and responsible for public order. How could one exercise control over them? The *sans-culottes* were quick to realize their imprudence. They had stood back in favour of an assembly that was to be chosen by an ill-informed country and a divided opinion. In their name, it would govern France and build a Republic that might not be theirs.

An outworn apparatus

The administrative framework set up in 1790 was as obsolete as the Constitution and was splitting at the seams, but its occupants held on to their sinecures. The Legislative Assembly, an integral part of that system, took the most urgent measures. After 'provisionally' suspending the king as chief of the executive, it entrusted his functions to an equally provisional council, the Conseil Exécutif, composed of three ministers already appointed on 13 June, Roland (Interior), Servan (War) and Clavière (Finance), to whom were added two newcomers on 11 August, Lebrun (Foreign Affairs) and Monge (Navy). Danton's presence at the Ministry of Justice was meant to reassure the Commune and the *sans-culottes*. This skilful blend suited the moderates and ensured continuity in government. But all these appointees were old hacks who had already compromised themselves. Danton shook them from their torpor and seemed to dominate them. In reality, the all-powerful bureaucracy, an inheritance of the *ancien régime*, controlled the ministries.

This complicated and cumbersome patched-up machinery turned out to be unadapted and inefficient. Roland presided alone over the equivalent of a dozen modern French ministerial departments, and the War Ministry comprised no fewer than 1,800 clerks. The volume of proceedings increased considerably during this interregnum. Ministers had to organize defence and elections, maintain public order, replace civil servants, and confront a situation that was getting out of hand. Anachronisms and inertia seemed all the more intolerable as the 'popular' authorities were more dynamic. Nonetheless, the latter participated in national government with a minimum of clashes during these forty days.

In fact, it was bureaucrats rather than the lack of administrative know-how that were the major source of complaints. The shortcomings of public services, communications and transport were criticized, as well as the uncooperative attitude of those employed in these areas. Many civil servants at the Interior Ministry came from the Contrôle Général and from the Direction du Commerce; some had occupied their posts since 1776. They did not conceal their attachment to the monarchy. The Postes et Messageries service had a nostalgia for the age of gilded carriages and tips, while the Ponts et Chaussées regretted the demise of bribes and gratuities. Old habits and prolonged subservience shaped political attitudes and delayed needed changes. Waste, negligence and malevolence all resulted from this tenacious opposition.

Opposition also manifested itself in local administrations. Those of the *départements* in particular aroused distrust and reservations. They were criticized both for their lack of civic spirit and for their overstaffing. The *conseils généraux* and *directoires* had each equipped themselves with four to six offices and a dozen clerks. Plurality and nepotism were common practice. In Sedan, the clerk of the Tribunaux de District and Tribunaux de Commerce was also in charge of the town records – in a town dominated by manufacturers, nobles and priests. Elected officials or civil servants used their modest salaries as a pretext for attending to personal business to the detriment of the public interest. A priest in a locality in the Poitou, who was also *procureur-syndic* (executive officer) there, deplored the negligence of legal officers, farmers and landlords, who, because of their almost total absence, failed to announce and enforce the measures they condemned. Hastily produced legislation lent itself to conflicting interpretations. Trivial breaches of the law provoked a flurry of protest. As Couthon stated on 22 September, there were conflicts everywhere between the municipalities, which were regarded as necessary structures, and the *départements*, which were thought of as harmful.

Decentralization meant the local authorities had acquired a relative autonomy and exercised their powers differently according to prevailing attitudes. In some places officials behaved like 'decayed remnants' of the old order, while in others they took a Jacobin stance. The weakness of the executive, troop movements and the enemy advance all made for confused and difficult situations. The municipalities, which were close to the population, were generally receptive to its initiatives. In the east, in Strasburg, Nancy, Metz and Sedan, in the Marne, the Indre and the Vendée, the *sans-culottes* took it upon themselves to stand in for the tottering authorities. Some electoral assemblies, convened in the *chefs-lieux** to choose the members of the Convention, also replaced – in part or *in toto* – the members of the *conseils généraux*, since they regarded dereliction of duty as treason.

However, competence became scarce when civic spirit became the overriding criterion for selection. Educated *sans-culottes* were a minority in the countryside, whereas there were many posts to fill. There was no choice but to appoint 'knaves and fools'. A fully fledged caste of scribes supported by humiliated notables perpetuated itself. It was proud of its skills and jealous of its functions. Taking advantage of the ignorance of the meek, it convinced them that life was impossible without a king and without priests. 'The people want the Revolution, but they are being held back by the revolting apathy and the intrigues of some of the rich, as well as by fanaticism.' They had to be educated and protected against their prophets of doom; the unity and indivisibility of the Republic had to be preserved.

Unity and indivisibility

On 25 September, at Couthon's suggestion, the Republic was solemnly proclaimed to be 'one and indivisible', a move that condemned in advance regionalist tendencies, secessions, and opposition to the capital. It was not a mere slogan but a weapon justified by the uncertain state

* Capital towns of the *cantons*, the second-largest administrative subdivisions of the *départements*, ranking below the *districts*. [Trans.]

of public opinion. After all, it has already been widely rumoured that the Assembly might be transferred to the provinces. The authorities of the Creuse advocated the creation of an 'anti-10 August' league, and the Var invited nineteen *départements* to examine together the measures that would destroy the pernicious influence of that *journée*. The right of insurrection was invoked against Parisian oppression. There was a genuine danger. Duperret denounced at the Jacobin club, on 17 September, a plan that aimed at setting up a coalition in the Midi and leaving the north to its own devices. 'Those who dare to say that the Assembly and the core of the administration should not remain in Paris are traitors who must be unmasked and punished. Paris started the Revolution; it kept it going; it will complete it.'

Once again, there was opposition between two concepts. One side advocated a federation on the American model, made up of provincial units that would be free to take any decisions at the local level and would be dependent on the capital solely for matters of national import. This notion stemmed from that of decentralization, dear to the members of the Constituent Assembly, and from persistent rural wariness of Parisian excesses. The supporters of this view stubbornly refused to recognize the reality of the democratic movement and its demands. The Commune and the Jacobins favoured a Paris-centred federalism instead, so that 'a single impulse would spread to all the *départements* of the Republic, and the shock wave, issuing forth from the Convention – its focal point, as it were – would jolt everyone at the same instant and in the same direction'. To achieve this, the *fédérés* were closely associated with the popular victory, and petitions and messages flowed in from all parts of the country to the Hôtel de Ville, where a central office of correspondence had been operating since 27 July. Provincial patriots who came up to Paris introduced themselves to the Jacobin club. The purpose of national unity, which was the foundation of the Republic, was to ensure the nation-wide enforcement of laws voted by the Assembly which were nevertheless the product of the people as a whole.

This role was devolved upon commissioners armed with full powers by the Commune, the Legislative Assembly, the Convention and the Conseil Exécutif. From late August 1792, these *commissaires de l'exécutif* toured the army of the Moselle and visited the northern and eastern *départements* – the most threatened – then the interior. The first contingent, appointed by Danton, included journalists such as Prudhomme and Carra, officers such as Westermann, Laclos, Parein, Ronsin and Jean Alexandre, scientists such as Giroud, and former priests. All were reliable patriots who were to take part again in the 'missions' of the Year II. Other participants included members of the Commune and the *comité de surveillance* of the Paris *département*, among them Clémence and Marchand. Anthoine, Billaud-Varenne, Bourdon de l'Oise and Fabre d'Eglantine, future *conventionnels*, also belonged to this élite, drawn from a wide variety of social origins. Their authoritarian character and decisiveness were what was needed in this dangerous emergency. Their ardent and disorderly zeal prompted them to observe every detail and embark on countless initiatives.

Their first objective was to raise volunteers, but they also had to provide food supplies and equipment, as well as inspect horses. They obtained arms by requisitioning those of the national guards and forcing blacksmiths to manufacture pikes. To rouse public opinion, they ordered domiciliary visits, had suspects arrested, and set up postal surveillance. Some municipalities protested against their powers; in the Haute-Saône, local authorities even imprisoned them. But many officials cooperated, as did the inhabitants. In Orléans, the assemblies of the *sections* declared themselves to be in permanent session. *Comités de surveillance* and patriotic clubs were set up spontaneously. There were massive contributions of personal belongings. Church bells and church silver were handed in. Nevertheless, some commissioners adopted extremist attitudes. At Bar-le-Duc, Gonchon wore the Phrygian cap (*le bonnet rouge*). The commissioners were accused of violating property, advocating radical land redistribution (the *loi agraire*) and violence, and demanding the gallows. Against the nation's enemies, they used the style and methods that the Terror was to legalize a year later.

Thanks to the commissioners, the democratic revolution found its way into rural France. In the Seine-et-Marne, Ronsin and Sebastien Lacroix enjoined electors to censure their representatives 'if they proved unworthy of their trust'. As the number of commissioners increased, their powers overlapped. A decree of 14 September imposed a limit by authorizing only delegations from ministers and the Assembly. They were entrusted with specific missions, in particular that of ensuring food supplies to towns and armies.

Economic contradictions

The obsessive concern among townspeople about the supply of daily bread was a potential source of further trouble. The *sans-culottes* demanded regulation, while the bourgeoisie held fast to 'peaceful liberalism'. To be efficient, the authoritarian intervention of the State would have to encompass production, consumption and prices. The Legislative Assembly could not take on such a far-reaching commitment, and it contented itself with an inventory of the harvest.

The crop was average but uneven. As it has not yet been fully threshed, municipalities were first asked to enlist farm hands, then, on the 16th, to collect growers' statements of crop yields. One part of the grain would be allocated to military stores; the other would be used to meet urgent demands on the market. It was thought that conflicts between the army and civilians would thus be avoided. Moreover, to ensure adequate supplies for regions in need and for large towns, control over grain circulation and trade was decreed. But these measures were thwarted by farmers' inertia and the connivance of peasants traditionally hostile to State interference and to the exorbitant demands of townspeople. The information requested was slow to arrive, while on the main supply routes the populace halted grain and flour convoys with no concern for the needs of the intended recipients. Sometimes the national guard actually protected looters.

On the whole, local authorities resisted attempts at a nation-wide distribution of supplies made necessary by troop concentrations and movements. The major producers and the merchants could not accept a restriction on the profits they were making thanks to scarcity and inflation. The steady rise of the paper currency (*assignat*) on the domestic market and foreign exchanges worked in their favour. The ensuing export boom created an artificial euphoria. While the trade balance ran a healthy surplus, the country was slowly going to ruin. The masses failed to grasp the inflationary mechanism and merely felt its effects. Even so, they came up with different explanations. In August 1792, the exchange rate for the *assignat* stood at 77 per cent of its face value, and cash was still used, together with paper money, to pay wages. Entrepreneurs were handicapped by the shortage of small banknotes, and the influx of promissory notes, which were meant as a remedy, conferred an even greater premium on coin. In the countryside, farm hands received a higher proportion than usual of their wages in kind, and farmers who worked small plots hesitated to sell their produce.

Humble townsfolk, whose purchasing power was dropping (when unemployment had not wiped it out altogether), refused to bear the total burden of inflation, which reached about 40 per cent for wheat compared to the previous year. During the same period, the price of the pound-loaf of white bread increased in a similar proportion, and brown bread, staple diet of the poor, rose by 33 per cent. But open markets, which were nearly deserted, would become entirely empty whenever price controls were attempted. Thus, municipalities adopted a policy of unilateral price-fixing for bread – a system that satisfied the small consumer without harming the producer or the middleman. In Paris, the Commune sold off its flour at a loss to bakers in order to maintain the price of bread at three sous a pound. Identical solutions were used in Tours, Orléans, Bordeaux, Rouen and Grenoble. The difference was financed by local rates, borrowing or levies on the rich. Subsidized distribution was meant to be restricted to the indigent, but the entire population and the surrounding areas wanted to enjoy the same advantage. The authorities contemplated localizing distribution by resorting to ration cards, producing a single type of bread, using the ovens bakers abandoned, or adding rye to wheat. These were all hybrid solutions that were unworkable except within the context of interventionism tempered by negotiations.

When the volunteers intervened, as in Châlons, they did not hesitate to use coercion to fill the markets. As soon as they were gone, the grain would be hidden again. The people, threatened with famine, displayed an equal loathing for producers and merchants, whom they regarded as speculators and hoarders. They were personally attacked, as were their homes and warehouses. The *crise des subsistances* thus revealed the balance of power that lay behind social strife. The democratic revolution provoked a hostile coalition of private interests, thereby strengthening the forces of reaction.

STRENGTHS AND WEAKNESSES OF THE REACTION

The reaction had been getting both stronger and weaker since the spring of 1792. It would be impossible, however, to assess its strengths and weaknesses accurately. Caste prejudice and blind allegiance to the old order were not the only factors at work. There were also disappointed ambitions, personal rivalries, family and friendship ties, the hope of material and moral gains and, lastly, the complexity of a situation that accounted for the varying degrees of counter-revolutionary commitment and helped to strengthen or weaken it. Alongside an organized and militant reaction, openly enjoying foreign support and domestic collusion, a passive and uncontrollable resistance was developing by stealth. It fastened onto the Revolution like a millstone that tended to impede its progress not by force of arms, but by its sheer inertia.

The conservatism that generated these attitudes took on varying

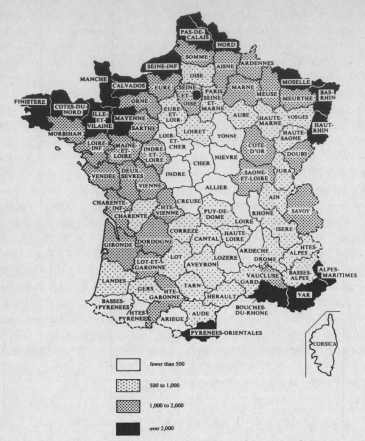

Fig. 1 Distribution of *émigrés* by *département* of origin. After D. Greer,
The Incidence of Emigration during the French Revolution (**25**)

shades of intensity and often resulted from scarcely reconcilable
motives. A small minority hankered after the society of orders and its
privileges. A larger group, which had fought against those values, feared
their return. Having assimilated itself into the society of 1789, it
defended the principles and gains of that society, including liberty and
property. Moreover, the nobility and bourgeoisie did not have an
identical concept of the homeland. The former equated it with the king
and religion, the latter with worldly possessions. They also disagreed
about 10 August. The nobles regarded it as a lost opportunity, while
property-owners and 'all thinking persons saw only the abyss in front
of them'.

The international aristocracy. The '*émigrés*'

Emigration, at first equated with absence, took on its true significance in wartime: it was a capital offence. By forsaking his homeland, the *émigré* ceased to be a citizen; by compromising himself with foreign powers and daring to fight alongside them, he condemned himself irrevocably. He was a traitor; all that he and his accomplices deserved was death. The fall of the monarchy and the banishment of priests prompted new departures, in particular to England and Spain. The total number of these *émigrés* was put at about one hundred thousand, of whom barely one-fifth were nobles, although public opinion thought they represented the majority.

The most illustrious names in France were to be found in Belgium and along the Rhine. These notables felt at home there and loudly proclaimed their titles and ranks. Did they not belong to the international aristocracy? Their solidarity was reinforced by common habits and a similar way of life, no less than by birth. One can describe that solidarity as caste ethos or class consciousness; its tangible existence and the high value the nobles attached to it led these *émigrés* to every kind of extreme. They were convinced that they alone represented the entire country and they refused commoners the slightest degree of authority. Noble *émigrés* regarded their 'homeland' to be wherever they settled down. 'Peoples can be divided into nations and be genuine strangers for one another, but the nobility is a single unit. No difference of climate, language or manners can divide it. It exists everywhere on the same foundations, on the same linchpin and by virtue of the same privileges, and when its foundations are attacked in one country they are in another as well.'

Thus, by ruining the French nobility, the Revolution had struck a blow against the nobility at large. The war that the Revolution had rashly declared was not just aimed at Prussia and Austria; it threatened time-honoured structures and traditions. 'This was not a war about trade, borders or supremacy, but an open war against all aspects of domination, monarchy, religion and ethics, and the hierarchy of rank, privilege and property. Every sovereign, every nobleman and every property-owner has the same reason for trying to stifle [the Revolution].'[3]

The French aristocracy issued a call to all its brethren for a crusade

[3] J. de Maistre, *Marie-Antoinette, archiduchesse d'Autriche, ou causes et tableau de la Révolution*, p. 15. Quoted by M. Bouloiseau in *AHRF*, 1958, no. 1, p. 66, and J. Jiru, 'Casanova observateur de la Révolution française', *AHRF*, 1959, p. 237.

against the principles of 1789 – principles confirmed by the 10 August rising – and against the abolition of the monarchy. The united aristocracy had to stop the epidemic from spreading. 'By its very nature the Republic was the enemy of every government; it aimed at destroying them all, so that every government had a stake in destroying it.' The September massacres shook foreign opinion. Across the Channel, it was said that Jacobins ate pies filled with human flesh. The Jacobins were depicted as bandits, heathens, possessed by the devil and capable of every crime. In the British Empire, French newspapers were banned and student leagues kept under surveillance. The governing classes were gripped by a full-scale 'Jacobinophobia' that spread to the masses through propaganda, caricature and fear. English liberals felt less and less sympathetic towards the Revolution as it revealed its democratic tendencies. The direst misfortunes were foretold for hesitant sovereigns. 'Before a century has elapsed, there will be not one regime left in Europe such as there are today.' The captivity of Louis XVI was an omen of more sacrilege, as the fate of the first *gentilhomme* of the realm was tied to that of his loyal nobility. The French monarchy had to be defended and its divine origins and hereditary privileges reasserted at all costs. Only a general coalition could restore the old society in France and peace in Europe.

No compromise seemed possible or desirable. It was all or nothing. The counter-revolutionary camp adopted the revolutionaries' attitudes and methods. 'That den of assassins must be expunged', an exemplary revenge had to be wreaked, and there had to be bloodshed. The spirit of the Brunswick Manifesto could already be summed up, according to Gouverneur Morris, in these words: 'Stand against me, every one of you, because I stand against all of you; put up a good fight, because there is no hope for you.'[4] Whatever these pronouncements were – verbal violence or boasts circulated by rumour – they left the Revolution with no choice but victory. The excessiveness of such threats was a serious miscalculation.

Admittedly, the *émigrés* did not doubt their coming victory. A dislocated country was the most vulnerable prey of all, and the Prussian advance seemed to confirm their assessment. Never were they closer to fulfilling their aims than after 10 August. With the king and his family in prison, the regency was open to the Comte de Provence. It would be easy to get rid of the d'Orléans branch, which was held

4 Quoted in A. Sorel, *L'Europe et la Révolution française*, vol. 2 (35), p. 310.

responsible for the insurrection. The *émigrés*, misinformed about the domestic situation, thought the country was ready to welcome them. They were sadly mistaken. Even when confronted with the facts, they continued to deny them. Despite their banishment from France, the *émigrés* refused to be integrated into the populations that granted them asylum. With their incessant recriminations and ever greater demands, they became a nuisance to courts and monarchs. They were spared no disappointment. The *émigrés* had to endure loneliness and a climate of suspicion, they wasted away in idleness, regret or envy, but they did not renounce their aggressive presumption.

These *enragés* of the counter-revolution and the princes they served kept the aristocratic plot alive, but not all *émigrés* shared their intransigence and blindness. They were weakened by petty rivalries as more conciliatory currents emerged. A confrontation developed between political and military factions. The military elements comprised disbanded guardsmen and foreign regiments, artillery and naval cadets, officers and soldiers; they were joined in September 1792 by hussars of the Bercheny and Royal-Allemand regiments. All had rallied to the Prince de Condé and Mirabeau-Tonneau.[5] For months on end, they had to curb their zeal in the camps before they were allowed to fight, as underlings. These poorly paid contigents were only a minority, perhaps about ten thousand, and they did not consist exclusively of nobles. In that same period of late 1792, more than half of the known *émigrés* were commoners who had fled from France for one reason or another. They belonged to all social categories, from chambermaids and lackeys to property-owners and tradesmen. As for prelates and priests – a quarter of the total – they vegetated alone or in groups and braced themselves for a long and shabby exile.

However, on the eve of 10 August some nobles, frightened by the threat that their property would be sequestered, went back to their lands and châteaux. They silently returned to their old habits, without giving up their principles and hopes. A distribution of roles was achieved: the counter-revolution displayed its adaptability and tried to organize itself. Revolutionaries were increasingly convinced of the collusion between 'foreign and domestic enemies'.

---

[5] The younger brother of the orator of the Constituent Assembly owed his nickname 'Tonneau' (barrel) to his paunch and drunkenness. After emigrating, he raised a legion that adopted black uniforms decorated with death's-heads. His regiment merged with the Prince de Condé's army, stationed on the Rhine around Koblenz.

The 'fifth column'

The 'fifth column' included, first of all, the *émigrés*' families, who were penalized by a measure of 12 September that made each relative responsible for the upkeep of two volunteers. Although the *émigrés*' families were known and vulnerable and were under a cloud of suspicion, the authorities hesitated to use force against them. Women and older members of these families took advantage of this leniency by protecting and managing family assets: money from farm rents, income from timber and grain sales, jewels and silver plate were sent abroad through well-tried channels. But stricter controls, as well as denunciations, provoked heavy losses. Increasingly, liquid assets were smuggled out through banks.

So long as the war remained a local affair there was no significant drop in the exchange rates. Letters of credit were drawn on Hamburg, Kiel and Altona against payment in cash or *assignats*. These letters soon became so expensive that the *émigrés*' families had to borrow in order to buy them. Pitt encouraged such behaviour and put London bills on the Paris market so as to drain off French gold. A favourite weapon of the reaction consisted in ruining the *assignat*, which was a symbol of the Revolution. The domestic collateral of the *assignat* was whittled down by postponing the sale of *émigré* property, and new *assignats* were issued to finance the war. An attempt was made to discredit the *assignat* by flooding the country with counterfeit notes. Forgery soon took on alarming proportions. Production centres established in Chimay and Rhineland towns put their forged notes into circulation in Chambéry, Mulhouse and Strasburg. From the border to the interior, peasants shunned paper money.

Another tactic consisted in confusing public opinion by spreading the wildest rumours. By September they had so proliferated that Gorsas complained about them in his *Courrier*. Moreover, the royalist press had not entirely disappeared. Although its major papers had been closed down, its style lived on in lesser periodicals. Witticisms, epigrams and gossip were all used to ridicule the patriots. Brissot and the Duc d'Orléans got their share, as did Marat and Robespierre. The royalists painted the situation in the worst light by exaggerating dangers and the ministers' lack of foresight; counter-revolutionary agents presented 'incendiary motions' at the Jacobin club. It was only in April 1793 that the *Feuille du Matin* ceased its sarcastic attacks on the Jacobins. The paper was probably then circulated clandestinely, like so many spiteful or vindictive tracts: the impact of this literature was all the greater for it. Informers volunteered or were paid to infiltrate the administration and the clubs. For the *émigrés*, it was worth paying for espionage so long as discussions about military operations remained public and could be reported on; later, royalist 'bulletins' carried hearsay along with serious news. Much importance has been given to the Comte d'Antraigues's bulletins, but they are noteworthy not so much for their credibility as for the attitude of the author and their impact abroad.

The forces of religion spared no effort to assist the nobility. Many non-juror priests who had stayed in France joined royalist networks, undertook missions, and risked their lives for the common cause. They assumed false identities in Paris and the large towns, or banded together in secluded mountain and forest areas, where they were protected and fed by the local population. In the Cévennes, in Brittany, in the Vendée, in Savoy and in the Pyrenean border regions, the non-jurors performed their religious functions in secret and 'kept fanaticism alive'. As for juror priests, who were compelled to take the oath of loyalty to the Constitution (*petit serment*), they complied less out of conviction than out of opportunism. Their publicly recognized role was considerable, both in the countryside and in the towns. With women as their intermediaries, the juror priests exerted their influence on husbands and gave instruction to children. They continued to occupy administrative posts and to take part in meetings of the *sociétés populaires*. Some juror priests, making a distinction between religious faith and revolutionary action, were genuine patriots. Most, however, adopted a cautious but reactionary attitude and in private linked the defence of the monarchy to eternal salvation – the temporal to the spiritual. The 'constitutional' or legally recognized church, which was maintained by the Republic in a hierarchical and disciplined structure, represented the single most persuasive force of the domestic counter-revolution.

Defenders of the throne and altar were therefore to be found in all strata of society, in the west and elsewhere, but their numerical strength varied because ideological solidarity was never total. Counter-revolutionaries resorted to open rebellion only when a strong leadership succeeded in imposing itself. This was how Baudry d'Asson led 8,000 peasants of the Vendée to capture Châtillon-sur-Sèvre on 22 August 1792; this also explains the royalist uprising in the Dauphiné. Nevertheless, the only actions one can describe as plots – that is, as planned undertakings with specific objectives – are the sporadic efforts such as those of the Marquis de la Rouërie in Brittany. But, however sporadic, such actions were more than just 'peccadilloes', as they have been called.

Moreover, unorganized and elusive resistance posed a threat that was all the more disturbing for being diffuse. In its desire to display its zeal, this resistance took needless risks. In the Yonne, 'liberty trees' were the object of public derision; at night, they were uprooted. The surviving correspondence testifies to the extreme thoughtlessness and fatally misplaced trust of the counter-revolutionaries. In these letters they openly stated their intentions and brooded over missed opportunities. The patriots who stumbled on such correspondence in the course of their searches became convinced that the enemy was lurking everywhere. Danger came to be seen as omnipresent: it could strike at any time and by whatever means. Spy-mania and the obsession with the 'foreign plot' inevitably led to preventive action and retaliation; these fears seem to be constant features of the revolutionary mentality.

The aristocracy of money

It was not enough to struggle against the aristocracy of birth and against fanaticism. Another peril threatened the Revolution of equality; it stemmed from the 'conquering' bourgeoisie. The patriots, who were aware of this danger, rejected the hegemony of wealth and the supremacy of notables. They increasingly regarded wealth, condemned in its outward manifestations, as a presumption of a politically suspect attitude. The term 'bourgeois', less current then than now, takes on its full significance in the context of the democratic Revolution.

Bourgeois businessmen, big merchants, bankers and shippers maintained a network of international relations comparable to that of the nobility, whom these commoners had for a long time copied and envied. Their reactions were watched by 'capitalists' abroad, in England and Germany. As soon as it had abandoned its liberal policy, the French Republic began to harass the moneyed bourgeoisie, whose golden rule was the free interplay between supply and demand. Their fortune, which already comprised a high proportion of movables, increased through currency speculation. For the capitalist bourgeoisie, the homeland was more of a symbol than a reality, since they were not tied to the land. In that respect, they differed from the big rural landowners whose wealth, like that of the nobles, was rooted in real estate and landed income rather than in capitalist profits. The sale of Church property provided the bourgeoisie with an impressive source of investments, and the payment by annual instalments constituted a legal form of agiotage. As for the 'bourgeoisie of talent', they possessed both a landed base and a function. The posts they occupied in the highest echelons of the State provided them with the money they needed to become a propertied class. They had expected the Revolution to offer them positions as lucrative as those bestowed by the monarchy and they did not conceal their disappointment.

Later, after 10 August, social conflicts were reduced to a stark confrontation between rich and poor, between 'the aristocracy of money and what used to be called the rabble'. 'There are two distinct groups in the Republic,' a speaker remarked at the Jacobin club in March 1793: 'the *sans-culottes* and the rich, the sybarites. We shall never live in peace so long as the latter group endures. We must therefore do our best to destroy the selfish rich. Another revolution is needed.' The 'rich' were the focus of resentment among the poor, who used the term to describe those who had enough to eat while the poor went hungry.

Economic and social problems were therefore seen as a consequence of 'the appetite for power of the rising class'. The notion that wealth posed a domestic threat to the Revolution thus became widespread by September 1792. Chabot even suggested that the rich should be treated just like the *émigrés*. 'If they do not want to share in the Revolution's achievements, they shall cease to belong to the great family; they shall no longer own property.' The rich were also to contribute – proportionally to their means – to the nation's expenses. It was right that 'revolutionary taxes' based on income should amputate capital in order to combat the bourgeois aristocracy. 'Had it survived', Collot d'Herbois and Fouché noted later, 'it would soon have given birth to a financial aristocracy, which would have engendered a nobiliary aristocracy, for the rich man is not long in regarding himself as made of a stuff different from that of other men.'[6]

The political attitudes of the wealthy bourgeoisie all came under the heading of moderatism, which revolutionaries saw as a scourge. In Rennes, which was 'crawling with supporters of the *ancien régime*', 'the moderates were considered a hundred times more dangerous than determined aristocrats'. However, in certain sections of rural France, the moderates' patriotism was not in doubt. On their own initiative, the moderates distinguished themselves from the Jacobins, with whom they were still confused. Moreover, there were degrees of moderatism; some moderates feared a return of absolutism as much as a social revolution. Such was the position taken by purchasers of nationalized

[6] Supplement to Aulard's *Recueil*... (2), vol. 2, 26 Brumaire Year II.

Church estates (*biens nationaux*) and by all those who, in one way or
another, had profited from the Revolution. These moderates had no
doubts about their civic virtue and jealously asserted it. An inhabitant
of Rouen objected to being called a *sans-culotte*, a term that fostered
pernicious distinctions: 'Citizens without *culottes* have come to be
regarded as the only friends of liberty, equality and the Republic; but
among the well-to-do, namely among those who do wear *culottes*, there
are many good citizens indeed who cherish a revolution founded on
civil and political equality.'[7] The commitment of the moderates did
not extend beyond that. For them, the defence of their homeland and
the safeguarding of property were one and the same thing. They did
not contemplate fleeing their country but were ready to fight an armed
battle against the aristocracy alongside the people, and to fight against
the people through the force of their inertia. There was massive support
for such views in rural communities where notables exerted their sway
through traditional patronage ties. Rural 'indifference' acted as a heavy
brake on democracy.

Other patriots of the 1789 vintage took a deliberately anti-Jacobin
stance. They accused Brissot and Pétion, as well as Marat and
Robespierre, of forming a faction, appropriating patriotism, and seizing
all the positions of power. For Du Pont de Nemours, the Jacobins were
'people...whose conduct in public affairs is guided solely by the
interests of the party to which they owe, or from which they expect,
posts, a share of authority and money'.[8] The Jacobins were increasingly
looked upon as seditious by the monarchists and 'constitutionalists'.
Robespierre was fully aware of the implications of such a threat, which
the 10 August insurrection defused without, however, destroying it.
A network of complicity allowed the 'bourgeoisie of talent' to take
refuge in the provinces or abroad. Although it disappeared from the
political scene and was kept at bay by the aristocracy, it continued to
further its own interests while biding its time.

The aftermath of 10 August can thus be defined by the varieties of
resistance that the uprising provoked. To the already explicit and
versatile opposition from the aristocracy and Church, one must add
that of the upper bourgeoisie and the genuine or feigned lethargy of
an unmeasurable section of rural France. With such a patchwork
character, the opposition's effectiveness was diminished. It hesitated and

---

[7] Reproduced in Claude Mazauric, *La Révolution à Rouen*, photocopy no. XII.
[8] Quoted in M. Bouloiseau, *Bourgeoisie et Révolution: les Du Pont de Nemours, 1788–1799*,
chapter 2.

manoeuvred instead of organizing itself and acting. Yet, by its very presence, it spurred on the revolutionary struggle. To attain victory, Jacobinism mobilized national feeling and the yearning for equality.

JACOBINISM

All good patriots were to assemble at the Jacobin club, and all those who were not good citizens were to leave it. National unity was rebuilt after 10 August around the Société des Amis de la Liberté et de l'Egalité. The Paris Commune treated the Société as a working partner, and the Jacobins also won the support of the Cordeliers. Every Parisian *section* was proud to imitate the Société. During the elections, it was regarded as the driving force behind public opinion. All 'momentous resolutions' had to emanate from the Jacobins, who acted like a sovereign assembly deliberating on the most serious issues. 'The nickname of Jacobin, which used to have something ridiculous and sinister about it', became a glorious title. Before setting out for the front, the volunteers asked for that badge of good citizenship – the Jacobin label – that would fill the enemy with dread.

The Parisian club and provincial 'sociétés'

The Parisian club was now open to all citizens, 'active' and 'passive'. But how could it tell if its members were sincere? There were calls for purges as early as 19 August. The *brissotins* gradually left to gather at the Réunion club but, while the Jacobin membership declined, the number of spectators increased. The crowed was so impatient that it was decided to allow the visitors' gallery to open before meetings began. The public participated in the discussions, which were noisy and disorderly. Often no agenda had been drawn up, and the chairman had to improvise one. Delegations would present themselves one after the other, taking oaths and petitioning for arms and assistance; the *fédérés* would submit their grievances and commissioners their reports.

The debates, which took place in the evening between five and ten o'clock, were filled with long speeches or would degenerate into a settling of scores. Neither the speakers, among whom Chabot distinguished himself more than Robespierre, nor the audience seemed prepared to take on their new, important role. The bureaucratic apparatus proved inadequate. The minutes of discussions were thought to be too succinct or inaccurate. A search was conducted for a reliable journalist, and new committees were set up, as the correspondence committee was overburdened. Contracts were developed with the *sections*. Since the meetings of the *sections* began at eight o'clock, the Jacobins were invited to address them. The Réunion *section* decided to meet only on the Jacobins' 'days off'.

Like the Parisians, patriots from the provinces and abroad would visit the club in the Rue Saint-Honoré. The Irish gave it their moral and financial support and asked for membership. To justify the 10 August rising, a message to the English was drafted. Civilians and soldiers would take advantage of a stay in the capital to denounce suspects to the Jacobins, provide information, and ask for advice. However, the affiliated clubs remained divided and few in number; they were often run by moderates. Some newly founded republican *sociétés* followed the Jacobin line before being recognized by the parent *société*. They were subject to harassment by local authorities, for example in Hyères and Marseillan, near Montpellier. In the towns, it was not unusual to find two rival *sociétés*.

Opposition was discouraged by the practice of taking decisions publicly by acclamation or show of hands. It was not majority that was being sought, but unanimity. Disagreement would be interpreted as a sign of weakness. Although the 'fine-mesh net', as it is commonly thought of, was extended only gradually to the whole of France, the Parisian club was seen even at the time as a rallying-point. Jacobin membership underwent a similar change in the capital and the provinces. The middle class and petty bourgeoisie came to the fore. Artisans and peasants were to be found alongside lawyers and priests. The 'first Terror' brought these groups closer to the people, who did not reject them. The poor remained in a minority, while the Jacobin ideal became that of the *sans-culottes*.

Jacobin ideology

What did Jacobinism represent at the time? In revolution, an ideology is measured by its effectiveness. Born of 'the passion for being right', ideology comprises a set of images and concepts, instruments of persuasion, and an emotional driving force, for it aims at convincing and leading to action. The climate of struggle fostered by ideology must provide both reasons for living and reasons for dying. The content of ideology is thus manifold: spiritual and concrete, personal and collective. By appealing to all these motivations, the Jacobin bourgeoisie succeeded in creating an amalgam whose roots go back to Roman history and the Enlightenment. Rousseau's influence is obvious, but Jacobinism simplified and implemented his ideas. Jacobinism derived its considerable strength from the dangers that threatened the Republic and from its own intransigence.

There was an element of mysticism in the Jacobin ideology, a religious character that manifested itself in its tenets and practice. It borrowed from Christianity its faith in the future and its striving for moral regeneration. Its dogmatism stemmed not from a rigid system, but from a handful of simple ideas that were commonly accepted and were capable of inspiring mass action. A carefully nurtured hatred of aristocracy and despotism constituted the key argument and favourite theme of Jacobinism. But Robespierre went beyond that hatred to proclaim the human dignity that was inseparable from freedom. Despotism corrupted morals, and it was corrupt men who supported it. For Robespierre, moral and civic conscience were linked, and this connection represents the first principle of virtue as he preached it in the Year II. He called upon the divinity to shackle the 'base and cruel passions', and appealed to reason to help man control his instincts and freely choose his way. The true republican had to respect himself before he could respect his fellow men, and he had to be worthy of his title of man and citizen. 'One does not count patriots; one weighs them...On the scales of justice, one patriot must outweigh a hundred thousand aristocrats.'

If the citizen could feel secure in his newly restored rights, he also had to carry out his duties. The citizen had signed a contract with the Republic, and could therefore appreciate the true significance of patriotism, which was no longer 'that exclusive love of the plot of land where we were born' but embraced the country whose laws embodied the general will. Homeland, liberty and virtue were inseparable. 'The place where virtue will flourish in the shadow of laws, where equality will reign among men, where the word "master" will be unknown, where man will be as nature made him, free and just – that will be the Frenchman's homeland.'[9] Hence the feeling 'of eternal and inexhaustible love for one's homeland' would suffice to commit the patriot to the Revolution. Patriotism, the mainstay and driving force of Jacobinism, would achieve its fullness in a society without barriers. For too long, patriotism has meant no more than blind allegiance to

[9] Quoted by A. Mathiez, *Annales Révolutionnaires*, 1921, p. 419.

king and clergy; but, beyond them, there now existed a national interest. The Revolution meant that there were no more *messieurs*, but only citizens who would address one another by the familiar *tutoiement*, as befitted their equal status.

As for the nation, which before 1789 had been defined as including only property-owners, it now comprised only patriots, who had to show unity in the face of the nation's enemies. Since the nation was striving to ensure the happiness of all its citizens, it required of them total selflessness. 'Men considered individually count for nothing!' The patriot did not exist outside of the nation, which was equated with the homeland; he owed the nation everything and achieved self-fulfilment through the sacrifices the nation demanded of him. When its existence was at stake, 'brothers, sisters, father and mother no longer counted; the Jacobins offered up all they had to their country'. A sort of neo-stoicism drove them to 'anticipate their natural fate'. In a society where 'egoism [had been replaced by] morality, chivalry by integrity, custom by principle', national unity depended on public trust. 'Brothers and friends' was more than a rhetorical phrase; it was a rallying-call and a profession of faith.

But whereas patriotism had once divided States and pitted them against one another, it now contained an appeal to unity among peoples. 'Mankind is one immense family to whom nature has given the earth as a realm and a home.' All men belonged to that family, regardless of colour or race, for they had to form a common front against their oppressors. National solidarity would guarantee universal brotherhood, and France showed the way. Despite deportation orders in eastern France, the Jewish people had won its place. The Midi celebrated the new-found understanding between Protestants and Catholics, and the Jacobins accepted a 'tribute' from a company of black volunteers. The threefold phrase 'Liberty, Equality, Fraternity', which Momoro had proposed in 1791, was soon engraved on the pediments of public buildings.

The longing for equality

'A State is close to ruin indeed whenever it offers the spectacle of extreme indigence alongside extreme affluence.'[10] Leclerc's dictum is an accurate expression of the patriots' attitude to social problems. Not

[10] Quoted in A. Soboul, *Les Sans-culottes parisiens* (5), p. 471.

only were such views held by eighteenth-century French liberals, Jacobins and *sans-culottes*, but they were to be shared by nineteenth-century socialists. A republic was inconceivable 'in a country where one class of individuals can devour the means of subsistence of several million men'. Robespierre, following Rousseau, condemned inequality in the name of moral principles and regarded opulence as 'the wages of crime'. He equated the struggle for social equality with the destruction of aristocracies, monopolies and privilege. But the democratic revolution demanded more: it sought equality of property, and threatened the very principle of property and its distribution.

It was vitally important for the republican State to avoid upsetting traditional patterns of ownership. The petty bourgeoisie, the peasantry, artisans and shopkeepers were aware of these policy constraints and accepted the tactfully presented compromises worked out by the State. Since perfect equality was just a utopian dream, and since the rich and poor were here to stay, a peaceful coexistence had to be devised. The notion of social rights according to which the community, as guarantor of individual rights, was entitled to control citizens' access to those rights gave the government the right to intervene in the distribution of wealth and goods. Public happiness depended on the law. Alongside equal opportunity, which allowed the citizen, within a certain time, to develop his faculties freely, there was the more immediately attainable equality of well-being, which could be achieved simply by destroying the 'extreme disproportion of wealth'. Equality would become truly meaningful when 'the immense gaps in happiness that separate men from one another' had disappeared. An appeal was made to the understanding and civic sense of the rich in order to carry out 'a gentle and peaceful revolution'. Saint-Just proclaimed this hope to mankind: 'Let Europe learn that you [the Convention] will no longer tolerate any unhappy man or oppressor on French territory; may this example multiply on earth; may it spread the love of virtues and of happiness. Happiness is a new idea in Europe.'

At the same time, the status of the poor was rehabilitated and distinguished from that of beggars and idlers. In a free country, poverty was respectable. The worker who obtained only his minimum needs while 'producing the rich man's gold' was considered poor; the worker who could not live on his earnings was considered indigent. Society owed them assistance and protection, as it did the defenders of the homeland in the form of aim and pensions, but there was a reluctance to enshrine broader obligations in law.

What we now call the 'living wage' the Jacobins proclaimed to be a matter of public policy, as they intended to make the rich support the poor. These intentions could have been interpreted with damaging consequences; the Jacobins preferred to assert as their principle the right to live and work, and this became the essential demand. Both Saint-Just — in his *Institutions républicaines* — and Robespierre stressed this first social principle, which took precedence over all others. In Hébert's works, 'one must eat, whatever the cost'. The people did not demand wealth, but they considered that in a Republic 'citizens ought to be able to live by their work'. Therefore, Hébert called for 'beneficent laws that will help to bring the price of food in line with the price of the poor man's labour'.

In fact, neither the Jacobins nor the *sans-culottes* intended to abolish individual property. On the contrary, they regarded it as a factor of emancipation and national cohesion as well as a guaranteed source of tax revenues. Robespierre defended property on the grounds that 'people own property primarily in order to live. It is untrue that property can ever be incompatible with men's subsistence.' For Billaud-Varenne, property was 'the linchpin of civil compacts', and could not therefore be exempt from the obligations imposed by circumstances. The State could impose limitations on land ownership and use. Far from being hostile to such restrictions, the peasantry had been calling for them for a long time. In late August 1792, it voiced its demands: farms were to have a maximum acreage of 150 *arpents** and the surplus, along with *biens nationaux*, was to be distributed among the indigent. By way of concessions to the peasantry, it was decided to allow the sale of *émigré* property in small plots and to divide up the commons. As for economic freedom, acceptable in 'ordinary times', it had to cease in times of crisis, when it might be carried to excess by 'homicidal cupidity'. There again it was enough to preserve the people against 'the monopolizer's brigandage'.

Principles and rights remained essentially intact even though, in the name of society, they were subject to what were felt to be temporary restrictions. It was necessary to 'be bold and accomplish as much good as possible' while respecting the traditional form of private property acquired by money. The Jacobin concept of democracy, shared by the vast majority of the people, was limited to a community of increasingly numerous small independent producers — peasants, artisans and

* About 150 acres. [Trans.]

tradesmen – among whom 'the State, through its laws, would ensure a rough equality'. Trotsky could thus, from this point of view, define Jacobinism as 'the highest degree of radicalism that bourgeois society can provide'. By playing on the working man's enduring hope of becoming a property-owner, Jacobinism was indissolubly linked to the revolutionary mentality.

The revolutionary mentality

The Jacobin, terrorist and *sans-culotte* attitudes, – all of which were characteristic of the patriots – were usually indistinguishable from one another. It was Jacobinism that shaped public opinion, forged collective consciousness, and guided the revolutionary struggle according to economic and social conditions. For revolutionary movements, Jacobinism provided leaders and objectives; for public opinion, it provided quintessential adversaries – the aristocrat and the rich egoist; for revolutionary dress, it provided emblems – the tricolour cockade and the Phrygian cap; for the crowds, it provided the slogans with which to voice enthusiastic support – 'Long live the Nation' and 'Long live the Republic'. The homeland had its altars, its priests were Jacobin, and its cult generated an infectious force. Propaganda, as well as the virtue of example, helped to create a common will and to 'condition the masses'. People listened more than they read, and acted more than they wrote. Speeches came to resemble sermons, and Jacobin societies became civic instruction centres. Crude popular reasoning, unused to political subtleties, sought simple and oft-repeated explanations. In the revolutionary phraseology, it adopted action verbs – keep watch over, pursue and punish; and vivid catch-phrases – 'War to the châteaux, peace for the cottages', 'Live free or die', and 'Better death than slavery'. The people adopted the 'Marseillaise',[11] the 'Carmagnole', and 'Ça ira', which were marching and victory songs. The secret of the Revolution lay in the creative activity of the masses. 'He who is not a revolutionary...is a nonentity.'

Private attitudes were changing along with collective ones. In this sense, the Jacobin Republic 'determined' the revolutionary. This shift has been interpreted as a return to animality and an unbridling of

---

[11] The first volunteers to sing the 'Marseillaise' were those of a battalion of the Rhône-et-Loire army in April 1792. The song was heard in Montpellier on 17 June, and on the 20th in Marseilles, from where the *fédérés* took it to Paris in July (J. Chailley, 'La Marseillaise et ses transformations jusqu'à nos jours', in *Actes du Congrès des Sociétés Savantes*, Lyons, 1964, vol. 1).

instinct. In any human society one finds weak elements who will cast off all restraints in order to conceal their true nature; but one also finds strong elements who preserve their self-control. Jacobinism, however, condemned excess and castigated corrupting and degrading behaviour. If the Revolution offered the spectacle of the best alongside the worst, it was because the two extremes are inherent in human nature. Moreover, revolutionary action involved the working population. In an age of low life expectancy, adulthood began early: a sixteen-year-old youth would regard himself as a man. From a very early age, the new generation was imbued with a sense of its future responsibilities. The intensity of commitments and the readiness to display enthusiasm and discouragement were the consequence of juvenile patterns of behaviour that persisted well beyond adolescence.

Besides, 'revolution' implies innovation, a break with traditions, customs and habits. The revolutionary, in his protest against the society around him, was in a minority position in that society. To impose his views, he resorted to force. 'It is through violence,' said Marat, 'that liberty must be established, and the time has come to organize temporarily the despotism of liberty.' The attitude of the revolutionary hardened as resistance stiffened. His feelings became more exclusive and intensified despite his own inclinations. Nevertheless, Jacobinism contained emotional ingredients that compensated for its coarse appearances: generosity, compassion and a certain tenderness towards the most destitute. The hope of a better world, the pride of helping to build it, and later the pride of belonging to it, stimulated the revolutionaries' imagination and resolve.

But discrepancies could exist between the private individual and the public figure who accepted civic duties, the first of which consisted in vigilance. Denunciation was not a sadistic pleasure, but an obligation. Concealing a danger through silence was reprehensible, and so was calumny. Yet, if paid informers were despised and women's gossip not taken too seriously, personal rivalries and expressions of impatience were given political significance. People were imprisoned on the strength of rumours and clapped in irons for trifling offences. Convinced as they were of the importance of their mission, the patriots claimed discretionary powers and often wasted time on pointless activities. It was easy to take advantage of their good faith, credulity and ignorance. Nevertheless, the malcontents expressed themselves more freely than has been thought.

By using threats and invective as a bogy and shield, the terrorist sought as much to frighten as to repress. Richard Cobb speaks of a 'demagogy of violence', and escalation at the subordinate level of those who carried out orders. Such excesses led to braggadocio and unreasonable behaviour verging on recklessness and absurdity. Thus braggarts far from home could secure at minimum expense their reputation as patriots, especially when that reputation was not impeccable. In the nation in arms, swords and pistols were used to display ferocity. The agents of authority – civilian and military – would surround themselves with an impressive retinue and take along the guillotine. In September 1792, the commissioners of the Commune were reported to have posted sanguinary proclamations in northern France: 'Put up the scaffolds; let the ramparts be studded with gallows; may whoever is not with us be immolated on them at once.' A few months earlier, it had been suggested that priests should be drowned in dredgers in the port of Brest. Other similar projects were discussed without being carried out, and Leclerc was criticized for having driven the Lyonnais to despair by his mad preachings.

Although he is not to be confused with a minority of 'cut-throats and brigands' who have passed into legend, the revolutionary was no saint. He indulged in useless cruelty and gratuitous brutality. For that matter, the other camp resorted to identical methods. Killing to avoid being killed is one of war's monstrous realities, but it can hardly serve as an excuse. Most revolutionaries were a far cry from the ideal portrayed by Saint-Just: 'The revolutionary is unyielding but also reasonable, frugal and simple without displaying an unnecessary false modesty; he is the irreconcilable enemy of every lie, of every indulgence, of every pretension.'

There was indeed a Jacobin puritanism, judging by written documents and public statements. The language of the *Père Duchesne* shocked the members of the club in the Rue Saint-Honoré. Jacobins condemned gambling, prostitution, stylishness, luxury and celibacy; they hunted down obscene pictures and books, which they saw as part of the aristocracy's arsenal, on a par with humour and *le bel esprit*.

On the other hand, there was considerable popular indulgence towards drunkenness; merrymaking was condoned. The high level of wine and spirit consumption undoubtedly influenced terrorist attitudes. The September 'slaughterers' were accused of having acted out of drunken excitement. They were sometimes tempted by their victims' cellars, and by those of the *émigrés*, which were pillaged with impunity by the guards assigned to watch over seized property. The volunteer demanded his brandy ration no less than his bread, the better to overcome his fatigue and his fears.

Having become national and revolutionary, the war at last enabled the individual to assert himself both privately and publicly. Whereas it 'had seemed about to confirm our downfall', the war saved France, for it 'kept the people alert, ardent and adamant'. Although the war was external to the Revolution, it reinforced Jacobin power and deepened the rift between rich and poor, between property-owners and the working classes (*les bras nus*).

VALMY

The war, presented by Isnard and Brissot's bourgeois supporters as the irresistible expansionism of liberty, fired the popular imagination. 'The French nation always believed that the eternal book of nature and reason was an infallible piece of propaganda, more powerful than its orators and pamphlets.' The Revolution infused the people with a new strength that made it invincible. 'Liberty's banner is that of victory.' In the excitement of its recent deliverance, France forged ahead to liberate Europe and mankind. This glowing picture masked a reprehensible state of military unpreparedness, and the first defeats were interpreted as acts of treason against the people, who were forced by the invasion to take the conduct of the war into their own hands. 'Come,' Robespierre was exclaiming by late July 1792, 'the [French] people must carry the weight of the world on their shoulders; they must be among peoples what Hercules was among heroes.' The issues at stake were no longer ideological, but had taken on an unforeseen social dimension. The conservative bourgeoisie joined the clan of sovereigns.

The new army

Of all the major institutions of State, the army had undergone the deepest but least spectacular change. It was no longer a frozen society, and on 10 August it had ceased to be the royal army. Had it become, at the same time, the army of democracy?

The emigration of officers and the integration of volunteers in 1791 had considerably modified the structure and ethos of the fighting forces. In mid-1792 the army's strength reached 300,000 men, of whom two-thirds belonged to line regiments. Barely one-tenth of petty officers and soldiers had taken part in the campaigns of the *ancien régime*. The vast majority, composed of young elements, had enlisted since

1789. Small peasants, journeymen and unemployed men, attracted by bonuses higher than the average yearly wage of a labourer with board and lodgings, were easily convinced by the 'recruitment sergeants'. They enjoyed the prospect of guaranteed meals, and hardship encouraged enrolments. Minimum height requirements were eased, and the legal age was lowered to sixteen.

Enlistments were prompted as much for family reasons as by the economic situation and lack of resources. All of France was more or less represented in the army. Peasants came to be in a distinct majority, although their numbers never reached proportions comparable to their strength in the nation at large. As for the humble townsfolk, such as shop employees and apprentices, they maintained their numbers, whereas foreign regiments shrank considerably.

The cavalry, which remained the noble arm, had a greater proportion of blue-bloods. It looked down on the 'rank and file' infantry, whose officers included more commoners than the cavalry, although there were still many *ci-devants* in the higher echelons. These officers still considered soldiering a privileged profession, and regarded themselves primarily as soldiers rather then citizens. Their professional experience and training acquired under the monarchy were precious assets. Some officers had risen slowly through the ranks; more than half of the captains were over forty years old. Most came from the towns and a fair number from the capital. They comprised a high proportion of lawyers, doctors, tutors and priests who preferred uniforms to cassocks. Noblemen and bourgeois were grateful to the Revolution for making promotion easier, but 'epaulette solidarity' militated against popular recruitment.

The volunteer, who had a reputation for inexperience, was still looked on by officers as a civilian. He had difficulty integrating himself and preserved his individuality by staying close to relatives and friends. Without warning, he did not hesitate to change units, disappear, then join up again. Regimental officers had some difficulty keeping track of troop strength. The volunteers' behaviour was ascribed to rivalry with the line, but not enough attention was paid to such capriciousness, which weakened military ethos and underscored the army's hybrid origins.

The volunteers of 1792

The army had not got over its growing pains when it had to make room for the levy of 1792, which brought its strength up to 400,000 men. The new intake, as specified in a decree of 12 July, included

auxiliaries for the line regiments and 42 battalions of volunteers, most
of whom were in fact conscripts: every *département* was required to
provide its quota of men, with each *canton* contributing its share. The
département of the Mayenne, for example, had to fill a quota of 1,100.
As the harvest was already under way, the rural population was less
than enthusiastic. Cash bonuses helped to persuade the poorest country
folk to join, and the rest were chosen by lottery or election. Those who
attempted to avoid conscription were liable to be executed just like any
counter-revolutionary. Property-owners resisted these inroads on their
manpower supply. Mental defectives, as well as men who were ill or
too short, were enrolled but later had to be discharged. Many conscripts
with wives and children worried about the fate of their families, who
sometimes actually accompanied them.

Yet such tepidness and reticence was no widespread. In regions
directly threatened with invasion, whole villages answered the call. It
was reported to the Jacobins on 14 September that a priest had put
himself in command of fifteen of his parishioners. In Paris, 15,000
volunteers signed up in a single week; the town of Saint-Denis offered
400 of its inhabitants. In large towns, municipalities and *sociétés
populaires* encouraged departures, which were celebrated with pomp
and with the population taking part. On the whole, the peasantry was
represented by labourers, domestics and sons of large families; the social
background of urban recruits was inferior to what it had been in 1791,
for both soldiers and national guard officers. Nearly half of the captains
were clerks, office-workers and artisans, but most were of rural origin.

Patriotism largely made up for lack of military instruction. These
were 'men of good will, brave and ardent'. They rushed at once to
the borders, without uniforms or weapons, led by officers whom they
had themselves just elected but who knew neither where nor how to
guide them. In a report dated 9 September from Châlons, Billaud-
Varenne described their advance as 'a single encampment extending
from the Place de Grève up to the armies'. Shunning the carts put at
their disposal, the soldiers marched singing 'Let us watch over the safety
of the Empire'* and, as they went through villages, shouted 'Long live
the Nation! Long live the *sans-culottes*!' They kept no account of their
time or their fatigue. Although they blocked roads and hampered the

---

* 'Veillons au salut de l'Empire' were the opening words of a well-known revolutionary
  song, later mistakenly believed to have been written during the First Empire. 'Empire'
  simply stands for 'France', and was frequently used in this sense by members of the
  Constituent and Legislative Assemblies. [Trans.]

movement of organized troops, they conveyed the impression of a massive and resolute levy. They did not seem concerned with order and discipline. Parisians proved to be the most unruly. Irregular companies were denounced for being filled with doubtful elements, publicans and suspects, who used this subterfuge to escape from the capital and avoid imprisonment. In order to survive, they did not hesitate to plunder, some of them indulging in 'excesses unworthy of soldiers of a free people'.

Legions too were created haphazardly. First came national infantry companies recruited among Parisian guards, together with Belgian, Batavian and Liégeois battalions topped up by French volunteers and compatriots who had deserted the Austrian army. Swiss members of former royal regiments also joined for a campaign. Some generals raised private armies in the provinces. All these formations tried to maintain their autonomy and the right to elect their officers. This anarchic trend posed a threat to army unity, and the authorities feared the intrigues of a handful of ambitious men. As for the *fédérés* who had taken part in the 10 August rising, some, like the Marseillais and the Brestois, went home, while others assembled in the Soissons camp.

The contingents assigned to join the line troops were integrated fairly quickly and their training began. The first attempts at brigading and amalgamation date from this period.[12] Apart from an increase in regiment strength, the regular army underwent no major change; only its ethos was altered. The army made closer contacts with civilian society and participated in patriotic demonstrations. The Paris Jacobins sent it newspapers. Although the army was wary of the volunteers of 1792 because of their extremist views, their presence accelerated the change of attitude. Soldiers everywhere called for patriotic leadership, the right to purge officers and choose those who inspired confidence. Lafayette's treason increased suspicions towards nobles. A proposal was made on 29 August to replace all the chiefs of staff, but the executive kept the right to appoint high-ranking officers on the sole basis of their military competence.

Similarly, there was no sudden change in tactics. A preference was still shown for deploying lines rather than massive columns protected by skirmishers and artillery. For a long time, the cavalry was regarded as inadequate. Officers hesitated to throw the full strength of their

---

[12] See J. P. Bertaud, *Valmy* (40), pp. 213–15 and below, chapter 4. Amalgamation combined line troops and volunteers at battalion level, while brigading brought together one line battalion and two volunteer battalions in a half-brigade.

ardently patriotic troops into frontal attacks. But mass combat soon imposed itself and transformed the character of the war. No less than the courage of the French troops, mass combat bewildered the enemy.

Supplies and transport

While the army was becoming the people's army, its non-combatant services were finding it impossible to cope with increased troop strength. If they were used to camps, stores and garrisons, they could not handle the constant troop movements. There was a shortage of war commissioners, quartermasters and travelling bakeries. Officers were given no marching orders; they took away plough-horses and confiscated weapons. On 4 September, the Conseil Exécutif authorized the purchase of supplies by private treaty and the requisition of transport. Volunteers would turn up in trousers and canvas smocks, sleep on the ground even in the rain, and have to be sent back. The army was short of everything – money, arms and ammunition. Even line regiments were lacking vital equipment. Dumoriez's 20,000 men had only two hours' worth of cartridges. Muskets stopped firing when triggers rusted and when grease and flintstones ran out. The bayonet then became, out of necessity, the only offensive weapon, like the wooden-handled pike that was given out to new arrivals.

The feeling of abandonment that ensued provoked uncontrollable collective reactions. The impatient recruits, who had come to fight, showed their disappointment, revolted against incompetence, and discovered treason everywhere. If gunpowder or food was soaked in a downpour, the authorities were to blame. Missed shots were ascribed to bad workmanship. The ruts that made roads impassable were caused by the negligence of the Ponts et Chaussées. The army's own couriers were suspected of communicating with the enemy and conveying French gold to him. Constant comings and goings helped to spread false reports.

Although the population did not traditionally welcome the arrival of troops, it made up for the shortcomings of the authorities. Thanks to local inhabitants, there were never any prolonged or total shortages of food. When the enemy approached, civilians waged their own combat. 'Their unbelievable enthusiasm and above all their exasperation against us are beyond all measure and exceed the means at their disposal,' noted the Prussians on 20 August. When the Prussians drew near, the people hid in the woods, set up ambushes, and hunted down isolated convoys and laggards. Soldiers and civilians were serving a common cause: that of the homeland and the Revolution.

Victory or mere cannonade?

In the flurry of this magnificent and disorderly onslaught, the exact position of the line regiments was unknown on 11 September, whereas Austrians and Prussians were thought to be everywhere. Nine days later, at daybreak, the troops led by Dumoriez and Kellermann, soaked by the rain and wading through the mud of the Argonne, took up positions on the heights of Valmy. Their objective was to cut off the enemy from the road to Châlons and Paris. They resorted to improvised tactics on unfamiliar ground. Company commanders, left to their own initiatives, showed their worth by creating diversions, occupying salients – including the windmill – and putting their field artillery in the right place.

Witnesses remembered a 'very heavy' cannonade that lasted four hours, the impeccable Prussian manoeuvre, and the unexpected resistance of French volunteers. The explosion of a powder convoy nearly provoked a panic, which Kellermann managed to avoid before launching a frontal attack, while on his right Stengel held the enemy in check. At the end of the day, the Prussian commander-in-chief – the Duke of Brunswick – and his king ordered a halt to the fighting, and their troops bivouacked on the Plateau de la Lune. Losses were put at some five hundred officers and soldiers and about one hundred horses, including Kellermann's which was killed under him. For a reasonable cost, in military terms, Valmy had achieved the desired result. Although Dumoriez could have made use of his victory, he hesitated to take advantage of the Prussian withdrawal and preferred to negotiate. 'We have fortunately marched three days without the enemy bothering to follow us; if it had, we should have had to abandon all our equipment', wrote one of Brunswick's officers. The Prussian army recrossed the border without being attacked, except by dysentery.

Because of these circumstances, Valmy did not immediately acquire the symbolic value later bestowed upon it by Goethe and other writers. Once the danger had been averted, the fighters congratulated themselves on having escaped it, then expressed a pride in their dead that was shared by the Assembly and the population. This first victory of the young Republic shook reactionary optimism and restored the patriots' confidence. For fifteen hours, an army that had been subjected to ridicule had held in check the world's best-trained army. An army of young men – two-thirds were under twenty-five – an army of peasants and unemployed weavers who were undergoing their baptism by fire, had overcome their fear just like old soldiers. Despite the number of troops engaged – nearly a hundred thousand – they had shown unity and discipline. The army of the revolutionary people had thus proved its efficiency, and had also revealed the secrets of that efficiency. However, the volunteers' zeal, courage and abnegation were sustained at Valmy by structures inherited from the *ancien régime*. The officers included a number of old-fashioned tacticians. National solidarity had merged with military ethos. In combat, the soldier-citizen became temporarily a mere soldier reduced to obeying orders. This imperative could not be applied to the 'democracy in arms', an unorganized and anarchic mass by definition. In the Year II, this lesson, along with the others, was to be remembered.

The enthusiasm of victory coincided with the first sessions of the Convention. A sense of relief and a more relaxed atmosphere followed the 'first Terror'. Now revolutionary 'legality' surrendered its prerogative to the promised Constitution. Volunteers continued to assemble in the camps, where they were settled and provided – as well as could be expected – with uniforms, an administration and a flag. The volunteers fell back into line.

2

The divorce of the bourgeoisies

The rivalry between the *Gironde* and the *Montagne*, which was at the centre of the political scene, is still seen as a partisan dispute. Modern observers measure the personalities and attitudes of the Revolution according to present-day standards and assume emotional stances more appropriate to factional quarrels; cut and dried judgements are made for or against each side. Generosity is attributed to one camp and denied to the other, categorically and without proof. The polemical exchanges between Aulard and Mathiez, which were not limited to Danton, encouraged this sectarianism. The verbal sparring and impassioned debates make one lose sight of the socio-economic context that affected the masses. Even the war itself, despite the weight of its presence, is reduced to a mere backdrop. So hard is it to discern the real factors at work that the *girondin* period of the Convention still remains very obscure.

The *girondin* Convention has never been studied as thoroughly as the popular movement. The forces acting on the established bourgeoisie assume, by contrast, an improvised character that foreign historians, unused to the term 'bourgeois', find surprising. Thus, the American historian George V. Taylor observes that the Revolution is no longer bourgeois if one defines the bourgeois as a capitalist, and Robert Palmer suggests that one should replace 'bourgeois' by a more clearly defined social grouping. Surely, in a given social category, there is room for opposing points of view that diverge from collective attitudes – room for leaders and camp followers.

There are a number of biographies that describe the background, education and occupations of the *conventionnels*; yet there has been no sociological analysis of the popular vote in the various elections, which were upset to a greater or lesser extent by events. What do we know about the relations between elected representatives and primary assemblies, the composition of those assemblies, the participation of former 'passive' citizens, the abstention of a portion of the electorate and its motivations? The re-election in November 1792 of administrative and judiciary bodies raises the same problems, and local returns, which have been insufficiently examined, are still very fragmentary.

One certainty, however, does emerge: in the universal suffrage contest social conservatives won the day, and the politics of the *Gironde* relied on that majority trend, which, although it was more visible in the provinces, also made itself felt in the capital. The electorate's patriotic choice did not rule out, in the minds of the elected representatives, the freedom to apply personal solutions to the problems at hand. Disagreements consequently arose over concrete issues: the king's trial, the European Coalition, the Vendée, high prices (*la vie chère*). These passions cannot be explained by the personalities of the 'ambitious puppets' usually regarded as the sole participants in the struggle. There was more than the conquest of power at stake. The people, who judged its representatives by their deeds, placed its trust in the boldest of them. The fall of the *Gironde* meant the temporary eclipse of the conservative bourgeoisie and the arrival of a new governing 'team' that enjoyed wide popular support.

Hence the distance between the two sides has to be evaluated on the basis of the solutions they put forward or accepted. Not only did the notables who supported the *girondin* government for nearly a year – from June 1792 onwards – prove incapable of resolving long-term economic problems, but they also allowed the situation to deteriorate to the point where half-measures could no longer work. In that sense, the social opposition unwittingly paved the way for a policy of rigour.

The democratic revolution proposed decisive solutions to the victorious people. The electoral system – the bedrock of political liberalism – was no longer adequate for choosing delegates who would faithfully express the people's will. The enemy invasion and the shortcomings of public officials justified special measures that the country would have accepted, but the decrees of 11 and 12 August preserved the old procedures. Universal suffrage thus became a symbolic gift. There was no need for an election campaign, for the patriots' unanimity could be taken for granted. But the patriots made their choices on the basis of civic merits and political attitudes displayed in circumstances prior to the insurrection. The resulting widespread confusion worked against the *sans-culottes*.

Predictably, the moderates regained their self-assurance and, with

Roland's support, sacrificed egalitarian hopes. The 'sovereign' people, victim of its own inexperience, surrendered to its notables. On the whole, the Convention represented neither the spirit of 10 August nor the popular will, but bourgeois society in all its diversity. No sooner had it met than it tore itself asunder.

THE 'NATIONAL' CONVENTION AND POLITICAL RIVALRIES

In the little time it had left, the Legislative Assembly tried to make up for the drawbacks of a wider electorate by instituting a two-tier franchise. The right to vote was now granted to Frenchmen over twenty-one who had a permanent residence and worked for their living (domestics included). Thus between three and four million 'passive' Frenchmen acquired overnight a citizenship for which they seemed unprepared. How many appreciated it for what it was worth, and how many availed themselves of it? The most ardent among them, who had left for the armies, were not there to lead the masses. An infinitesimal proportion turned out at the primary assemblies from 26 August onwards – barely one-tenth of the electorate, or 700,000 out of seven million, a figure close to the number of voters under the 'franchise monarchy'. For the first time, however, the humble folk took part, even though the true turn-out is hard to evaluate.

Electors and representatives

The 'working class' that spoke up in the urban *sections* often refrained from doing so in the countryside. The prevailing impression, as described by Jaurès, was one of bourgeois preponderance, the first signs of which were manifest in the choice of electors. They had to be over twenty-five, and their number was determined, as in 1791, by the *département*'s population: in the Haute-Marne, there were 405, in the Marne, 540. The electoral assemblies that met in each *chef-lieu* after 2 September comprised between 300 and 600 members. The selection of representatives was therefore in the hands of an insignificant minority, but one determined to save the Revolution and establish the Republic.

Who composed this minority? The civil service bourgeoisie, free professionals, landlords, wealthy farmers and entrepreneurs exerted their sway over intimidated artisans and peasants who had little time to spare. In the interior, procedures were slower: assemblies evaluated candidates' merits, weighed criticism and blame, and insisted on an absolute majority and a secret ballot. Sometimes polling continued beyond 20 September. But in northern and eastern France, the alarming news, the influx of volunteers, and the fear of famine shortened the elections. The assemblies voted to sit in permanent session, then melted away during the final days. The censure of candidates, voting by acclamation, and relative majorities all helped to keep away nobles, priests and the rich. Electors obeyed the watchwords circulated by the Jacobins as early as 22 August. Apart from proven patriotism, candidates had to display the 'triple features of commendable talent, a strong will and a blameless life'. Few *sans-culottes* felt educated enough to run for office, or competent enough to hold one.

In the capital, the situation was identical. The Paris assembly, which had no more than 525 voters, sat at the club in the Rue Saint-Honoré in order to be accessible to a wider public. Robespierre, who was the first to be elected, did his best to influence the vote, which was conducted orally under public scrutiny. Chabot supported Marat's candidacy, which was approved, as was that of the Duc d'Orléans, while Kersaint, the *feuillants* and Brissot's clients were eliminated – but they triumphed in the provinces.

The rules required one alternate (*suppléant*) for every three representatives – eight for twenty-four in Paris, almost all of them Jacobins. The final number of candidates elected was 1,080, of whom 780 were called to the Convention, but multiple elections reduced that figure to 749. Carra, who was so unpopular with the Commune, won a majority in seven *départements*, Condorcet in five, Dubois-Crancé and Thomas Paine in four, Sieyès and Brissot in three. At the national level the electorate proved remarkably stable and confirmed its earlier choices.

Over a third of the *conventionnels* – lawyers, *notaires*, solicitors and former public prosecutors – already held public office. Many had sat in the Constituent and Legislative Assemblies. There were also some nobles, including Philippe Egalité and Lepeletier de Saint-Fargeau, and about fifty clergymen, including seventeen juror bishops and three Protestant ministers.[1] Whereas Saint-Just was barely twenty-five years old, most representatives were middle-aged and propertied family men. The doyen, an Auvegnat, Rudel, was seventy-three years old. Several

[1] In 1791, Louis Philippe Joseph, Duc d'Orléans, secured a decree from the Paris Commune allowing his family to use the name 'Egalité' in perpetuity.

of the bourgeois members were wealthy, like Cambon and Oudot, who had about one hundred thousand *livres* each in 1780. The *conventionnels*, who had been initiated in Latin language and culture by Oratorians and Jesuits, had no trouble reliving the happy days of the Roman Republic.

Despite universal suffrage, the nation's representatives boasted only two workers, Armonville, from Reims, and Noël Pointe, a gunsmith from Saint-Etienne. Jacobin propaganda did not achieve the expected results. By 5 October, only 113 representatives had joined the Paris club and the provincial *sociétés* were getting worried. Couthon reprimanded the 'false friends' and stressed the need for unity. The conquest of power by legal means constituted the key objective and it required the support of popular forces. The Jacobins were not 'gentle visionaries' nor was Jacobinism a romantic ideal. Patriots already had their eyes on positions of power and did not conceal their aims. These posts were already occupied by 'clever and very ambitious men' who 'wanted the Republic only because they enjoyed the support of public opinion and counted on the Republic to perpetuate their influence'. With the stakes thus defined, any compromise between *girondins* and *montagnards* became unthinkable. On the left- and right-hand sides of the Salle du Manège, they were already facing each other like adversaries. Their fight could cease only by the total elimination of one of the two currents.

'*Girondins*' and '*montagnards*'

The two groups belonged to the same professional categories, shared a similar education, and had a comparable outlook and way of life. These 'enemy brothers' possessed the attributes of integrity, courage, abnegation, authority and perseverence in equal measure. They had the same means at their disposal. Blood was not a frightening prospect for them provided it was usefully shed. Strenuous attempts were made to label them as political parties and to read a disciplined pattern into their votes, whereas in fact they confined themselves to voting as their conscience dictated. Whatever tags were stuck on them, the *conventionnels* were die-hard individualists. Their discordance manifested itself through attitudes rather than doctrinal imperatives.

Patriots, republicans and revolutionaries only gradually expressed their differences of opinion. Their respective positions had first been asserted over the issue of the declaration of war. As *Le Courrier extraordinaire* of 4 April 1792 observed: 'M. Robespierre had some enemies among the Jacobins; MM. Isnard, Guadet and Basire gave the impression of climbing half-way down from the summit of the *Montagne*.' Although the two groups were still united in their hatred of aristocracy and their love of liberty, personal rancour embittered their relations. Disputes over prestige between Danton and Roland and rivalries for influence with Robespierre were exploited by Manon Roland, an intelligent, assertive and possessive woman.[2] She manipulated 'Barbaroux, with whom she was thought to be in love, Buzot, whom she did love, and Louvet, who was privy to that passion'. The *rolandiste* clan haunted her salon and that of Valazé, the *philosophes* and foreign liberals gathered at Condorcet's, and the correspondents of *Le Patriote français* met at Brissot's.

However, one cannot overstress the class politics that the *girondins* were led to adopt by their constituents. 'Just look at how the rich are rallying to their support...Well, they are the *honnêtes gens*, the respectable people of the Republic; we are the *sans-culottes*, the rabble.' Robespierre had no trouble identifying himself with the people, whom Vergniaud regarded as a 'herd race' whose fate it was to be led. *Montagnards* and *girondins*, along with their electors, split after 10 August over the question of the nature of democracy. 'I think that M. Brissot is a republican', observed the journalist and representative Robert, 'but not in the same way as the Jacobins. There are different kinds of republics.' Brissot, who invoked 'free America', made room in his republic for 'an elected king' and 'the aristocracy of property'.

To consolidate their influence, the *girondins* were not afraid of resorting to the monarchy. They corresponded with d'Antraigues's friends and invoked the name of Liberty the better to conceal their designs. The plans they were working on in private reflected their desire to strengthen the executive. They wanted a Republic of notables, strong government and economic liberalism. Their notion of public credit and wealth was predicated, as that of Calonne had been, on appearances. The *girondins* claimed to protect the value of the *assignat*, which was financing their ruinous war, while the *Révolutions de Paris* denounced the scandalous profits of army contractors, 'true vampires' who, under Servan's protection, 'would shortly reduce the French Republic to a bare skeleton'.

Although they did not personally belong to the world of big merchants, the *girondins* supported their views and those of shippers,

---

[2] Marie Jeanne Phlipon, who had married the minister Roland de la Platière.

manufacturers and 'money men', not for political reasons – for they had no coherent policy – but out of conservatism and, perhaps, because of certain sympathies with the physiocrats. The *girondins* regarded landed wealth and commercial capital as the only factors of social consolidation; they clung, as if to a lifeline, to the principle of property, the only confiscation they tolerated being that directed against declared enemies of the nation – the same confiscation as practised by absolutism. Any authoritarian restriction, however justified, however necessary, was anathema to them for it could set in motion a disastrous process.

Couthon momentarily shared this fear when he deplored the presence in the Convention of 'excessively opinionated persons whose weakness was conducive to anarchy'. Chabot put the number of these *enragés* – including himself and Marat – at about fifty. The *girondins*, using the *loi agraire* as a bogy, won the support of the propertied bourgeoisie and spoke in its name. As for the *montagnards*, they identified with the Jacobins and Jacobinism. Their supporters included rural artisans and smallholders. To improve the condition of the poor and of consumers, they did not hesitate to challenge the rights of the producer and the capitalist. The *montagnards*, who displayed both opportunism and boldness, were cautious realists and looked with favour only on initiatives compatible with the national interest. These defenders of the people's cause remained bourgeois and steered clear of extremes. If they dominated the Paris club and the Commune, they did not represent the capital alone; for the most part, they were provincials, like the *girondins*.

Too much has been made of the antagonism between Paris and the provinces – a friction that served as a propaganda and combat weapon. The resistance of the *départements* to centralization was symbolized by the desire to reduce the capital of the Revolution to its one-eighty-third share of influence. Much as the *Gironde* wished to remove the Assembly from a city dominated by 'agitators and flatterers of the people', it did not at the time encourage an aggressive federalism that would have run counter to its political ambitions. To be more specific, the 'party struggle' had a dual aspect: hatred in the pursuit of private vendattas, and blindness in the defence of class interests.

Parliamentary struggles and propaganda

After a 'three-day truce', the conflict between the *Gironde* and the *Montagne* broke out with immoderate violence, both in the Assembly and in the country. The power to draft a new constitution put immense means in the hands of the majority party. But each camp had roughly the same number of representatives. The undecided members of the *Plaine* (or *Marais*) – the Convention's centrists – had to be wooed. Their politics and social background drew them towards the *girondins*, with whom they voted at first, thereby ensuring *girondin* chairmanship of debates. The centrists were impressed by the eloquence of *girondin* speakers like Vergniaud and by Dumoriez's military successes. With the approval of the *Marais*, the special powers inherited from 10 August were abolished, the Commune was deprived of its *comité de surveillance*, and the *commissaires de l'exécutif* were recalled. The special tribunal that had failed to condemn the defenders of the Tuileries was dismantled.

Although centrist support remained conditional, it did enable the *Gironde* to gain control of parliamentary committees. Condorcet chaired the Constitutional Committee, and Brissot the Diplomatic Committee. Only the Committee of General Security came to the Jacobins to declare, through its spokesman Hérault de Séchelles, 'that it wanted to act only with them and in accordance with their policy'. It is true that by then the *girondins*' slanderous and heavy-handed attacks were antagonizing the Convention and the *sans-culottes*. For example, the *girondins* demanded of Danton – who was not hostile towards them – an account of his secret expenditure, and accused him of having profited from a theft from the national furniture depository. Louvet tried in vain to prove Robespierre guilty of dictatorial schemes 'so absurd that even those who did not want to know the full story were reduced to silence'. The *girondin* members from Paris condemned the 10 August rising.

Instead of cleansing the political atmosphere, these first weeks furthered the confusion of public opinion. Thanks to Roland, the *girondin* newspapers had talent, experience and ready money. They borrowed the methods and arguments of the royalist pamphleteers, heaping equal scorn on 'Marat the *septembriseur*' and 'Robespierre the dictator'. Manon Roland contributed her impassioned ardour to this 'shaping of public opinion' and drafted her husband's proclamations, whose poisonous content spread freely and penetrated into the *sociétés populaires* with the help of civil servants. The parent *société* lacked the financial means to strike back; it asked its affiliated clubs for a supplementary contribution to pay for correspondence and leaflets. In order to 'smuggle out the truth', Robespierre, in mid-October, launched the *Lettres à ses commettans* (Letters to his constituents).

Gradually, the *Plaine* grew weary of the bombast and verbal violence that it seemed to be endorsing. Several of its members – and hardly the least influential – Cambon, Carnot and Barère, chose the *Montagne*. The *girondin* plan for surrounding the Convention with a guard from the *départements* was scrapped. The *girondins* became the Republic's 'schemers' and 'seditious elements'. Some ministers broke with Roland, who was expelled from the Jacobin club along with Louvet, Lanthenas and Girey-Dupré, editor of *Le Patriote français*. Pétion finally lost control of the Hôtel de Ville. The moderate Chambon was flanked by Chaumette and Hébert, the 'Père Duchesne'. Public opinion in the capital had punished the *girondins*, and it was hard for the *sans-culottes* to bear the high price of foodstuffs. In the countryside, wealthy farmers were worried by *girondin* set-backs and contradictions.

However, the war seemed to prove the *girondins* right, and the evacuation of enemy troops from French territory helped to preserve confidence in their policies for a time. The processions of foreigners that filed past in the Assembly expressed endorsement by the subject peoples. There was a widespread notion of a French Republic surrounded by sister nations delivered by her and voicing boundless gratitude. Savoy welcomed Montesquiou as a liberator on 24 September and Anselme entered Nice on the 29th. The Rhineland welcomed Custine and the Austrians lifted the siege of Lille. Dumoriez routed them on 6 November and occupied all of Belgium. The victory of Jemappes, won by sheer numerical strength and repeated assaults, was regarded as a happy omen by the Convention, which learned the news three days after the event. The army of the Revolution was living up to the promises of Valmy.

CONFRONTATIONS

As the *Gironde* felt power slipping from its hands, it hardened its attitudes and moved closer to moneyed interests, which saw the war as a source of profit. In addition, for all moderates, the domestic and foreign situation depended on the fate in store for the king. Was there not a danger of provoking an uprising in rural France? 'Sparing him would have saved the Republic from many woes.' But could the Republic be established without the king's disappearance? To absolve him would be to condemn 10 August and repudiate Jacobinism. 'Louis must die because the homeland must live.' Thus the issue at stake went far beyond the safeguarding of a dynasty and a constitutional principle.

It posed a painful moral dilemma for representatives, citizens and all Catholics. The determination, logic and self-confidence of a minority carried the day.

In the revolutionary process, this episode was a decisive step. The execution of Capet involved the responsibility of the entire nation, which thus implicated itself both in a brutal break with the past and in a huge conflict with Europe all of whose consequences it had to accept.

The king's trial and the 'sacrilegious' execution

Jacobins, patriots and *fédérés* were convinced of Louis XVI's guilt. The betrayed people called for justice. In Strasburg, his portrait had been veiled, and by 27 August the Mont-de-Marsan club was demanding the punishment of the 'crowned traitor, criminal and faithless'. For the Commune, which was guarding him, the king was the nation's hostage. The insurrection had marked the opening of his trial: 'His sentence was his fall from power; his punishment was that required to ensure the people's freedom.'

After the king's collusion with foreign powers and the counter-revolution had been revealed, the 'Committee of 24' set up to examine the charges stalled for one full month. Valazé's report, presented on 6 November, convinced the *montagnards* and public opinion that the legal problems invoked – royal immunity and parliamentary incompetence – concealed a determination to save the king by every possible means. Roland was unwise enough to order the opening in secret of the iron chest of the Tuileries,[3] thus exposing himself to the charge of having made off with compromising documents. In any event, the remaining papers were damaging enough for Dumoriez and the *girondin* leaders. Now Jacques Roux at the Gravilliers *section*, followed by all of the forty-eight Paris *sections*, demanded that Louis XVI should be tried by the Convention, which finally decided to do so on 3 December after a memorable speech by Robespierre. The *sans-culottes*, whose feelings he expressed, accompanied him in triumphant procession to the club in the Rue Saint-Honoré, where he was greeted by a tremendous ovation. The debates continued without a break until 7 January and were marked by many vicissitudes.

---

[3] In this secret chest, installed in a corridor wall by the locksmith Gamain and Louis XVI himself, the king kept in particular his correspondence with his fellow monarchs and *émigré* brothers.

As it was expected that incidents would be provoked and blamed on the Jacobins, proceedings had to be swift. 'The people do not try like courts of justice, they cast lightning; they do not condemn kings, they plunge them back into oblivion.' Nevertheless, legal precautions were taken at the trial. The king appeared, he was questioned, and his defence counsels were given a hearing.[4] Such an act had to appear impressive and solemn to the world; it was also necessary to allay the scruples of representatives who, against their will, were about to set themselves up as judges.

Nor could the Convention remain indifferent to the pressures that were being put on it. A host of brochures were circulating with descriptions of the royal family's misfortunes and of the king's nobility of soul, patience and dignity. In eastern France, priests openly linked his cause to that of religion. In every province, manifestations of sympathy called for clemency. The idea of an armed force to protect the Assembly from agitators was revived. At the theatre in Bordeaux, spectators asked for mercy for 'Monsieur Veto'. In Rouen, in the Place de la Rougemare, the public signed a petition containing the same request. There were gatherings in the Ardèche, the Vendée and Brittany, but their importance was exaggerated. Although afraid to side with the royalists, part of the population took pity on the man who still represented some notion of eternal France.

Much has been made of the attempts by foreign courts, including those of the Spanish Chargé d'Affaires, Ocariz, to buy representatives' votes. Public opinion was astir with rumours to that effect. There is greater reason to believe, however, that his wealth was used to prepare a vast uprising in the southern rural areas, where the reaction seemed very powerful. According to statements made by Talon during the Consulate, Pitt is supposed to have denied Danton any help from London, where the prevailing opinion was that if the king were sentenced, civil war was certain.

The Jacobin counter-offensive, for the most part confined to the capital, nevertheless paid off. Robespierre and Saint-Just's speeches and Hébert and Marat's articles convinced the *sans-culottes* of the need for an exemplary verdict. 'Clemency is a crime when it endangers the people's safety.' Opponents were threatened with reprisals. Undoubtedly, intimidation by the *sectionnaires*, like royalist manoeuvres,

---

[4] Louis XVI's first choice was Target, who refused; Tronchet then accepted unenthusiastically and Malesherbes also volunteered. The Comte de Sèze was appointed to assist Malesherbes.

influenced the representatives' behaviour. The weight of Paris opinion, which was more immediate and perceptible, carried along the hesitant members. Michelet emphasized the hostile attitude of spectators in the Assembly and the Jacobins' grim determination: 'The blood of 10 August began to boil again.' Popular insurrection was not far away. The *fédérés* who had come up to Paris joined the delegates from the *sections*. The *Montagne* established with the *sections* the decisive contact that the *girondins* had not wanted to seek.

And yet the debates were endless, with adversaries fighting each other every inch of the way. Why not banish all the Bourbons? Would the primary electoral assemblies be convened? A call to the people and a secret ballot might alter the outcome of the trial. By a public and explicit vote, each *conventionnel* had to assume his reponsibilities towards his country and himself. The *girondins'* attempts to obstruct proceedings seemed infantile when compared to the commitments they had taken on.[5] The first roll-calls, begun on 15 January, appalled the moderates. Louis was found guilty by an almost unanimous vote and – thanks to Barère, who carried the *Plaine* with him – he was denied, by 424 votes to 287, the right of appeal before the people. In the course of twenty-four long and painful hours, everyone then pronounced an opinion on the sentence, either by voicing qualms and anxiety or by expressing conviction. The death sentence was voted by 387 representatives, of whom 334 asked for conditions, including a stay of execution. On 19 January, a clear-cut majority of 70 emerged in favour of an immediate execution, which was carried out two days later.

'Condemning a man to death – of all the sacrifices I have made for my homeland, that is the only one that deserves to be recorded,' admitted Roger Ducos, echoing the view of many of his colleagues. Some felt that this useless cruelty was a blot on the Revolution. The regicides, in varying degrees, experienced remorse, a desire to justify themselves after the fact, and a feeling of having transgressed divine law. A sense of solidarity now united them. 'He who has led the tyrant of the French to the scaffold must now count as his enemies all those who secretly hanker after a king.' The royal 'murder' brought the regicides closer, and Lepeletier de Saint-Fargeau, the 'scapegoat victim', was sanctified by the Jacobins.

[5] In his unpublished notes, Romme recounts how 'the right-hand side managed to take up as much room as possible on the benches, thus making it difficult for the representatives of the *Montagne* to move about'.

In the deeply shaken country, grief was concealed and gave way to resignation. Women wore mourning clothes in private, but public displays did take place on rare occasions, as in Lyons and Orléans. In Paris, schoolmasters read out edifying texts on the king's death to their pupils. The relative calm of the provinces reassured the notables. As for the *émigrés*, they were suspicious of Philippe Egalité, whom they imagined to be on the verge of ascending the throne. However, a martyr-king could be useful: accordingly, the *émigrés* prepared his legend, circulated his will, and fed foreign sovereigns with accounts of his sorry fate. Finally, the *émigrés* tried to dissociate the French people from its deputies, who were alone guilty of 'the sacrilegious assassination'.

Even the *montagnards* were worried about the future. They now had to forge ahead and ward off every danger in order at last to establish the Republic. 'We are on our way, and the roads are cut off behind us', wrote the *conventionnel* Le Bas. Soon the patriots withdrew their confidence from the *appelants*, who included nearly all the *girondins*, rightly suspected of provoking Europe.[6] As Brissot put it: 'We shall never be at peace until Europe, all Europe, is aflame.' War with England, which was predictable by November for reasons other than national defence, became a reality.

The European Coalition and the 'great levy'

The conquest of Belgium coincided with the king's trial and popular demonstrations, which triggered off the subtle mechanism of *girondin* diplomacy — the dominant influence in the recently created Committee of General Defence. The sensational announcement of successive liberations spread the idea that town gates were being opened in the name of the Rights of Man. Consequently, on the right bank of the Rhine, the feudal regime was abolished, although the old tax system was preserved. The bishopric of Bâle, renamed the Republic of Rauracia, put itself under French protection.[7] Geneva revised its constitution. Everyone spoke of emancipation, autonomy and independence, even though the freedom promised could only be French and the army of occupation had to finance the war.

---

[6] The representatives who had voted for an appeal to the people were expelled from the Jacobin club on 1 March.

[7] On 23 March 1793, the region was named the *département* of Mont-Terrible; see J. Suratteau, *Le Département du Mont-Terrible sous le régime du Directoire*, Paris, 1965.

At first the Revolution seemed to adopt the traditional objectives and the old dreams of the monarchy in its struggle against Austria and in its colonial wars. However, it did add a new objective: the conquest of 'natural' frontiers. Custine's plan was to push the boundaries of national territory up to the Rhine and Dumoriez wanted to continue his northward advance. By 26 October, he was writing to Kellermann: 'The Rhine must be the only boundary marker in our campaign from Geneva to Holland, and perhaps to the sea.' The minister Lebrun and Danton were also of the same opinion. It was the *girondins* who had developed this policy, but the *montagnards* did not reject it.

Nevertheless, the *montagnards* intended to abide by the principles of 1789, to consult the local populations, to suggest rather than impose measures. They foresaw resistance to the levies that would have to be made for the garrisoning and upkeep of French troops. Proselytism and taxation hardly went together. 'Nobody likes armed missionaries.'

Moreover, the authorities could not but notice how the zeal of the conquered peoples had dampened – and Belgium was a case in point. Its bourgeoisie deserted the Jacobin societies that Dumoriez had promoted. The inhabitants hesitated between their desire for freedom and their fear of coming under the Austrian yoke again. They were unhappy with the seizure of Church property and the abolition of the tithe and seigneurial dues. The arrival of French commissioners provoked irritation and provincial assemblies had to meet under the protection of French bayonets. Only an isolated minority of the Belgians took part.

The extension of the war suited the *girondins* not just for ideological reasons, but as a means of keeping the mass of *sans-culottes* busy. The *girondins* made no mystery of their aims. Roland is said to have declared: 'Our thousands of soldiers must be made march as far as their legs will carry them, or else they will come and slit our throats.'[8] Although they were aware of the navy's weakness, the *girondins* fanned the flames: on 1 February, Brissot suggested a break with England and the Stadtholder. The Convention raised no objections to the move, nor to the severing of relations with Spain and the Italian States. By March 1793, the divided Republic seemed at the mercy of an almost universal coalition.

Each member of the First Coalition, fortunately, had its own weaknesses: Prussia, Austria and Russia, for example, were squabbling over Poland. Moreover, their objectives were not identical: the

[8] Quoted in A. Sorel (35), vol. 3, pp. 155, 279.

European aristocracy was fighting a class war, dispossessed sovereigns were out to reconquer their thrones, and the British government aimed at economic and colonial supremacy. It was the British who, in April 1793, organized in Antwerp the joint struggle on land and sea. That campaign ruined the hopes of French traders and shippers and deprived the country of imported foodstuffs. Even fishing became dangerous. With only its domestic resources left, France was obliged to regulate them and centralize its administration despite *girondin* opposition.

National defence raised the same problems for the army and the country as it had in August 1792. The lessons of the intervening months had not been learnt: the army was still suffering from the dual nature of its recruitment that even the amalgamation enacted on 21 February failed to eliminate. The army was also handicapped by the deficiencies of its supply corps and the reluctance of its high command. But the most urgent need was to increase troop strength. The volunteers of 1791, who had joined for one campaign, went home after Jemappes despite the efforts of the Convention, which decreed a levy of 300,000 men on 24 February and another of mounted troops on 16 April. Arrangements were left to the local authorities. In such a crisis, the results were likely to be disastrous. The representatives sent on mission – two to each *département*, and others to inspect the armed forces, in accordance with a well-tried method – averted a catastrophe. The *montagnards* who were chosen enlisted the help of the Jacobin *sociétés* and the national guards. They managed to check abuses in the lotteries established by most municipalities, and also cut down on gatherings and long queues. On 6 May, the Convention increased the representatives' powers.

Resistance stiffened and there were few volunteers. Nevertheless, thanks to civic-mindedness and unemployment, quotas were in some cases exceeded. In the Landes, 'female citizens galvanized their husbands'. In Ruffec, ninety-six recruits were offered instead of thirty-two; in Bouchemaine, near Angers, eighteen instead of four. The peasants of the Ardennes sometimes left without sowing their fields. A levy on the rich financed bonuses and the *étape*, which attracted 'many soldiers'.[9] By late June 1793, the objective of 500,000 men at arms had been met.

Although riots broke out in the regions of Clermont-Ferrand and Montauban, in the Côte-d'Or, the Yonne and the Saône-et-Loire, they

---

[9] The *étape* was the right granted to recruits and soldiers to obtain supplies from military depots along their route for a small sum that was the same for all the men.

were spontaneous and ceased with the arrest of a few ringleaders. Suspects were taken into custody, except in the west, where they were not paid sufficient attention: there the premeditated and organized disturbances turned into civil war.

The Vendée

The rebellion in the Vendée had been smouldering for a long time, but the criminal courts had shown extreme indulgence, and preparations continued with the help of priests. Religion and allegiance to the king were decisive in uniting peasant rancours against the townspeople who had bought 'their' seized Church lands, had filled the positions of authority created by the Revolution, but had proved powerless to provide unemployed textile workers with the means of subsistence. Parochialism, age-old customs and religious fervour made the Vendée impervious to Jacobinism, and it was now 'ripe for unrest'. Recruitment served as the pretext, all the more so for its being reminiscent of the raising of the militia by lottery.

In the first days of March 1793, the tocsin rang in the belfries of 700 to 800 parishes. According to Choudieu, the nobles tricked the abject sharecroppers into supporting them. Bonchamp, d'Elbée, Lescure, Charette and La Rochejaquelein, followed by Cathelineau, 'as pious as he was narrow-minded', commanded this 'Catholic and royal army', which never became a standing army. In Brittany and the Poitou the representatives on mission succeeded in maintaining order but, in the Vendée, whole villages of peasants joined the rebel army and set out followed by their wives, who egged them on and stopped them from deserting. The recruits were escorted by gamekeepers and poachers. Foreign deserters, to whom the Convention had unwisely granted a pension, also turned up. The Vendée's improvised armoury was soon upgraded with captured 'republican' weapons. On 12 March, the *vendéens* occupied Les Mauges, the Bocage, the Marais up to Clisson, and the island of Noirmoutier, where the British could have joined forces with them. But the Coalition did not respond to *vendéen* appeals, thereby passing up one of its greatest opportunities.

The rebels failed to take immediate tactical advantage of the region and instead stormed the towns in waves of tens of thousands. The speed and size of this mass movement took the garrisons by surprise: after Cholet, it reached Parthenay in the Thouet valley and, on 9 June, Saumur in the Loire valley. The patriots, who were described as 'clumsy' and given rough treatment, made a pretence of giving up, but only a minority openly collaborated. In fact, in these outlying areas, many families were so divided that their members were fighting against one another. Those who had gone astray or had not yet taken sides might still, it was believed, come over to the patriots' camp.

The Convention entertained such hopes and hesitated. On 24 March, at the Jacobin club, Tallien denounced the uprising and ministerial inertia: the Jacobins demanded fuller information. The two armies dispatched to the Vendée under the command of Canclaux and Biron were not organized until May. The announcement of their arrival forced the *vendéens* to abandon Chemillé, Noirmoutier, then Saumur. They ended up at the gates of Nantes on 29 June, but their strength had not been impaired. Against them, the Republic waged an exhausting struggle.

Meanwhile, on the borders, the Coalition scored its first successes. Coburg took Aachen on 2 March, then Liège. Dumoriez, defeated at Neerwinden, left Belgium and went over to the enemy on 5 April, provoking a patriotic outcry comparable to the reaction following Lafayette's betrayal. The *girondins*, who were compromised with Dumoriez, were further discredited. Public opinion criticized them not for having started the war, but 'for having been incapable of waging it'.

Inflation ('*la vie chère*')

While Custine was retreating along the Rhine, and the enemy was invading home territory in the north and east, the economic situation, a cause for concern since September, was deteriorating rapidly, adding to the general unrest. By the end of the winter, grain circulation had stopped completely and grain prices doubled from one region to another. Despite Saint-Just's advice, vast quantities of *assignats* were still being put into circulation. In February 1793, they had fallen to 50 per cent of their face value, when they were not actually refused. The depreciation of legal tender provoked inflation and speculation by producers, who created 'artificial dearth'. The scarcity of foodstuffs did not affect the rich and the poor equally. The poor, who were unable to purchase essentials, found themselves obliged to take to the streets. But the possessors of consumer goods increased their profits. The Revolution's survival was therefore contingent on ending inflation. 'The same factors that induce famine will lead to the break-up of public administration.'

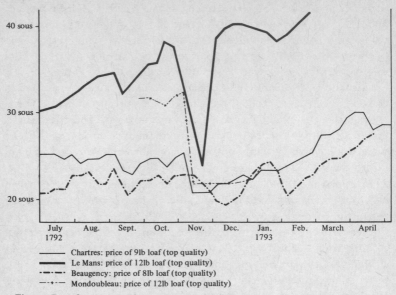

Fig. 2 Bread prices in the Beauce and bordering areas. After M. Vovelle, 'Les Taxations populaires...' (22)

The *sans-culottes* also blamed inflation on army contractors, who were making competitive purchases. Requirements had not increased significantly, but troop concentrations made it necessary to concentrate supplies, conclude large transactions, and engage in large-scale transport. In rural France it was customary for families to bake their bread at home with their own wheat. Peasants and soldiers were more fortunate than townspeople, whom the government still left to their own devices. In Le Havre, unemployment was compounded by an influx of outsiders and the fear of a British landing. Never had the price of bread risen so high: nearly five sous a pound for brown bread and ten sous a pound for white bread. The price of brown bread reached eight sous in Clermont-Ferrand, where the employees of the *district* administration earned only twenty-five *livres* a month. In Grenoble, where – as during the *ancien régime* – there was a great consumption of fine wheaten bread and *grèche* (a type of *brioche*), the new municipality adopted an 'assistance plan' financed by the rich. Elsewhere, the authorities hesitated and took emergency measures with limited means. Instead of declining, unrest spread throughout the countryside.

In the Beauce, in late 1792, bands of workers and foresters had set out from the forest of Vibraye for Chartres, Châteaudun and La Ferté-Bernard, moving on towards the Loire as far as Beaugency and proclaiming a freeze on wheat prices along the way. They were supported by petty bourgeois and artisans and sometimes protected by the national guard. This vast movement embodied a basic demand of wage-earners – the right to live by one's work. No distinctions were made between categories of producers: the smallholder was no more spared than the big farmer. In these traditionally well-provided, cereal-growing areas, workers in small local industries – particularly glass – and non-propertied village artisans came to realize that their interests diverged from those of the peasantry.

In Paris, the Commune kept the bread price fixed at three sous a pound despite the tremendous financial burden, which the Convention hesitated to share. The same procedure was followed in Rouen and Bordeaux. Then colonial goods disappeared from the grocery shops and Pitt ordered the inspection of grain shipments. The requisition of wood by the navy caused the price of firewood in Brest to rise from twenty-two to thirty-six *livres* a *corde* in one month.[10] Forests were devastated and shops looted. On 24 February, Paris laundresses complained before the Assembly of the exorbitant price of soap; the next day, groups of men and women from central Paris went to the outskirts, where they requisitioned sugar, candles and wax at a very low price – or simply walked off with them. Such disorders, which flared up again at Les Halles on the 26th and were swiftly put down, testified to the staunch determination of consumers to impose fair prices. The rioters included wage-earners and artisans but also prosperous individuals or their servants, *agents provocateurs* and profiteers. Women called the police and the national guard 'knaves, fops and mischievous hoarders' and shouted 'down with the bayonet'.

The embarrassed Jacobins accused the counter-revolution, stressed the non-participation of the 'worthy *sans-culottes*' and 'honourable indigent' inhabitants of the Faubourg Saint-Antoine, and expressed their disapproval of the excesses of the women. If the Jacobins seemed to underestimate the true significance of popular action, they certainly took it into account. The *montagnards* voted on 11 April to make the *assignat* the sole legal tender; on 4 May, in conformity with the *sectionnaires*' wishes, they voted to fix a maximum grain price in each

---

[10] The *corde* was an old unit of measurement generally equal to four steres.

département. The fall of the *girondins*, who had opposed these measures, was hastened by *la vie chère*.

THE TRAGIC SUMMER

Eight long months had been squandered in 'scandalous' debates that discredited the national representative body. France had been expecting its Constitution; what it got was civil war, invasion and a crisis so deep that it was shaking the nation to its foundations. 'Everywhere people are tired of the Revolution, the rich detest it, the poor have no bread and they are being persuaded to blame their troubles on us.' Was this then the Republic? Public opinion was increasingly nervous and confrontations became more dramatic. Pétion appealed to the wealthy bourgeoisie for help: 'Your properties are threatened and you close your eyes to this danger...You can see all respectable men of means leaving Paris...Parisians, shake off your lethargy at last and drive these poisonous insects [the anarchists] back into their dens.' Robespierre, on the contrary, deplored the fact that the people 'had not yet reaped the fruit of their labours. They are still being persecuted by the rich, and the rich still are what they always were – hard and merciless.' The *sociétés populaires* were the scene of chaotic meetings, disrupted by contradictory motions, petty squabbles and resignations. As in the summer of 1789, social fears fanned the flames of hatred; suspicion was spreading.

The Jacobins were proposing two attitudes: sacrifice or all-out struggle. 'We will know how to die, we shall all die', preached Robespierre, while Marat drafted this fiery exhortation: 'Friends, we have been betrayed. To arms! To arms!...To arms, Republicans! Rush to Paris, for that is where France must meet.' 'Patriotic frenzy' was out of place. Victory was required and one could no longer skimp on the means to achieve it. Whereas the *Gironde* was losing ground, the *montagnards*, more realistically, consented to 'compromise themselves' with the *sans-culottes*. 'The people must save the Convention, and the Convention in turn will save the people.'

The fall of the 'Gironde'

The *Gironde* remained solidly established in the State bureaucracy and the provinces. It was because of the *Gironde* that the Assembly tempered the rigour of measures that local authorities pretended not to know about. At no other moment – except perhaps in the autumn of 1792 – did the government have less influence and authority. The ministers, hardly any of whom had been replaced, surrounded themselves with intriguers. The Committees dithered. Under Beurnonville, the War Ministry slumbered. 'We observe', said the Jacobins, 'that the more we advance the less attention is paid to putting individuals in their proper place.' The Jacobins proposed decrees that the Convention took several months to enact.

But authority was imperceptibly passing into the hands of the fifteen hundred *montagnards* delegated to the *départements* and armed forces. The *Gironde*, which had thought it would be rid of the *montagnards* by sending them on missions, saw its influence decline in the interior and the number of anti-Brissot petitions increased by late March. The *montagnards* took generally well-advised initiatives and they were recognized to be efficient. Wherever they went, the *comités de surveillance*, created on 21 March, filled up with *sans-culottes*. Rebels caught under arms, who were liable to the death penalty under a law of 19 March, were executed and their property was seized along with that of the *émigrés*, whose 'civil death' was decreed on the 28th. The criminal courts were roused from their torpor and flanked by special commissions. 'Minds were revolutionized.'

The hunt for suspects, nobles, priests and hoarders was being revived. The Revolutionary Tribunal, established on 10 March, judged political crimes without appeal. Its five judges and twelve jurors were chosen by the Convention, as were the nine members of the Committee of Public Safety, which, on 6 April, began to coordinate government action and spread Jacobin watchwords. Despite difficulties encountered in enforcing its orders, and despite the vagueness of its mandate, the Committee was well briefed, made all members live up to their responsibilities, and singled out forceful personalities. National sovereignty was thus safeguarded by a delegation of power that prepared for the Year II and the 'despotism of Liberty'.

The *Plaine* had gradually become convinced of this necessity. However, it still dreamt, like Danton, of bringing together the extremes so as to avoid a predictable disintegration of the Assembly. The *girondins* hounded Marat, who was acquitted on 24 April, while the *Montagne* espoused the views of the *sans-culottes*. At the Assembly, the curtain was rising on the last act, which had begun on 3 April with an attack on Dumoriez's accomplice Brissot. Robespierre, who kept up the pressure until the end, exhorted the Convention at the same time not to give up the 'search for means...to alleviate the people's misery'. The deputation from the Paris clubs and *sections* kept reminding the Convention of the social dimension of the conflict. Robespierre took them up by proposing a very democratic Declaration of Rights and restrictions on property that *Le Patriote français* greeted with sarcasm, describing the progressive tax as 'absurd and ruinous for industry'.

In the trading cities — Bordeaux, Marseilles and Lyons — the *girondins* made common cause with the counter-revolution, imprisoned the Jacobins, and took over local administration. But in Paris the volunteers mobilized against the Vendée demanded the elimination of the entire right wing of the Assembly. 'If the Convention will not march, we will make the Convention march.' The Cordeliers and the *Républicaines révolutionnaires*, led by Claire Lacombe, added their voices to the appeal on 19 May. The capital could abandon neither its Commune — which had been attacked by Guadet — nor Hébert, arrested on the 24th along with other popular militants. There was a real danger, as there had been on 10 August, of a right-wing *coup d'état*. The 'Bishop's Palace Committee', composed of delegates from the *sections*, therefore decided to prepare an insurrection.

On the 26th, Robespierre summoned all patriots to the Bishop's Palace and proposed to the Assembly a decree bringing charges against *girondin* leaders mentioned by name. 'If the decree is not enacted, we will enact it ourselves,' Marat had threatened. A first demonstration on the 31st lacked conviction. The following day, it was decided to surround the Tuileries;[11] on Sunday 2 June, the *sections* obtained satisfaction. Without bloodshed, twenty-nine representatives and two ministers — Clavière and Lebrun (Roland having resigned earlier on 22 January) — were ordered to be arrested; but they were only placed under house arrest and several escaped.

Thus the *Montagne* had conducted a 'purge by ballot' (*scrutin épuratoire*) of the representative system. Although it had secured a majority in the Convention, the *Montagne* had to contend with the federalist movement and force timorous citizens to 'stand up in these critical circumstances'. One of these 'worthy people', Jean D'Yzez, a representative from the Basses-Pyrénées, observed in June: 'I know the innumerable reproaches levelled at over-zealous patriots, but I believe that moderatism is causing us infinitely greater harm. It is insufficiently realized that centuries-old habits must be eradicated and that we have

---

[11] Since 10 May, the Convention had met in the Salle des Machines, where it remained until the end of the session.

a long way to go before we see the end of old rancours that reach down into hell.' The *Montagne*, now on its own, had to assume before the country and before Europe the responsibilities of its victory.

The Constitution of the Year I, or of 1793

In the circumstances, voting the Constitution represented both an obligation and a danger. The slowness of the Assembly was interpreted as an error and an admission of powerlessness. Were so many endless arguments necessary to establish the republican regime? There were some who went so far as to deem it unworkable. Indeed, there was a confrontation between two political concepts and two radically opposed modes of government. Here again, legal forms masked contradictory social concerns. The interminable project presented by Condorcet on 15 February not only instituted a 'kingship of ministers', but also pitted against each other the executive and the legislative, both to be chosen by universal suffrage. Despite its democratic look, the project provided for an ingenious electoral districting that would neutralize the urban *sans-culottes* and keep basic powers in the hands of the *départements*. Moreover, the *girondins* were anxious for an early decision in order to proceed to elections that would strengthen their position.

The Jacobins, on the contrary, kept enjoining prudence. They felt that a Constitution, which would require a popular endorsement, could wait until the end of the war and the conscripts' return. They formed their own committee to examine projects and collect suggestions. The Jacobins agreed on one point that Saint-Just had set out on 24 April: 'A weak Constitution now can cause great misfortunes and new revolutions fatal to liberty. We need a lasting document.' Criticizing the importance attributed to the 'executive power', Saint-Just suggested replacing it by a sovereign council – ministers would be reduced to implementing its decisions. Plurality seemed inevitable to him, but he felt that it was a matter best left to the people. Saint-Just may already have felt that the Republic could ensure the common good only by merging with a society politically organized as a single party.

The discussions that began on 15 April concerning the articles of the Declaration of Rights were the occasion of a bitter clash between defenders of individual rights and defenders of society. The Declaration solemnly reaffirmed the nation's indivisibility and the great principles of freedom of the press, equality and resistance to oppression. It went far beyond the Declaration of 1789, adding to it the right to public assistance, work, education and insurrection. No man could impose his will on others. All political and social tyranny was abolished. 'The only permissible contract between worker and employer is one that calls for care and gratitude [on the part of the employer]' (article 18). Although the Convention did not adopt the social limits on property suggested by Robespierre, this text was regarded as the Jacobin charter; and although the *montagnards* had refused to be led further down the road to democracy, the Constitution became the bible of all democrats.

After the elimination of the *Gironde*, the Convention suddenly seemed in a hurry to adopt the Constitutional bill, which was drafted mostly by Saint-Just and Couthon, presented by Héraut de Séchelles, discussed from 6 June onwards, and voted in its entirety on the 24th. Out of hostility to liberalism and the parliamentary system, it vested all powers in a single assembly devolving from the people, who were to exercise legislative control also by referendum and were to judge their delegates' conduct when their terms of office expired. A compromise was struck between the popular notion of direct democracy and the bourgeois concept of representation. In the event, the primary assemblies were asked to vote on certain laws only and, first of all, on the Constitution.

The provinces and armies gave it nearly unanimous approval. The results, proclaimed on 10 August 1793, showed only an infinitesimal proportion of nays – 17,000, or less than one per cent of the votes cast. The French population thus committed itself to the Jacobin Republic, one and indivisible. However, it was never intended for a single moment to put into practice – under the then prevailing circumstances – the form of government prescribed by the Constitution. Instead, the document was kept in a cedar box, its provisions not to be enacted before peacetime, although it served as a symbolic inspiration for the decisions of the Assembly, which perpetuated itself and endorsed *montagnard* policy.

Federalism and counter-revolution

An immense task awaited an apparently disoriented Convention, still reeling from the brutal purge it has experienced. Seventy-six representatives bravely protested against the 31 May action.[12] Others,

---

[12] By 6 June there were 52 protesters, joined by 19 more on 19 June and by 5 others later on; they have been inaccurately called 'the 73'.

like Grégoire, also expressed their disapproval. The Jacobins 'strayed from one issue to another' without concentrating on the major problems, but then regained their determination. Robespierre complained of fatigue and contemplated resigning. The possibility of a *girondin* counter-offensive was not ruled out.

The news of the fall of the *girondins*, which reached the provinces between 5 and 15 June, caused a shock wave throughout *départemental* administrations. The Jura demanded a meeting in Bourges of the alternate representatives, and Montpellier the summoning of the primary assemblies. Correspondence from local officials substantiated the idea of a massive opposition, whereas in fact the population was only partially involved. The moderate bourgeoisie rallied to political federalism in order to safeguard its social advantages. In regions where the representatives on mission enjoyed support and armies were vigilant, a few dismissals of local officials put an end to bourgeois ventures. Local governments all deserved to be replaced, observed Dartigoeyte in the south-west. 'The enemies of equality must cease monopolizing positions of authority.' In the towns of the Gers, where 'petty legal officers and *procureurs*' clerks' hankered after the *Gironde*, silence was maintained about the civic spirit of rural areas.

Thus opposition to the government was fostered by its own officials. Every isolated act – a hostile cry. here, an inconsiderate gesture there – was magnified to excess. The Convention and the Jacobins registered these warning signs, which the *sans-culottes* took as proof of a vast plot against the Republic. Even in the thirty-odd *départements* loyal to the Convention, some *sociétés populaires* had let themselves be outmanoeuvred by their officers. The Rouen *société*, for example, broke with Paris. Auch, Agen, Pau and Tarbes banded together in defence of 'legality'. But they soon changed their minds and by the end of June about eight hundred *sociétés* were reckoned to have 'endorsed 31 May'. That number was to increase, and the action of the *sociétés* was to be decisive in the struggle against the provincial reaction.

There was a difference between federalism and rebellions fomented and organized by the counter-revolution, but both were a stab in the back for France at a time when its borders were being overrun. Both types of risings were a betrayal of the nation and the Republic. Federalism, the product of *sectionnaire* movements in the large towns in late May, was especially strong in Normandy and the south-east. In its bid for power it used Jacobin methods – purges of local authorities, the arrest of patriots and their trial before 'popular'

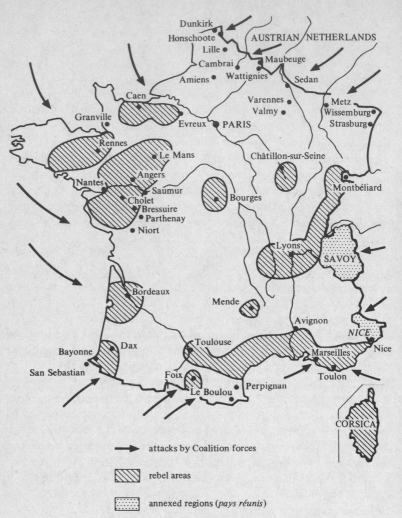

attacks by Coalition forces

rebel areas

annexed regions (*pays réunis*)

Fig. 3 The Republic under siege (July–August 1793)

tribunals, conscription and 'revolutionary taxes'. Invoking the right of
resistance to Parisian oppression, the federalists refused to comply with
decrees and banished or expelled delegates sent by the Convention, but
their movement was in no way a spontaneous mass phenomenon.
Moreover, its disparate recruitment made it vulnerable. Supporters of
the *ancien régime* and of the non-juror clergy fought alongside

anti-Jacobins. Troops were mustered to march on Paris, and appeals were made for foreign support, except in Caen, where Buzot, Pétion and Barbaroux had taken refuge.

The central assembly of the six Norman *départements* secured the aid of Wimpffen – Jacobin for a day – who commanded the Côtes de Cherbourg army. But the countryside did not follow suit; the Orne and Seine-Inférieure refused to help and the insurgents fled in panic near the forest of Bizy at the approach of the republican battalions. In the region of Marseilles, the federalists had seized power in the towns that acted as centres for the revolt, but peasant support was uneven,[13] making Carteaux's advance all the easier. He took Aix on 21 August and Marseilles on the 25th – before the arrival of the British; then laid siege to Toulon, which was protected by Admiral Hood's squadron and thus managed to hold out, not without difficulty, until mid-December. But Lyons, where the royalist Précy had called for help from the Sardinians, fell by 8 October.

It was still believed that there would be a general invasion of the Midi. The enemy had been prodigal with false news and money. Forces had to be deployed from Bayonne to Nice. The Spanish could rely on many friends along the Pyrenees. Plots were unmasked in the Ariège, in Perpignan and in Cette; Paoli opened up Corsica to the English. In the Lozère, Charrier's bands seized Mende and Marvejols, cut down liberty trees, ordered the celebration of mass, and executed prisoners in the name of the Comte de Provence, regent of France. 'New Vendées' were born, while the first, far from disappearing, resisted victoriously.

Anti-national and anti-patriotic federalism, confused with royalist plots, was considered an unforgivable crime. Despite the protection of dissident representatives by Robespierre and Saint-Just, a merciless repression bathed both Marseilles, 'City-without-name', and Toulon, 'Port-of-the-Montagne', in blood. After the capture of Lyons nearly 2,000 rebels were shot in the plain of Les Brotteaux. Admittedly, an identical number were spared, and Robert Lindet, in Normandy, acted humanely. Although the general aim of the Convention was to strike at the leaders and impress public opinion, it was unable to avoid local excesses 'that drove from their homes... individuals whose talents could have contributed to the defence of the State'. The rich and the innocent were sometimes unjustly accused of federalism, but the

[13] See M. Vovelle in *Atlas historique de Provence*, maps on pp. 70–1 and 155–7.

girondins were eliminated from the power structure and replaced wherever possible by Jacobins, whose hegemony was thus reinforced in the provinces thanks to federalism. The petty bourgeoisie of small entrepreneurs and shopkeepers took over local government and the *comités de surveillance*.

Public opinion, however, remained generally passive. In the Tarentaise, an observer noted that 'public opinion remained as ice-cold as one could imagine'. Inns were closed and the army had to subsist on its rations alone. In the Bas-Rhin, 'barely a third of the inhabitants were for the Revolution'. Populations caught in the cross-fire were as frightened when the enemy retreated as when it advanced: at its approach, patriots would flee; when the Republic scored a victory, 'collaborators' would escape abroad. In the Anjou, there was naturally a sympathy for the Vendée. The correspondence of representatives in every region confirmed this reprehensible indifference. The people had to be 'enlightened as to where their true interests lay'. The task fell to the purged or newly founded *sociétés populaires*. On 22 August, the Paris club demanded the death penalty for anyone who suggested that the *sociétés* should be disbanded. The *sans-culottes*, traumatized by the assassination of Marat, second 'martyr to Liberty', as well as by invasion and deprivation, called for the population to express its unconditional commitment. Whoever did not proclaim his support for the Republic was against it.

Such intransigence was justified by the mortal dangers that threatened the Republic. The Convention seemed unable to handle the situation. Danton was negotiating. Instead of waging war, the generals were quarrelling; the army's morale was ebbing. In late July, the Prussians captured Mainz and the Austrians laid siege to Maubeuge. Having invaded Savoy, the Sardinians were threatening Nice; the Spanish were closing in on Bayonne and the Roussillon. The government's weakness was patent; the Committee of Public Safety was revamped. Confronted with the continuing food crisis, the Committee decided to accede to the demands of the *sans-culottes*. The popular vanguard forced the *montagnards*' hand and compelled them to a definitive break with the liberal bourgeoisie.

THE POPULAR MOVEMENT AND THE 'ENRAGÉS'

The popular movement, which pre-dated 1789, followed an autonomous course. The 10 August and 2 June *journées* were its proof that daring was enough to attain victory: the strength of the popular movement lay in numbers and in unity of action. The dangers facing the homeland gave the movement renewed vigour; it rallied to Jacobinism but remained vigilant and took up the initiative again as soon as workers' living conditions worsened. Misery, injustice and the inability to satisfy basic needs were more effective incentives to action than factional disputes. Malcontents of every kind tried in vain to exploit the popular movement; all they achieved, between June and September, was confusion.

The anonymous and latent force of the movement did not spring only from the lower ranks of society, as those who feared it pretended; it was neither ignorant nor stupid. The collective mentality was shaped both by the concerted efforts of intelligent individuals and by a gradual spread of ideas. The pre-capitalist outlook of the popular movement asserted itself according to the degree of affluence or poverty. 'It is above all in Paris that the poor are too poor.'[14] The movement was an urban phenomenon, which rarely expressed itself in class terms, given the highly disparate nature of its constituent elements. The young played an important role and infused the movement with their passionate ardour. Faced with everyday problems, women poured out streams of caustic remarks in the queues and at home, thus shaking men from their torpor. Directly or indirectly, women participated in social movements.

The relation between the popular movement and its vanguard has been equated with that between instinct and knowledge. In actual fact, popular demands had been framed before the militants took them up. Militants did not discover popular protest, but used it and gave it impetus. Their contact with the masses remained fragile and vulnerable to the most trifling disagreement. The militants acted as the intermediaries between the masses and the authorities.

The vanguard; male and female militants

Much attention has been focused on the *enragés*, whose enthusiasm, or ambition, placed them in the limelight. They spoke out at the Jacobin and Cordelier clubs before 10 August, then at the Commune and the Convention, where they were sent by their *sections*. It is in these terms – as a movement rooted in the people – that the *enragés'* action must be evaluated. Apart from the well-known figures, there were many anonymous ones who shared their sentiments and spread their

---

[14] Chaumette, speaking to the Convention on behalf of the Commune, 27 February 1793.

influence. The *enragés* were backed up by a hidden 'micro-élite at neighbourhood level'. If one abstracts them from the context of the suffering urban population and its problems, Jacques Roux, Varlet and Leclerc in Paris, Chalier in Lyons and Taboureau in Orléans lose their substance. Their existence was due solely to that environment. The 'creative genius' of the movement belonged to the collective mentality; the *enragés* had but to understand and take advantage of that mentality.

They acted as spokesmen in keeping with their quick-temperedness and generous disposition, but their bourgeois origins and superior education had left them with traditional patterns of thought. Although they were gifted with common sense, social awareness and talent, they lacked stature and confined themselves in the short term to improvised solutions. One cannot speak of the *enragés* as a party with a programme or system. But because they were able, at a given moment, to adopt common attitudes, they could defend with courage the *sectionnaire* democracy whose cause they espoused. A priest from the Angoumois, Jacques Roux, had come up to Paris in his forties. Embittered and disappointed, he established himself in the Gravilliers *section* as if in a 'fortress' and devoted his violence and imagination to the popular movement. 'I am quick-blooded,' he admitted. Outstripping Marat, his hero, he called for hostages, fetters, victims and scaffolds. The term *enragé* was appropriate for him, and so were *exagéré*, extremist or anarchist – labels applied to his friends.

Yet Jacques Roux did understand the art of persuasion. As a confessor of the poor, he influenced husbands by indoctrinating wives. In spite of the fact that women were legal minors deprived of civic rights and excluded from national sovereignty, they had their militants, who met in *sociétés patriotiques*. On 17 August 1792, the *fédérés* had proposed at the Jacobin club that women should be given the right to vote, but the Jacobins did not take up the suggestion. The *Républicaines révolutionnaires* held their meetings in the library adjacent to the Jacobin club, under the presidency of the pretty young actress Claire Lacombe, who was a born speaker. Other women's clubs were formed in the provinces, at Porrentruy for example, and they did not confine themselves to shredding linen for dressing wounds. Pauline Léon married Leclerc, and the female militants followed the *enragés*, denouncing the mercantile aristocracy, keeping a watch over markets, purging their own ranks and flogging the adventuress Théroigne de Méricourt. Men regarded their disorganized activity with some disdain, but feared them all the same.

This contagion of violence manifested itself especially after the king's execution. Jacques Roux prided himself on having accompanied the king to the scaffold, and compared Capet's crimes to those of hoarders: 'It is cowardly to tolerate those who appropriate the fruits of the earth and of industry . . . who subject the pauper's tears and impoverishment to usurious calculations.' Because the *girondins* rejected a controlled economy, the *enragés* launched an all-out attack against them, bringing into the political struggle the crucial problem of food supplies; the *enragés* then applied the same method against the *montagnards*, whom they considered too faint-hearted. On 25 June, speaking for the Cordeliers, Jacques Roux inveighed against the *montagnards*: 'No, no, you shall not leave your work unfinished . . . You shall not end your career in disgrace.'

How did the *enragés* view the Constitution? As no more than 'a pretty but one-eyed woman' if it did not impose the death penalty on those who starved the people. Jacques Roux made an obsession of this leitmotiv of the hungry: 'He talks of nothing else at the moment.' He was held to blame for the soap plunder in the port of Saint-Nicolas and for disunity among patriots. The Cordeliers expelled him with Leclerc at the end of June; the two leaders were disavowed by the Commune and treated as seditious elements who insulted the dignity of the national representative body!

But in six months the *enragés* had won the sympathy of the Parisian crowds. The Observatoire *section*, among others, voted to listen to a speech by Jacques Roux twice a week. *Enragé* newspapers and pamphlets were best-sellers. The *Père Duchesne*, the *enragés'* 'sounding-board', increased its circulation. The *enragés* were potential rivals for the Jacobins in public opinion and posed a permanent threat to the *montagnards*.

'Sans-culotte' democracy

The *sectionnaire* militants did not espouse the hard line of the *enragés* without some hesitation. Even Hébert advised caution: 'Do not pluck the fruit before it is ripe.' After the assassination of Marat, Jacques Roux, his 'shadow' (*Ombre*), moderated his stance, while Leclerc, a 'genuine' *Ami du Peuple*, still preached insurrection. The movement to impose price controls, while united on principle, split over practical means and over the evaluation of their consequences. One of the many merits of Albert Soboul's thesis is that it traces the development of *sans-culotte* power from 2 June onwards. The *sans-culottes* did not take over the capital at once and for two months they had to contend with the moderates.

Neither in the general assemblies – in which less than a tenth of eligible voters took part – nor in the *comités civils* or the *comités révolutionnaires* did the proportion of wage-earners exceed a quarter of the participants, most of whom were artisans, office-workers and shopkeepers. Many of these *sectionnaires* were Jacobin sympathizers and attended club meetings. They believed that the wage problem was a consequence of the high cost of living, that the right to property should be based on work, and that limits to ownership were imposed by necessity. In its social policy, Jacobinism largely reflected popular attitudes. However, it was in the service of representative government and hesitated to condemn commercial capitalism, to which the *sections* were hostile. The *sections* warmly applauded Jacques Roux when he spoke out against 'senatorial despotism, as terrible as the sceptre of kings, for it generally puts the people in bondage without their realizing it'.[15] Naturally enough, the *sections* advocated direct democracy, predicated upon popular censure and the people's right to recall their delegates. The Convention was provisionally vested with an authority that belonged to the people. On 21 August 1793, Leclerc exhorted the Assembly to return to its place: 'Officers of the sovereign, step off the tiers, for they belong to the people; take up the floor of the amphitheatre.' Such anarchist tendencies hampered the efforts to consolidate the government.

Gradually it also came to be accepted that the means of production, as well as the products themselves, belonged to the Republic. The possessor was merely a depositary, and the farmer had a free right only to a surplus; all the rest had to be accounted for. Profit was reduced and excess profit eliminated. Was it wise, however, to alienate shopkeepers, entrepreneurs and above all smallholders without having fulfilled their just hopes – the total abolition of seigneurial dues and a ban on the plurality of farm tenure? Was it wise to limit social protest to 'paltry commodities' and to townspeople?

The Parisian clubs and the *sociétés populaires* showed in their debates a keen desire to preserve unity and gather the widest possible support. From the outset, they often endorsed and enlarged upon motions drawn up by *section* militants on a variety of issues: the arrest of suspects; slow justice; the trial of the *girondins*, Custine and the queen; the

---

[15] *Discours sur le jugement de Louis le dernier* ... (Bibliothèque Nationale, Paris, shelf mark Lb⁴⁰ 2014).

'revolutionary army' and mass mobilization (*la levée en masse*). The provinces sometimes took the lead over the capital and scored points. The spirit of the Revolution thrived on boldness and perseverance. Terrorist propaganda, which one cannot dissociate from the foreign threat, began in July, when the *fédérés* from the provinces were flocking to Paris to commemorate the 10 August rising. They joined the Jacobin club, where violence was spreading: proposals were made to arm citizens with scythes, to purge all ministerial personnel, and to place a row of chained suspects in front of troops on the firing line. This movement became nation-wide before reaching the Convention and finding its way into law. Once again the problem of food supplies strengthened revolutionary will and forced the *montagnard* bourgeoisie to overcome its fears before it was too late.

The battle for bread

'The people must have bread, for where there is no bread, there are no more laws, no more liberty, no more Republic.' Caught up as it was in total war, the Revolution resorted to the *assignat* to finance its outlays. Galloping inflation set in. Despite the fact that the *assignat* had been decreed as the sole legal tender and that the stock exchange had been closed, the *louis* was being traded at a hundred paper *livres* – and paper currency was falling in the east and in Savoy to a quarter of its face value, well below the official rate pegged in August at 39 per cent. Among the repercussions was a doubling of textile and meat prices within almost three months, whereas wages remained stationary. Anxiety about bread became the daily plight of the urban population, not just because of its price, but because of its scarcity: it reached twelve sous a pound in the Nièvre, sixteen in Clermont, eighteen in Limoges and Guéret and twenty in the Pyrénées-Orientales.

The first *maximum* (price controls), far from easing the situation as had been expected, sparked off a series of genuine small-scale economic wars between municipalities and *districts*. Not only did the market supply areas not coincide with administrative divisions but, above all, the price lists, drawn up by *département*, contained unacceptable disparities, which were in fact greater for the lower-grade grain consumed by the people. It is hardly surprising that grain should have disappeared from places that offered the lowest prices. Some regions were deprived of grain, while others were supplied well beyond their needs and jealously held on to their stocks. The representatives on mission were even more agreed than in the spring on the artificial character of this dearth, from which only towns and border areas suffered. 'The poor have no bread and there is no shortage of grain – it is just being held back.' Hence the *enragés'* fierce attacks on hoarding, which was decreed a capital crime on 26 July.

The decree soon proved as ineffective as price controls. These measures provoked a host of complaints from landowners, officials and the population at large. To feed the army and the towns, transactions by private treaty were conducted at prices above the official ceiling, but sellers were increasingly afraid. Was it not better to pay a high price for bread rather than be deprived of it altogether? The capital, which had depleted its reserves, looked like a besieged city. Several bakers closed their shops. Sentries were assigned to maintain order at distributions, which had become irregular owing to the depletion of stocks between harvests, drought and the Normandy rebellion. The crisis was blamed on Garin, head of the Paris food supply administration. The Gros-Caillou *section* produced ration cards to be accompanied by the assignment of consumers to specific bakeries – a system already in use in several provincial towns. But the authorities had to wait for the new harvest before proceeding to the necessary requisitions.

There were renewed outbreaks of violence in Montargis, in the Gonesse *district*, at Jagny, in the Oise and in the Somme, where the agricultural proletariat was well represented. At Nesle, near Péronne, it was suggested in early September that legions of workers divided into companies should be raised 'to ensure the grain supply' and that men, women and children should be paid a reasonable wage to speed up threshing. The overwhelming majority of *fédérés* demanded the abolition of price controls at the very moment when they had to be extended to all basic commodities. 'Price controls must be applied to all goods if you want the agricultural worker to survive; better still, cash must be banned.' The *société populaire* of Saint-Florentin added its voice on 13 August, calling for a realignment of wages as well.

The Convention hesitated between two policies: to freeze the bread price at three sous a pound throughout the Republic and make up the difference between that price and the purchase price of grain by a tax on the rich, or to create barns for storing grain, similar to army storehouses, to be filled by requisitioning and payments in kind. L'Ange, in Lyons, had thought of setting up a popular and national authority to supervise the second solution. On 9 August, the Convention adopted Barère's proposal to create a barn in every *district* and public ovens. The

Commune issued a decree on 15 August setting the grain requirement for Paris at four quintals per plough in the traditional food-supplying areas, to which it dispatched commissioners. But the results were slow in coming and the Committee of Public Safety granted cash advances. By early September, dearth had spread to nearly all the towns.

The September storm

From late August onwards, Paris police informants reported alarming rumours. There were bread queues sometimes lasting seven hours and it was said that bread supplies would run out on the first Saturday in September, the 4th. Hébert published ever more venomous attacks on the merchants: 'The eaters of human flesh have armed their servants and errand-boys against the *sans-culotterie*... at present they are opening the ports of Toulon and Brest to the British.' The news – which was not true for Brest – reached the Jacobins at the same time as disturbances broke out starting, so it seemed, in the arms factories and spreading to the Place de Grève. Behind the workers, led by young militants like the typographer Tiger, one could feel the weight of female recriminations.

'It is not promises we need; it is bread, and at once,' demanded the crowd that broke into the Commune's assembly room. The crowd decided to meet the following day in front of the Convention. Chaumette and Hébert voiced their support for the proletarian movement of the *sections*. The Jacobins sponsored it discreetly and managed, with Robespierre's help, to make it change course and focus its attacks on suspects: 'The enemies of the people have for a long time been provoking them to revenge. The people have risen up, their enemies shall perish.' Somewhat reassured, the Convention welcomed the petitioners on the 6th. Once again, the Jacobin slogans of 'War on tyrants', 'War on aristocrats' and 'War on hoarders' rallied the *sans-culottes* to the Assembly. Unity – so necessary to the cause – was maintained.

But at one point it was feared that the militants, outflanked by their troops, might be irresistibly caught up in a political rising for which they were unprepared. They realized that public authority required men versed in parliamentary practice and that after all the *Montagne* was the lesser evil, provided it became 'a volcano whose burning lava would destroy the hopes of evil-doers and reduce their hearts to ashes'. The *enragés* wanted the Convention to identify itself with the people and lend it assistance – to 'change its tactics'. 'Start acting and stop talking,' Royer also told the Jacobins. 'Terror must be put on the agenda.'

But was it wise to endorse *enragé* violence? As early as 5 August, Robespierre had denounced 'these upstarts, patriots for a day who want to make the people lose their oldest friends'. Even at the Gravilliers, Jacques Roux's action encountered opposition. Hébert had condemned him at the Jacobin club. Roux was arrested and papers found on him proved that he was counting on women and mass conscription to spread the insurrection in the provinces. His newspaper and Leclerc's, which kept their readership, demanded the Constitution. The *Républicaines révolutionnaires* thundered against prostitutes and wives of *émigrés*. Together with the *sections*, they campaigned for the wearing of the tricolour cockade to be made compulsory.[16] They joined the Cordeliers in harassing the Convention on the most diverse issues. Varlet protested against the decree of 9 August that forbade the *section* assemblies from sitting in permanent session and abolished the beggarly allowance of forty sous granted to their members. Varlet, and then Claire Lacombe, were also imprisoned.

Sweeping measures

Wartime conditions and pressure from the Paris *sections* made it necessary to enact 'revolutionary' legislation founded on a new social contract. The moderates of the *Plaine* and the provinces gradually agreed to comply with 'the force of circumstances'. Public opinion accepted Jacobin explanations.

In September, when the tide could have turned against it, the *montagnard* majority was consolidated. On the 6th, it decided to raise among the *sans-culottes* a 'revolutionary army' of 6,000 infantry and 1,200 gunners to ensure food provisioning. The project had first been discussed the previous winter; it was put forward at the Jacobin club on 18 March and backed by Robespierre. The same suggestion had been made almost simultaneously in Lyons and Montpellier, then in Châteauroux and Bellac. In fact, enrolment began in Paris in early June, when the federalists were organizing themselves. Many *sociétés populaires* had proposed regional projects. In the Midi and Le Havre, there were attempts to carry them out by late spring. Richard Cobb records more than fifty detachments raised here and there, in anarchic fashion. The

---

[16] On 20 September, the Commune made it compulsory to wear the cockade; on the 21st, the Convention voted to punish women who refused to comply with the order.

Parisian army, created on 9 September in accordance with Carnot's
plan, restored the initiative to the Convention. The preservation of
republican unity ruled out improvisation.

The *levée en masse*, 'permanent requisition of all Frenchmen from
eighteen to sixty', was not a new demand either. To adopt such a
measure and send to the border – as Hébert imagined – legions of
poorly trained, poorly armed and poorly dressed *sans-culottes* would
have been sheer madness, and Robespierre spoke out against it on 29
March: 'You have been invited to leave all together. But our army
has more soldiers than it needs...Turn down any idea of removing
from this city either your arms or your citizens.' For several months,
Robespierre held fast to his position, despite the fact that public opinion
was in favour of a general mobilization of patriots. In July the idea
was given irresistible impetus. The Jacobins, the Commune and the
fédérés convinced the Convention on the 16th, and the Committee of
Public Safety, on the 23rd, set down in unforgettable terms the
conditions of a progressive levy, young men under twenty-five being
the first to go.

This involvement of an entire people entailed the nationalization of
the economy. The general control of prices and wages, adopted in its
broad outlines on 4 September, was widely debated and was accompanied by a string of partial measures between 11 and 29 September.
Fuels, as well as grain, were subjected to controls. To overcome the
resistance of producers and retailers, they were made subject to punitive
measures as were those who henceforth dared to impede the Revolution's progress. Mass opinion called for more repressive measures to
annihilate opposition forces, not just at the political level but in all
spheres. Leclerc, acting as spokesman for the masses, harangued the
Commune in these words: 'Why are you so slow in getting rid of your
enemies? Why are you afraid of shedding a few drops of blood?'

On 5 September, the Convention recognized the need for the Terror,
while reserving the right to organize it. That was the aim of the law
of the 17th against suspects, who were turned over to the *comités de
surveillance*. Leniency was no longer in order; hesitation meant retreat.
'It is weakness towards traitors that is fatal to us.'

Yet it took a whole month and much adroit manoeuvring for the
montagnard government to impose its will on the *sans-culottes* and the
Assembly. The Committee of Public Safety was criticized for its
dominant role and its increased powers. There was even an attempt,
on the 25th, to appoint dubious individuals to it, like Briez, and to

frighten the provinces, as in the autumn of 1792 and spring of 1793, by brandishing the threat of a popular tidal wave.

The threat was so real and so strong that the revolutionary bourgeoisie, fearing a point of no return, marshalled its Jacobin contingents and invited them to wipe out the after-effects of the *girondin* and federalist movements, to eliminate the moderates from public administration and take over as the State's new agents. The representatives and *sociétés populaires* drew up lists of patriotic candidates from which government agents were chosen. The Paris club stepped up its propaganda and correspondence; from 8 September onwards, the *Moniteur universel* opened its columns to the Jacobins. Unity of public opinion – the driving force behind government action – depended on Jacobinism's persuasive force. It was even suggested that all citizens who did not espouse Jacobinism should be massacred. 'I think', wrote Dubouchet, 'that we shall not have peace and harmony on the home front until we have put away all the *honnêtes gens.*'

This derogatory expression was used to describe the 'bourgeois', who were responsible for domestic perils. Had they not 'done everything to put the people under their yoke and make all the defenders of the Republic perish on the scaffold'? By isolating themselves from the people, they abandoned the revolutionary cause. *Montagnards* and Jacobins, who remained faithful to the Revolution, denied that they were bourgeois and claimed to belong to the great family of the unfortunate, of which Robespierre was proud to be a member.

'To defeat the bourgeois, one must rally the people.' By following that course, the Jacobin Republic was taking a serious risk. Its socially divided people could not long share a joint destiny. A temporary dictatorship obliged the people to do so in the name of common dangers. France turned into a gigantic national enterprise.

3

Revolutionary government

The history of the revolutionary government coincides with that of the Year II and of the country at war. Hence, in textbooks, the narrative of events and the history of institutions have often obscured economic and social aspects. It is not that those aspects have been neglected but, where they have been studied, the dictatorship, the class struggle, the controlled economy and the terrorist repression have been judged in doctrinaire terms that have precluded true discussion. Moreover, historians have dwelt on memoirs in which survivors of the Terror vented their spleen – accounts that their descendants exploited to give credence to a number of persistent legends.

One must depoliticize these issues and remove the emotional obstacles to a proper understanding of them. For no other period as short as the Terror is there such a mass of primary sources and studies. Official records, made available only years later, are gradually revealing their treasures. As first-hand accounts by contemporaries, they have become standard references. The study of the popular movement has shed new light on Paris, and that of the 'revolutionary armies' has revealed provincial diversity. The balance-sheet of the Republic is no longer completely negative. Beside the tally of ruined or sacrificed lives, there is now a tally of individuals who managed to improve their existence.

Indeed, the authorities and artisans of the Year II had promised social happiness; they tried to ensure it by using the institutions, policies and ideas of their time. Often they were forerunners, and often the weight of inertia slowed their action, but they never gave up. The general impression they have conveyed to us leads to the inescapable conclusion that economic imperatives took precedence for them over all other aspects of the revolutionary struggle. Public safety, which was the government's objective, required that the people enrolled to defend it should be fed and armed.

I consider, as those authorities did, that their overriding duty lay in organizing and safeguarding an enterprise of unprecedented magnitude. The State, as manager of the firm called France, had to mobilize all the human and material resources of the nation. The State introduced both vertical and horizontal economic integration – before the terms existed – and tried to work out their smallest practical details. Jacobin cadres provided the State with technical officers, controllers and agents at every level, and they were kept to a strict compliance with orders. The State acted as partner, supplier and client.

The employer–State distributed wages, bonuses, relief and pensions to an enormous mass of citizens: in all, perhaps one million civilians and one and a half million military or para-military men owed their livelihood to the State, thus linking self-interest to patriotism and civic spirit. This was the Republic's true clientele – and another of its contradictions. The relations between the State and individuals became those of an employer with his employees. In the name of the people, the revolutionary government became their oppressor; patriots enslaved other patriots in the name of a general interest that they did not always understand.

The government of France, which had been on a provisional footing since 10 August, was supposed to follow a normal course after the Constitution had been voted by the Convention and ratified by the people. On 10 October 1793, however, the government was declared to be 'revolutionary until there is peace', and it lasted, *de jure* if not *de facto*, as long as the Convention, that is, until Brumaire Year IV (October 1795). The revolutionary government was the work of genuine democrats committed to liberty, justice and order. They assigned it a double task, which they believed would be short-lived: the elimination of domestic enemies and the pursuit of foreign war until total victory was achieved.

There were no limits on the authority of the revolutionary government, for it combined a constituent power – encompassing all other powers – with revolutionary dynamism, which made those powers effective. The government was vested with those powers by the people, whom it represented. It legislated and enforced laws in the name of the people and ran the country on new lines and with exceptional means. Against the wishes of its founders, who were incensed by the mere reference to the 'Roman magistrature', it was a dictatorial regime, based on 'the holiest of laws, public safety; the most irrefutable of principles, necessity'. A determined minority of *montagnards* and *sans-culottes* imposed this regime on the reluctant masses as long as the state of emergency remained in force in the beleaguered Republic. This minority espoused Jacobin ideals, intensified the patriotic impulse, and informed collective attitudes with its enthusiasms and apprehensions; it accepted economic constraints and applied them on a large scale by resorting to the Terror. Later, its militants, who had become civil servants, were tempted to exceed their powers. When the dictatorship encountered resistance, it became more radical.

'The fiercer the storm, the more vigorous and unflagging must be the hand that steers the rudder.' The government's hand came down heavily on individuals in its excessive desire for control. As a force in the service of the Revolution, directed against the Republic's adversaries, that heavy hand struck out right and left against patriots who objected to its demands. The Ventôse and Germinal purges, which guaranteed Jacobin supremacy, were ultimately fatal to the Revolution: the tide had begun to ebb.

THE 'CENTRAL IMPULSE'

'A movement led by the masses, which took them spontaneously towards direct democracy, and a strong government that relied on petty bourgeois support' seemed incompatible. The improvisations of 1793 – those of September in particular – were ineffective as long as a single will was unable to coordinate them. 'Unity is our fundamental maxim; unity is our anti-federalist defence; unity is our salvation.' Billaud-Varenne, Saint-Just and Robespierre gave the revolutionary dictatorship its theoretical foundations.

Their conception was based on the supremacy of the Convention, whose long-term survival had to be ensured at all costs. With the help of the *sans-culottes*, the *Montagne* had secured its parliamentary majority and its political positions. The decree of 14 Frimaire Year II (4 December 1793) fleshed out and codified existing institutions. The centralized structure built around the Assembly was extended from Paris to the country at large and its armies thanks to the representatives on mission.

Parliamentary government

'The Convention governs alone and it alone must govern.' It symbolized revolutionary continuity and national unity. Both as a whole and in each of its sections, it was a sovereign body. All of its members were tied together by joint responsibility; they remained subordinate to their constituents and were liable to their censure. 'A people who deserve their freedom do not idolize their representatives; they watch over them and in respecting them respect their own dignity.' Robespierre shared this belief with most of his colleagues.

Did the Assembly maintain its representative character in the Year II? From early 1793 to early 1794, thirty-five representatives resigned and a hundred or so died. Not wishing to resort to by-elections, the Convention filled its ranks with alternate representatives whose civic merits were closely scrutinized. These replacements did not modify the Assembly's social composition or political character. Although often unobtrusive, the *suppléants* were imbued with a sense of their exceptional duties and did not shirk them. Collot d'Herbois judged the representatives in these terms: 'They do not bear an exact resemblance to one another; Nature does not cast two men in the same mould, but all those who sit in it [the Assembly] are well intentioned and have positive hopes.'

During the winter of 1793, the parliamentary debates, which took place every day from ten a.m. to four p.m., were attended by 250 members at most — less than a third of the total — for the twice-weekly renewal of the Assembly's officers. It has been assumed that members were unenthusiastic and that the Convention confined itself to registering decrees. But that is a misconception of the nature of the Convention's legislative activity and the variety of issues with which it dealt. Petitions and messages, many and varied, arrived every day by the hundreds directly before the Assembly, for the people turned to 'the good Lord rather than his saints'. A division of labour became necessary. On the one hand, the decision-making power of the Assembly gave rise to constant discussions reported on by journalists; on the other, the groundwork was entrusted to specialists in the committees, of which there were nineteen.

The committees drafted bills and reports, sometimes jointly, and were reluctant to change or discard them. Committee members were swamped by administrative details and paperwork and to a great extent they acted for the ministers. It has been said that the representatives of the *Plaine* took refuge in committee work, striving through legislation to tone down revolutionary ardour — but in fact only the bureaucratic routine of the committees' departments deserves such criticism. On the contrary, the thoroughness with which committee members carried out their obscure and little-known task deserves our tribute. Camille Desmoulins observed in Frimaire: 'They have all been so busy and caught up in the whirlwind of events...that they have had no time to read, I should even say to meditate.' The pre-eminent role of the two 'government' committees helps to explain why the others have been neglected.

The 'great' Committee of Public Safety

The team that took charge of the Revolution during the Year II was assembled between 10 July and 20 September. It comprised eleven members, after the elimination of the fair Hérault de Séchelles, and occupied centre stage for ten months.[1] Robespierre contributed his experience and political intuition; Barère, his lively prose; Jeanbon Saint-André, Carnot, Lindet and the two Prieur brothers, their expertise and methods; Couthon, Saint-Just, Collot d'Herbois and Billaud-Varenne, their zeal and boldness. All belonged to the hard-working and thrifty petty bourgeoisie of the *ancien régime*. The eldest was just under forty-eight and the youngest twenty-six. Their strong personalities and temperaments, as well as overwork, were a source of clashes. Their differences of opinion were genuine: Lindet and Carnot, who were social conservatives, refused to join the Jacobin club, while Billaud and Collot had *sans-culotte* leanings. But they set aside their concerns, sentimental, family or professional, to devote themselves unremittingly to their homeland.

Their capacity for work and their extraordinary activity were astonishing. At seven in the morning, they would already be reading the first dispatches and discussing in detail all manner of questions. In the afternoon, several members would attend the Convention and, in the evening, the Jacobin club. At about eight o'clock, they would meet and their discussions would go on late into the night. Overcome by sleep, they would sometimes steal a nap on the camp beds set up in the committee room itself. There was no real intimacy among them – no common leisure or amusement. They spurned the 'showy trappings' that usually accompany power and were content with their parliamentary allowance of eighteen *livres* a day, paid in *assignats*. When they did eat at the nearby restaurant, they would have a meal for eight sous.[2]

---

[1] Hérault de Séchelles, a former *avocat général* (assistant public prosecutor) at the *Parlement* of Paris, was related to the Polignac and Contades families and had been a protégé of the queen. He was arrested on 18 March 1794 (27 Ventôse) and executed on 5 April with the *dantonistes* (see below, p. 117).

[2] 'Révélations...', published in G. Bouchard, *Prieur de la Côte d'Or* (**86**), pp. 433–57, and reproduced in M. Bouloiseau, *Le Comité de salut public* (**83**), p. 41.

The number of cases submitted to them – over five hundred a day – precluded their examination by the whole Committee. Instead, after being registered, they were handed out among the Committee's departments, whose staff was increased from 67 to 252 in the three winter months. The department heads, known as the 'examiners' (*les gens d'examen*) – Carnot for the War Department, Prieur de la Côte-d'Or for Weapons and Gunpowder, Lindet for Supplies – had greater responsibility for practical arrangements, but the power of decision was essentially collegial and orders needed at least three signatures. The 'overseers' (*les gens de la haute main*) – Robespierre, Saint-Just and Couthon – who were in charge of major policy issues, did not stand apart from the 'revolutionaries' – Billaud and Collot, responsible for correspondence. Their concerted or individual actions were marked by the same doctrinal rigour. Until Thermidor, institutional unity was maintained and proceedings kept strictly secret.

In theory, the Committee remained 'closed and inaccessible' to personal intervention, but it continually asked for the Convention's endorsement and used the Assembly as a cover. '[The Committee] is a portion, a summary version of yourselves; one cannot accuse it unjustly without attacking every one of you,' Barère declared to the representatives, who, every month, confirmed the Committee's powers. Until the first victories in the autumn of 1793, the Committee's existence was no less vulnerable than that of a government in a parliamentary system. Like those of the other committees, its proposals were circulated, commented upon and debated before being enacted in decrees; it was not enough for the Committee to make suggestions for the Assembly to submit. Couthon, Barère and Collot – more often than Robespierre – defended before the Convention the policies of a government that refused to call itself one: 'We are the arm set in motion by the Assembly.'

Even though limited to policy implementation, the Committee's influence was considerable. It controlled the ministers, who reported to it every evening to receive their instructions. The ministers, confined to looking after administrative details, were conscientious, upright, but opportunist, like Bouchotte at the War Ministry and Monge at the Navy. They accepted the Committee's tutelage as a form of protection. Public opinion recognized the Committee's authority, which the enemy believed to be absolute. Such subordination does not appear in the relations between the individuals involved. Representatives behaved as 'colleagues', spontaneously conveying information and offering suggestions to the Committee, which took them into account and was always attentive to local situations. Although Robespierre and Barère did not leave Paris, the other members, particularly Jeanbon Saint-André, Prieur de la Marne and Saint-Just, were often away. Just like the *montagnards* in the Convention, they went on long and trying missions. Thus all of them together constituted the government and contributed to its greatness.

Delegation of power

The Convention made a practice of delegating power. That practice has been compared to that of the *commissions d'intendants* under the *ancien régime*, but wrongly so, for the representatives never ceased regarding themselves as fractions of the sovereign people.

During the winter of 1793, more than one-third of the Assembly's members were away on mission in the *départements* and the armies. Whether assigned to a limited task or vested with unlimited powers, they displayed initiative and their orders showed that they interpreted the Convention's decrees with considerable latitude. They have also been portrayed as 'proconsuls of high and low lineage', but only a minority fit the description. Some, like Baudot in Strasburg, surrounded themselves with an impressive retinue and insolent pomp. Fréron and Carrier were said to have numerous mistresses. Several representatives, including Boisset, were gullible, while others were exceedingly rigid. Charles Alexandre considered Javogues 'a real lout who has just cast off his shackles'. However, they all felt that they were living up to their mission and behaving like true *montagnards*.

Every ten days they sent in a summary of their operations and copies of their orders to the Committee, which generally expressed approval. But some missions overlapped, exacerbating personal rivalries harmful to public order. Such was the case in the Moselle between Faure and Lacoste, and in the Lozère and Ardèche between Solon Reynaud, Chateauneuf-Randon and Boisset. Many representatives remained absent from Paris for a long period and acquired considerable freedom to manoeuvre in their regions.

The slowness of communications was an incentive to such initiatives. It took between eight and twelve days to get from Paris to Marseilles, and fourteen to reach the Ariège, while Lacombe-Saint-Michel in Corsica was practically cut off from the mainland. The representatives remained outspoken with the Committee, and warned it against intrigues – it was not being told the truth about events in the Vendée, nor about the army outside Toulon. 'You can remedy the situation', Ricord and Augustin Robespierre ('the younger') assured the Committee, 'by relying on our prudence'.

However, divergences were to be feared. 'You who have been entrusted with the same mission and the defence of the same interests, and who are committed to the same goals – you must act in step.' This reminder was all the more urgent as the 'missionaries', who could hardly be ubiquitous, were delegating their own powers in turn. 'That is one of the greatest abuses of our provisional government', observed Pocholle on 6 Brumaire; on the 13th, the representatives were prohibited from resorting to such methods. Envoys sent by the ministers were recalled and so the Committee had nearly all the *grandes missions* at its disposal before the decree of 14 Frimaire.

The decree of 14 Frimaire Year II

The 14 Frimaire decree, a fully fledged charter of the revolutionary government, included in a single text all the measures that accompanied the government's gradual development. The eleven-day discussion over the decree revealed a desire to 'simplify the intermediate cogs' of the State machinery. The Committee was entrusted with the task of achieving 'an identity of views, maxims and wills'. Only the Committee had the power to interpret decrees and spell out their details. There was already talk of abolishing the Conseil Exécutif. 'All constituent bodies and civil servants' were obliged to 'undergo immediate inspection' by the Committee. It took charge of 'major diplomatic operations' and submitted nominations of army chiefs and members of other committees to the Convention, which ratified them. The Paris Commune came under its control and the institutions dear to the *sans-culottes* were neutralized. The Committee assumed responsibility for the conduct of the war, provisioning, and order in the streets.

The *districts*, municipalities and *comités révolutionnaires*, cogs in the official machinery, applied the measures of public safety demanded by the *agents nationaux* chosen by *scrutin épuratoire* and invested with powers by the Assembly. These intermediate structures cooperated closely with the Assembly in achieving administrative centralization. As they were responsible on pain of death for carrying out orders, the lower echelons merely obeyed. Carefully drafted circulars enjoined them to do so. The Committee issued the following injunction to the *districts*: 'The law has drawn a circle for you; never overstep its bounds'; to the town administrations: 'Disregarding the passions of others and your own, you must strive to deserve by your virtue the right to punish crime'; to the *agents nationaux*: 'Just remember... that other eyes are watching ...The axe of justice is hanging today over the judge's head.'

'As workers of the Republic, we are each manufacturing the part that has been assigned to us in this vast construction.' Subjected to the national will and not to a handful of men, the 'workers' could, without losing their dignity, submit to the law. Such precautions were useless: the *montagnard* dictatorship, having acquired institutional status, now fed on a monotonous and obsessive propaganda that dominated public opinion.

Propaganda and dictatorship of opinion

'The *sans-culottes* have only good will. They could do with the constant presence of an electrical stimulus.' In their passion for unity, the men in power did not regard the masses as capable of looking after themselves. 'The people are sublime, but individuals are weak.' The Revolution therefore had to transform the individual mind and shape public consciousness. Opinions, which remained free, nevertheless needed to be 'guided towards what is good and useful'.

The Convention devoted its *Bulletin* to these aims, printing speeches and narratives dealing with civic actions. The *Bulletin* gradually reached every town, village and army. The major reports presented at the Convention, which were widely circulated, had 'a beneficial effect that one cannot evaluate at a distance. They won over everybody's hearts and filled them with hope.' The Committee of Public Safety had its own printing presses for emergencies. It sponsored patriotic journalists and financed their publications. After the fall of the *Gironde* Fabre d'Eglantine went so far as to concoct a vast scheme: three groups of newspapers (for rural areas, towns and armies) written by thirty *montagnard* representatives, printed in 45,000 copies, and distributed free. The nationalization of the press followed a different course. The subscription system that covered owners' costs was maintained, but ministries took out a great number of subscriptions to the *Antifédéraliste*, the *Feuille du salut public* and the *Père Duchesne*. Some papers disappeared and others were founded; fifty or so new publications were launched in the year II, including the *Journal de la Montagne*, mouthpiece of the Jacobin club.

Most members of the Convention regarded the club as its necessary adjunct. Representatives would report to the club on their return from missions. Robespierre devoted special attention to it and spoke there more often than at the Assembly. The Jacobins kept a close watch over purge proceedings and opposed every exception in favour of nobles. In order to act as the 'guide of public opinion', the Jacobins had to be distrustful of the 'fanaticism of immoral men', Cordelier excesses and *sociétés sectionnaires*. Through the affiliated clubs – which 'regenerated' themselves – and the *sociétés populaires* established in small towns, the Jacobins propagated their circulars throughout the country. The number of such circulars has been underestimated and their impact in the provinces is hard to assess. The Jacobin influence was stronger in the provinces than in Paris, for rural notables used it as a palliative.

In a largely illiterate France, the people's ignorance ensured that they were kept under guardianship. National unity and training for citizenship demanded an improvement in education, which was proclaimed to be a constitutional right. Lepeletier's education plan, revived by Robespierre, is worth remembering for its doctrinal boldness (education was to be compulsory, secular and free) and pedagogic innovation (physical, moral and social instruction to prepare for community life). The war effort consigned the project to oblivion and the government confined itself to waging a struggle against dialects: 'Let us destroy these instruments of harm and error.' On 8 Pluviôse, Barère obtained the appointment of French teachers, but their training remained inadequate and primary education stayed in private hands. As a makeshift measure, the *sociétés populaires* were invited to become 'schools for Liberty'. In the name of Equality, Latin was banned, on the grounds that its mysterious character fuelled the fanaticism of humble folk.

The use of a single language contributed to political unity and was a weapon capable of 're-creating the people by revolutionizing habits, morals and dress'. The new calendar, introduced on 5 October 1793, broke with the traditional system of dating. Weeks were replaced by ten-day units (*décades*) and months were renamed to reflect the seasons and agricultural work.[3] The introduction of the metric system, which unified methods of reckoning, gave rise to a proposal for a decimal division of time which, however, was not adopted. An effort was also made to abolish old customaries and replace them with a civil code.

---

[3] Romme's report was submitted to the Convention on 20 September, and Fabre d'Eglantine's report on the names of months was presented on 3 Brumaire Year II (24 October 1793).

On 22 August, a first draft was begun, but work proceeded slowly. The introduction of divorce, rights for natural children and equal inheritance rights – described as a 'land-carving machine' – made inroads into existing family structures.

There was also the question of whether the Jacobin ideology and traditional religious beliefs could coexist in a republican society. On 18 September 1793, Catholicism ceased to be a public religion and priests lost their status as civil servants. The closure of churches was ordered on 3 Frimaire. The increasing number of patriotic celebrations gave widespread publicity to Jacobin slogans by attracting vast crowds in Paris and other towns for processions, speeches and choruses where familiar tunes would be sung.

These forms of propaganda had a greater effect on popular attitudes than did theatre performances. Young writers were commissioned to produce plays inspired by Greek history and Spartan simplicity. One free performance a month was planned. Hassenfratz even suggested *montagnard* banquets where one could eat one or twice a week for thirty sous. One could imagine the *sans-culotte*'s new day of rest (*décadi*) thus:

We find him first in the temple of Reason, in a peculiar psychological state, as if fascinated, hypnotized by the ceremonies taking place there. He is about to lose his conscious personality. He goes out with his co-religionists. He talks. He gets excited. Where is he going? To the club. There his exaltation reaches its peak; he vehemently supports the most violent motions. Where will he spend his evening? At the theatre, in another environment of *sans-culotterie*... The triumphs of the Revolution, the Republic and Democracy are celebrated to every kind of rhythm; patriot saints and republican husbands are extolled.[4]

Thus were produced the 'mustachioed worthies' who 'walked with a firm stride down the path of Revolution'. The force of their convictions was contagious. Couthon wanted fifty of them to indoctrinate Lyons. A hundred would perhaps have sufficed to dethrone 'Pitt and the British tyrant'. Their presence stimulated a collective consciousness already exacerbated by its hatred of the *ancien régime* and the foreign invader, as well as by its obsession with plots and treason. The people's safety required 'the extermination of all the schemers who are stirring up the Republic'. It was to thwart these schemers that the Terror was legalized.

[4] M. Dommanget, 'Le Symbolisme et le prosélytisme révolutionnaires...', *AHRF*, 1929, p. 373.

Up to this point the Terror had been conducted at random. The will
to punish and summary justice – both inseparable from the
Revolution – were spontaneous outgrowths of troubled times. Far
from being arbitrary and tyrannical, the Terror that had been 'put on
the agenda' was meant to be both preventive by instilling fear of the
gendarme and repressive by being directed against the sworn enemies
of the Republic. The Terror conferred an awesome power on the
revolutionary government that wielded it. Billaud-Varenne depicted
the Terror as 'fearsome for plotters, coercive towards the agents of the
State, stern for corrupt officials, formidable for the wicked, a protector
for the oppressed, relentless for oppressors, well disposed to patriots,
and benevolent for the people'.[5]

The Terror demanded intelligence, steadfastness and objectivity of
its agents. Their civic sense was meant to guide them more than their
degree of education. The true impact of the Terror ultimately depended
on their temperament.

The terrorist apparatus

The Committee of General Security, the second 'government Committee', served as the 'ministry of revolutionary police'. As successor
to the Legislative Assembly's *comité de surveillance* – one half of whose
members it inherited, along with their expertise – it came under heavy
attack during the crisis of September 1793. On the 8th, the Convention
asked for the Committee's renewal on the grounds that the Committee
was easily influenced and was being hoodwinked. The 'corrupt'
members – Basire, Chabot and Julien de Toulouse – were eliminated.
The new membership comprised twelve representatives, including
Vadier, Amar and Le Bas, who remained in office until Thermidor.
Like the Committee of Public Safety, the Committee of General
Security was a 'great' Committee and it played a major role.

It exerted its influence over individuals by exposing subversive
opinions and actions. Its police functions empowered it to exercise
surveillance, carry out searches, and seize documents, including mail.
The security of the State rested with the Committee, whose discretionary powers extended to all of France and beyond, since it was

[5] Speech of 28 Brumaire Year II (18 November 1793), quoted in J. Godechot, *Les
Institutions de la France...*, 1951 edn (**82**), p. 258.

also in charge of counter-espionage. Civilian authorities and generals were also subject to its control.

The Committee's members were distributed among four sections, each of which handled a geographical division, conducted investigations and interrogations, confronted witnesses, and prepared the cases that led to the release or arrest of suspects. Principled, unbending and jealous of their power, the Committee's members resented the sort of guardianship exercised by the Committee of Public Safety, which summoned them all together once a week. The task of the Committee of General Security was an unpleasant one in such dangerous times, when denunciations – sometimes outlandish, often petty – were flowing in. Decisions were collegial and would be taken in the evening; sessions dragged on. Every case had to be settled by a vote of half the members present, who later excused themselves for having turned into 'signature machines'. However, their personal responsibility was at stake and they submitted a monthly report to the Convention, which paid for their considerable secret expenses. The Committee employed numerous observers in Paris, supervised by Maillard, as well as agents in the provinces, including Héron, Sénar, Dossonville and the dubious Nicolas Guenot, who took part in André Chénier's arrest. But were they typical of the Terror as a whole and was their behaviour identical to that of all the members of the *comités révolutionnaires*?

Under different names, the *comités révolutionnaires* had been set up in several towns as early as 10 August 1792 by popular demand. The decree of 21 March 1793, which provided for one *comité* in every municipality, initially entrusted them only with the monitoring of foreign residents. The *comités* were composed of twelve elected officials – *ci-devants* excluded – and were subjected to a succession of purges. Their members received an allowance and were recruited increasingly from among the *sans-culottes*. After 14 Frimaire, they were made responsible for enforcing revolutionary measures in conjunction with the municipalities and *districts*. The urban *comités* displayed a sometimes excessive and chaotic zeal in issuing passports, identity papers (*certificats de civisme*) and arrest warrants, destroying the traces of feudalism, and inspecting prisons. In the countryside, they were less active and their objectives questionable. The rural *comités* were created later and were hard put to avoid entanglement in village rivalries. Nevertheless, by their mere presence, they served the Republic by discouraging resistance. They were rightly regarded as 'the mainsprings of the Terror'.

The 'revolutionary armies' obtained, at the local level, more spectacular but less durable results. Their martial appearance and the guillotine that accompanied them emphasized the repressive character of their mission.[6] These armies had not been created to 'string beads', proclaimed the *Père Duchesne*, but to 'sever heads'. Their soldiers and officers, who wore Phrygian caps, were paid at the highest rate, forty sous a day. They were loath to observe strict discipline and made trouble where they were supposed to maintain order. Their excesses often shocked public opinion and the authorities, but they were 'neither demons nor saints'. The government was apprehensive about their anarchic behaviour; it recommended to the representatives that they should disband the armies and the Convention, on 14 Frimaire, did so with the exception of the Parisian army – which, however, did not survive the fall of the *hébertistes* and was abolished on 7 Germinal.

Although the 'revolutionary armies' were violently criticized, especially after Thermidor, one must admit, with Barère, that 'if they aroused [counter-revolutionary] fanaticism by committing some abuses, they put down some disturbances by their resolute action'. Their efficiency was hindered by their fragmentation. In some instances they carried out the directives of the Committee of General Security and followed a consistent course, while in other cases local authorities used them to carry out police tasks. However, it is more their verbal violence than their 'crimes' that helped to stifle the counter-revolution and neutralize suspects.

Suspects and prisoners

The notion of 'suspect' followed from the basic distinction established among citizens by the revolutionary government. Those who collaborated in its policies deserved protection by the law; the enemies of the Republic deserved only death. However, it was necessary to introduce finer distinctions. The decree of 17 September 1793, which recapitulated earlier measures, attempted unsuccessfully to set out a comprehensive definition, which was diversely interpreted. Some officials regarded an unfavourable comment on the *maximum* as proof of a subversive attitude, while others prosecuted only crimes of *lèse-nation*. Returned *émigrés* and rebels caught under arms were subject to capital punishment

---

[6] On his return from the Vendée, Parein, addressing the Jacobins, demanded a second guillotine in order to 'cast all the aristocrats into the void'.

after a mere identity check. Agitators and federalist leaders also came under the heading of 'suspects' and were treated as outlaws.

The case of nobles and priests, on the other hand, was never fully settled. Despite the people's wishes, they were at first merely disarmed. Later, those who were denounced were imprisoned, placed under house arrest, or brought before a tribunal, along with foreigners and deposed officials. In those cases there were still precise motives for legal action. But how can one assess today accusations arising out of often unknown circumstances? Besides the 'traitors', 'plotters', 'federalists' and 'hoarders' whose misdeeds are not specified, how many 'schemers', 'tyrants', 'fanatics', 'egoists' and 'charlatans'! How many unfortunate individuals who got into trouble for having infringed decrees they knew nothing about! Could one treat as guilty 100,000 inhabitants of the Gironde, 50,000 Normans and as many Bretons, Marseillais, Savoyards and Alsatians? The representatives on mission who were confronted with these problems were acutely embarrassed. Nearly all of them turned a blind eye and punished only the ringleaders.

The number of suspects has been variously estimated at between 300,000 and 800,000, that is, between 1 and 4 per cent of the population.[7] That one portion of France was suspicious of the other is a certainty, but that one half hounded the other like 'animals at bay' hardly bears up to examination. Moreover, there were degrees of suspicion and of constraints upon freedom.

Ordinary prisons were so quickly filled up that old convents and other hastily converted buildings had to be used. The prisoners, who 'would be held until peace returned', were crammed into these quarters and fed, as well as could be expected, at their own expense; deprived of medical attention, they were decimated by epidemics. But detention conditions were not the same everywhere: in the Maison Belhomme, at the top of the Rue de Charonne in Paris, the wealthiest prisoners led a relatively peaceful life, communicated with the outside world, met in the courtyards, and organized a semblance of social life. Although there were very few guards, detainees did not attempt to escape, for fear of being turned in at once. Some inmates managed to keep out of the limelight, while others sent in a flood of petitions to the authorities, who were also besieged by their relatives. The authorities realized the need to conduct a thorough review of arrest

[7] See J. Godechot, *Les Institutions de la France...*, 1951 edn (**82**), p. 320.

warrants, to ensure 'the triumph of innocence', and to redress errors. Couthon did not object, on 17 Frimaire, to the 'Clemency Committee' called for by Danton, who divided prisoners into three categories: 'Some who deserve death; a great number whom the Republic must keep in custody; and a few who can be released without harming the Republic.' Robespierre himself considered that 'one must be lenient towards certain offences that result from human weaknesses'.

The fact of the matter was that the Terror, under the impulse of the terrorists, was in danger of overreaching itself. From Brumaire to Germinal, the number of political prisoners doubled in Paris and at the time its twenty-seven prisons held over 6,000, not all of them Parisians. The national total was put at 90,000.[8] A general study has yet to be made to determine the rate of arrests, their motives and duration, and the social origins of detainees. It already appears that there were some releases before September 1793 and that the *comités de surveillance* stepped up their activity during the winter, rounding up both men and women, nobles and priests, bourgeois and artisans, rich and poor – most of whom, in fact, were spared and released.

Revolutionary justice

Jacobins and *sans-culottes* demanded 'swift, stern and unbending' justice. The Revolutionary Tribunal in Paris still followed the procedures laid down by the Constituent Assembly: it was composed of a public prosecutor who presented the charges, jurors who passed verdicts after hearing witnesses, and judges who handed down sentences based on laws still in force. Until September it handled 260 cases and pronounced 66 death sentences (26 per cent of the total). Later, it was swamped with the sheer numbers of accused persons and came under attack for its slowness. Questions were raised about the integrity of Fouquier-Tinville, a judicial bureaucrat of no real standing. The will to punish imposed urgent demands. Gaston de l'Ariège even suggested to the Convention that it should 'lay its hands on all suspects and lock them up in places that would be set on fire in case of a royalist insurrection'. To stop this excess of violence, the Tribunal's efficiency was quadrupled by appointing more members and speeding up procedure. Death sentences were handed down in greater numbers: until 10 Nivôse (30 December) there were 177 for 395 accused persons

---

[8] At the end of the Year III, Boudin, a representative from the Indre, put the number of suspects incarcerated during the Year II at 80,000.

(45 per cent). In the Place de la Révolution, the guillotine provided strollers with regular free shows.

But the great trials did not satisfy the Parisian crowd. Hébert had spent three months asking for the trial of the queen, who was executed on 16 October. The *girondins'* trial opened on the 26th and looked as if it would last for ever, prompting this comment by Chaumette on the Tribunal and its methods: 'It tries plotters as it would try a pickpocket.' The *girondins* were admired for their courage at their execution, which drew a vast crowd. 'National vengeance', too long in the making, exacerbated unrest and passion instead of assuaging or satisfying public opinion. 'Too many laws are being made, and not enough examples', noted Saint-Just.

In the *départements*, the criminal tribunals proceeded with the same precautions for they were composed of *hommes de loi* trained under the *ancien régime* and faithful to its practices. Hébert denounced their weaknesses and fondness for money and pretty women. 'The Revolution has changed the situation and men have remained the same; unfortunately judges are only men.' Most of them carried out their duties conscientiously and maintained their independence, sentencing outlaws but displaying leniency towards crimes of opinion. The performance of the Blois Tribunal in 'making three heads fall in Brumaire' was considered exceptional; the guillotine set up in Metz ceased to function in Frimaire.

'Our repressive laws are made for a people no longer living in a revolutionary crisis; they are certainly not suited for the present moment.'[9] This remark, made sixteen months previously, was still topical. Could one 'manage revolutions through judicial pettifoggery'? Special tribunals were established in Rochefort, Brest and Nancy to try without jury royalist sailors and hoarders. The Strasburg Tribunal, made famous by one of its members, the defrocked priest Euloge Schneider, pronounced more confiscations than death sentences. Elsewhere, a dozen commissions, reduced to three judges and sometimes called 'popular', ordered the execution of rebels caught under arms in Lyons, Marseilles, Nîmes, Toulouse and the west. They also acquitted suspects, whereas the military commissions – not to be confused with army tribunals – handed down only death sentences.[10] There were about sixty military commissions, named after their presidents, and often the exact number of their victims is unknown.

[9] Comment recorded at Douai on 22 August 1792 and quoted by G. Aubert, *AHRF*, 1924, p. 74.   [10] See below, p. 148.

This anarchic proliferation — the work of representatives on mission — weakened government control over the Terror. The 14 Frimaire decree forbade special courts and gave absolute priority to the Paris Tribunal. Yet special courts survived in several towns and operated after Germinal with increased rigour. Hence it is hard to provide more than approximate figures for executions, suspects and prisoners; moreover, such figures cannot be established before Thermidor. Nevertheless, one can already note that although many persons were arrested on economic charges, few were executed for economic crimes.

RUNNING THE ECONOMY

Administrative and economic centralization went hand in hand. The state of siege forced France into autarky; to save the Republic the government mobilized all the nation's productive forces and reluctantly accepted the need for a controlled economy, which it introduced extemporaneously, as the emergency required. Far from implementing a social policy, as has been claimed, the government was chiefly concerned with efficiency alone. While outwardly rigorous, government policy lacked a constructive programme and was reduced to a flurry of annoying measures reminiscent of the royal *régies* (economic agencies). These measures were frustrating to those who were expecting laws that would bring prosperity and they caused those whose interests were harmed thereby to band together against the Revolution. Despite these manoeuvres and obstacles, the Committee of Public Safety managed through sheer energy to supply troops and save urban populations from famine — a miracle that astonished the world.

The Food Commission

The Food Commission (Commission des Subsistances) was established on 1 Brumaire (22 October 1793) and placed under the direct supervision of the Committee of Public Safety. Its three members were carefully picked top civil servants, and the best specialists in their fields.[11] Young, 'upright, enlightened and, above all, revolutionary patriots', they were experts in 'law, commerce and navigation'; they also knew how to handle men. From the outset, they were assigned an inhuman task.

[11] Raisson, *secrétaire général* of the Paris *département*, Goujon, *procureur-général-syndic* of the Seine-et-Oise, and Brunet, an official in the Hérault.

Their authority extended to all sectors of the economy, from production to transport and commodity distribution. They oversaw foreign purchases and domestic requisitions, set prices, and ensured the provisioning of the armies and Paris. Apart from these immediate tasks, there were more long-term objectives: the improvement of agricultural techniques, yields and husbandry; forestry and mining development. Far from duplicating the activity of the Convention's Agriculture Committee, which drafted decrees, the Food Commission presided over their enforcement. It made forecasts, put forward proposals, and took decisions with the approval of Robert Lindet – recalled from Normandy – and the counter-signature of the 'great' Committee.

Such prerogatives required a permanent staff and occasional outside assistance. There were soon over 500 employees working for the Commission in three departments – production, distribution and accounting – as well as a host of agents sent to the provinces. In addition, specialists like Hassenfratz, military and civilian officials like Pache, the mayor of Paris, and civil servants from the Treasury were invited to meetings of the Commission, for it controlled its own expenditure and was empowered to requisition armed forces. For help in commercial matters it relied on an advisory council composed of a former banker, Moutte, a well-known seed merchant, Vilmorin, and a Parisian wholesale grocer, Lesguillier, who had been president of the Tribunal de Commerce. Later, two more sections were created, one for the cadastral survey, the other to supervise operations in the *districts*, with whom the Commission corresponded directly. This public service, set up in one month and turned into a gigantic machine, was surrounded by technical experts whose advice it heeded and applied.

The government first displayed its authority in the area of production. The Commission's members, imbued with physiocratic theories, believed that the earth – the nation's soundest asset – should be worked rationally. The *ancien régime* had channelled the development of agriculture towards capitalism, but the initiatives of the notables had been hindered by community traditions and family-run mixed farming. The need to step up wheat production was taken as an excuse to attempt to regulate and develop basic crops and shake off old habits.

A search was launched for available lands as a concession to the wishes of the peasantry. By early winter, parks and pleasure gardens, including the Luxembourg in Paris and those belonging to the Liste Civile, were turned over and sowed in spectacular fashion. It was decreed somewhat unrealistically in Frimaire that marshlands should be drained and ploughed. 'We are all taking part in the plot against carp, and we are for the reign of sheep,' Danton commented ironically. Heaths, moors and copses were cleared. Recommendations were issued to restrict the size of vineyards and meadows so as to make room for wheat fields. The cultivation of potatoes, turnips, carrots and plants yielding oil and fibre was encouraged. Attempts were made to improve livestock by purchasing merinos and good breeding-stock. Private individuals flooded the 'plant' and 'animal' sections of the Commission with countless projects about the use of fertilizers, farming without fallowing land, agricultural education, the struggle against bunt and epizootic diseases, and the use of the scythe and rake. Unquestionably, rural France was awakening and growing aware of its backwardness. Agronomy was becoming revolutionary and held out the hope of increased profits to all farmers.

This innovative spirit, which mobilized a portion of the peasantry, has failed to receive due notice. Historians have confined themselves to analysing the Commission's reports, which are a fairly distant reflection of that spirit. Moreover, the Commission's circulars rarely had a compulsory character. The Commission behaved like the old agricultural societies, but its propaganda was not without effect. Obsessed as they were in the short term by cereal production, the authorities devoted scanty attention to vegetables and especially to the potato. However, the notion of planting potatoes caught on as soon as it was realized that they could make low-grade soil worth farming and provide an extra source of food. If attempts at crop regulation were limited, they nevertheless helped to hasten technical progress and increase the amount of arable land.

To achieve an equitable distribution of production, the Food Commission examined the resources and needs of the Republic. It made available the latest data and survey findings to a special department, forerunner of modern statistical services. Census techniques, already used by the Contrôle Général under Terray and Turgot, acquired new dimensions. They were applied not only to the population and tax revenues, but to all the products of farming, husbandry and industry. On 9 Brumaire (30 October), municipalities were asked to provide figures for cereal supplies and inhabitants; on 15 Brumaire (5 November), the Convention asked the Minister of the Interior to prepare a comprehensive report on the harvest. Although they were 'personally responsible' for their surveys, local authorities confined themselves to reproducing farmers' statements. Obsessed by the possibility of higher taxes, the farmers, despite threats, were loath to disclose their assets and it would have been too expensive to verify their claims thoroughly. The results obtained with such difficulty were therefore not considered particularly reliable. Forecasts were adjusted slowly, whereas the circumstances required immediate solutions.

Requisitioning and hoarding

The national monopoly of commodities suffered from these uncertainties. Requisitions were carried out on the basis of estimates that were often erroneous. Decisions to redistribute supplies from regions with a surplus to areas in need were taken somewhat at random; quotas seemed arbitrary and excessive despite a bumper crop.

But the Commission centralized orders and put an end to rival missions. It coordinated the activities of its agents and those of the war commissioners. The provisioning of civilians came second as the Commission gave the armies and the capital top priority. However, in dealing with emergencies, it sometimes took away stocks from certain *départements* and resupplied them later. Some *départements* close to where troops were stationed had to put up with constant requisitioning, while others, far removed, suffered less. Economic centralization was not completely enforced and distribution remained very unequal.

As the centre-piece of the system inaugurated on 14 Frimaire, the *district* enjoyed a measure of autonomy, but its means were limited. Each *district* theoretically lived on its reserves and was forbidden to encroach upon its neighbour. The authorities did not take into account the discrepancy between the boundaries of the *district* and its traditional markets, where growers were required to bring their produce. At most the *district* was allowed to requisition in its own *arrondissement*. The situation thereby created was responsible for isolated cases of dearth, which were hastily relieved by representatives on mission. The Commission refrained from ordering the supervision of mills or nation-wide rationing. The Convention merely fixed quality standards for bolted flour on 25 Brumaire (15 November); later, it prescribed the ingredients for the 'bread of equality'. Hence, depending on local conditions, the authorities resorted to ordinary expedients: municipal bakeries, family ration cards for bread, control of private stocks and a ban on pastry.

Hoarders – the *bêtes noires* of the *sans-culottes* – benefited from official leniency. The commissioners of urban *sections* and the members of *comités de surveillance*, who had to contend with the merchants' bad faith, were allowed to conduct searches and seize surplus commodities. But the government forbade domiciliary visits and local requisitions. The Convention abolished capital punishment for profiteers and replaced it with fines and imprisonment. The Revolutionary Tribunal, which was authorized to try crimes against the economy, combined them with political charges that came within the province of the law on 'suspects'. After 12 Germinal (2 April 1794), only wholesalers were required to submit an inventory of their stock to the authorities and post it outside their warehouses. Compared to the number of denunciations, there were few legal proceedings. Fraud became practically universal, with regard not only to price and weight but also to quality. Its effects were especially noticeable on bread and wine, but textiles and soap were affected as well. A clandestine market where prices exceeded the *maximum*, and which was therefore accessible only to the wealthy, flourished without being discouraged by the Terror. Moreover, the mixed system of distribution at a fixed price to the poor alongside freedom of purchase for others prevailed in most cities, where it limited the municipalities' financial burden.

The Commission had envisaged filling the reserve granaries with levies and farm rents in kind, but it failed in its efforts to institute this scheme through a succession of circulars. Stocks were depleted as soon as they had been built up, leaving no choice but requisitioning. However, the representatives were meant to use requisitions as a last resort and with the utmost care after having informed the Committee of Public Safety. Soon the entire grain harvest, including the family reserve, was deemed to belong to the nation. Although the Convention abolished the family reserve on 25 Brumaire (15 November), citing its alleged misuse, the practice did not disappear altogether, for seed had to be preserved.

Furthermore, requisitions, while threatening to deprive the farmer of the fruit of his labour, fell short of meeting the nation's needs. Tradesmen, frightened by the climate of suspicion and by popular insults, gave way to inertia or grudgingly performed their traditional functions. The government tried to stimulate trade without sacrificing consumer interests. In order to meet these two requirements, existing economic controls had to be reviewed.

The 'maximum général'

The *sans-culottes* had welcomed the announcement of the extension of controls to the entire range of prices and wages (*maximum général*), calling it a 'great blessing', an 'act of justice' and a 'victory'. But producers and possessors of consumer goods did not share that euphoria. They wanted by whatever means to escape from a law that reduced their profits. Frenchmen, for whom tax evasion was a time-honoured custom, applied their intellectual skills to the task. One would almost have had to assign an inspector to every farmer and tradesman. In addition, the decrees of 11 and 29 September, drafted in haste, created only a semblance of uniformity. Although scales had been fixed at the national level by the Assembly, each *district* administration adjusted them as it saw fit and according to local conditions. Moreover, transport charges were not taken into account, so that it was in the seller's interest to deliver his goods to the nearest market. Finally, the one-third increase in prices over the levels of 1790 favoured the producer and penalized the small retailer, who had to bear the cost of damages and losses.[12] .

'Thus, colleagues', wrote Albitte, 'a good deed poorly prepared does harm.' Barère denounced the *maximum* as 'a trap laid for the Convention by the enemies of the Republic', a ploy by Pitt and the counter-revolution. But there was room for improvement. By imposing controls 'at the centre' and remunerating wagoners and shopkeepers – a 'class of good republicans who purchase and live from hand to mouth' – one could bring the circulation of foodstuffs back to normal. On 11 Brumaire, the newly created Food Commission was entrusted with this heavy responsibility. The general price list would be calculated on a precise basis, starting with production prices at 1790 levels, increased by one-third, to which would be added packaging costs as well as 5 per cent for the wholesaler's profit and 10 per cent for the retailer. A sliding allowance would offset transport charges. Twelve commissioners chosen in the provinces and Paris were assigned to four departments – food; textiles; chemical products and hardware; metals and fuels – that acted as clearing-houses for information sent in by municipalities and *sociétés populaires*.

This massive undertaking was not completed until 2 Ventôse (21 February 1794), a delay that caused widespread apprehension and

[12] See above, p. 81.

prompted schemers to circulate a false document in Paris on the 4th. The people grumbled outside the shops and tradesmen grew irritated. Requisitions continued in accordance with previous laws and, to assure army provisioning, representatives on mission were granted many dispensations. They bought above the *maximum* and paid in cash – procedures that did not help to clarify the situation.

The general price-scales were made public in the capital on 5 Germinal (25 March). *District* officials were responsible for determining retail prices in their region by adding profit margins and local expenses to the 'general' price. Barère proclaimed that no nation had ever carried out such a task. But his optimism was unwarranted. Although discrepancies had been reduced, prices still varied from region to region; they were also lower on the lists than in practice. As for wages, they had been heavily cut. While they had been unregulated before the law of 29 September, they had risen – despite controls – owing to the pressures of mass conscription and wartime production. In fact, entrepreneurs were torn between self-interest – which led them to comply with the new scales – and their manpower needs. Labourers and skilled workers in particular demanded up to three times the regular wage. Faced with the violation of food price controls, workers banded together in *coalitions*, obliging the Committee of Public Safety to take action against them. In the countryside, the law was circumvented by increasing payments in kind.

Domestic trade picked up when requisitions were eased. The authorities turned a blind eye to minor infringements and the practice of cash compensations, which guaranteed settlement of transactions. The *maximum* was applied to requisitioned items, but purchases by private treaty were still allowed for certain products and for livestock. Traders' profits were held within reasonable limits, but no trader operated at a loss. Paper manufacturers, among others, boasted of selling at a quarter above earlier prices. The tanning industry was revived at Montauban.[13] Although State orders and private consumers' needs provided firms with guaranteed outlets, foreign trade became a necessity.

[13] See D. Ligou, 'Cuirs et chaussures à Montauban en l'an II', in Commission d'Histoire Economique de la Révolution Française, *Mémoires et Documents*, vol. 13, 1958, p. 79. A shoe factory run by the State was even created.

Foreign trade

The sea blockade reduced foreign trade without interrupting it altogether. But the Committee of Public Safety, alarmed by the rivalry among government missions, put the Food Commission in charge of purchases, payment and merchant fleet activity. The Commission was flanked by an Agency whose five members were to decide on imports and exports, henceforth placed under State control. British merchandise was sequestered. The Navigation Act – which had been modelled on Cromwell's and restricted trading to ships flying the national flag – was suspended; French ports were opened to neutral ships. In Nantes, Bordeaux and Marseilles, French agents dealt with Sweden, Denmark, the Hanseatic States, the United States and Genoa. The agents were also offered privateers' spoils for sale. Horses and arms were obtained through Switzerland.

The government dispossessed traders who were 'too corrupt to deserve the trust of a free people', but it enlisted the help of patriots and took their advice. It bought up the Compagnie d'Afrique and benefited from its traditional relations with the Barbary Coast pirates. The government also had official suppliers abroad, including Haller in Leghorn. On 21 Pluviôse (19 February 1794), it ordered the seizure of commercial bills payable abroad and forced Paris bankers, including Perrégaux, to sign bills worth fifty million *livres*. This measure helped to increase food imports, but in return it made the outflow of specie increasingly ruinous.

If the 'revolutionary policy' of the Food Commission was oblivious to 'mercantile calculations', only the lure of gain attracted foreign merchants. They shied away from danger and financial risk, refusing to be paid at *maximum* prices and in *assignats*, or in bills of exchange that were often protested. The French authorities resigned themselves at first to cash payments. However, neutral ships, which could not set sail again in ballast, wanted freight for the return journey. The Commission provided them with the luxury goods that France had in plentiful supply: fine fabrics, lace and silk, all exempted from price controls, followed by fine wines and spirits, which the *sans-culottes* did not drink. The authorities made extensive use of sequestered assets: the *émigrés'* silverware, gems and furniture, now national property, paid for French imports.

From the spring of 1794, the volume of exports increased considerably. Private merchants were allowed to export colonial produce, including sugar and coffee. Barter agreements ensured a healthy trade balance. Without returning to total freedom, the State gave an increasingly free hand to those who agreed to help it, and it benefited from their experience. The State also took advantage of their credit while it lasted; and, as long as controls were maintained, the flight of capital was reduced. But these businessmen collaborated without enthusiasm and often without making a profit: 'Our duty is to submit.' They did not forgive the Republic for their humiliations and led an underhand campaign against the *assignat*.

Budget and currency: 'revolutionary taxes' and 'loans'

Foreign countries, whether enemy or neutral, condemned the French monetary system to isolation. The *assignat* was worthless abroad unless it remained negotiable for cash on the open exchange, like sterling. Moreover, it posed a double-edged threat since, whatever its exchange rate, the mechanism of exchange premiums was likely to drain off cash from neighbouring States into the French finance market. Bankers and traders in Bâle were submerged with these speculative demands.

Cambon, who controlled the French Treasury, agreed with Saint-Just on the need to reduce the amount of fiduciary currency in circulation. This inflation has been attributed to war expenditure, but ordinary expenditure, which was not fully covered by taxation, was also a factor. The payment of *biens nationaux* in annual instalments did not generate as much revenue as had been expected. Moreover, the Revolution had generously assumed pensions, stipends and debts left over from the *ancien régime*. When added to emergency expenses, these outstanding charges overburdened the budget, which ran a deficit of nearly 200 million *livres* a month during the whole of the Year II. The State was therefore in no position to stop producing *assignats*, which saved it from bankruptcy. The State, in turn, supported its paper currency.

As the *assignat* was a standardized currency that served as the sole legal tender, its stability guaranteed contracts. The problem of the *assignat* concerned not just finance and the economy, but society at large. Confidence in the currency was a political imperative and a safeguard for public order. The government and the legislature understood that and agreed first to make the rich pay, as the *sans-culottes* had wanted. 'Revolutionary taxes' were levied locally for specific purposes: troop kits, food purchases and poor relief. These taxes, which were variously designed and yielded little, were abandoned after

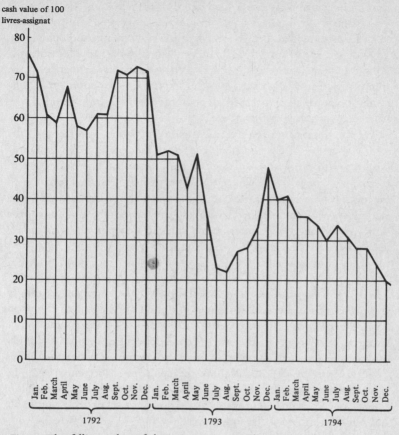

cash value of 100
livres-assignat

Fig. 4 The falling value of the *assignat* in Paris (1792–4). After P. Caron,
Tableaux de dépréciation du papier-monnaie, Paris, 1909

Frimaire, because of their adverse effect on ordinary tax revenues. The
'forced loan' of 1,000 million *livres* – a scheme approved in May
1793 – was put into practice in December. It was a progressive levy
that hit incomes above 1,000 *livres* for single individuals and 1,500 for
married couples. Any extra income above 9,000 *livres* was due in its
entirety. It took time to draw up tax rolls – indeed, they were not
completed until the Year IV.

Furthermore, debt funding soon came to compete with payment of
the forced loan. Cambon's Grand Livre de la Dette Publique, voted
on 24 August, combined withdrawal of *assignats* and stabilization of

liabilities. Old bonds were converted into perpetual loans, while interest-bearing voluntary subscriptions were opened – an investment that capitalists used as a loophole. All the same, these measures produced immediate results. The Caisse de l'Extraordinaire burned a considerable volume of paper currency – nearly 2,000 million *livres'* worth by the time *assignats* stopped being issued on 11 Ventôse (1 March 1794). The total money supply, estimated at 5,000 million *livres*, was less than the value of available *biens nationaux*.

For the duration of the Terror, the *assignat* stood, according to the region, at between 35 and 50 per cent of its face value. Gold remained hidden and had no adverse effect on paper money. There is no proof for the assertion that the *montagnard* bourgeoisie preferred inflation to taxation. Nor did it want the cost of the war to be borne by the people, whom it protected from hardship. The economic policy of the *montagnard* bourgeoisie nevertheless helped to split the *sans-culotte* movement.

THE VENTÔSE DRAMA

The role of the capital in the Revolution was becoming increasingly disproportionate. Because it housed the brain and engine of the great national enterprise, it arbitrarily determined the fate of the entire country. Pressure from the masses could endanger the painstakingly constructed edifice of the revolutionary government, which wanted to avoid that risk at all costs. Neither the democratic movement nor the parliamentary opposition had given up. The administrative machine, which was not yet running smoothly, did not consist entirely of reliable men. It was known to be vulnerable.

Like a border outpost, Paris deserved care and attention. It was provided with food and jobs; most of its *sans-culottes* were usefully employed. Later, to tighten its grip on the great city, the government treated it like an entrenched camp. The republican State, whose chief concern was to safeguard its achievements and pursue its task, treated its citizens like subjects, punishing their slightest deviations. It regarded its line of action as the only valid one and forbade anyone to stray from it. But by removing those who stood in its way and stifling popular protests, the State emasculated the Republic.

Paris and its 'sections' in the Year II

Paris under the Terror preserved its customary appearance: there was still the same overcrowding in the central quarters, the same encroachment by the countryside on the outskirts, and the same stability of the professional categories that formed the city's infrastructure and met its consumption needs. The distribution of *rentiers*, shopkeepers, artisans, workers and idlers did not change noticeably, nor did the total population, which remained stable thanks to the influx from the provinces. On the whole, however, the number of wage-earners increased, particularly in certain neighbourhoods. The traditionally aristocratic Faubourg Saint-Germain took in the armourers of Maubeuge as employees in the *section* workshop. The war had little effect on Parisian demography – still characterized by a high percentage of young persons – but it influenced inhabitants' behaviour and stimulated social mobility.[14]

Paris was a stop-over for troops on the move, military transports and messengers. Envoys from the provincial *sociétés* and visitors bearing gifts came for brief stays to imbibe the civic spirit of the Convention and Jacobin club. The police had difficulty keeping track of visitors, refugees and meetings, and had to keep watch on lodging-houses and inns, as well as check passports carefully. Paris, always a proud and restless city, became even more so in these troubled times; always a poverty-stricken town, it flaunted its poverty without shame. More than elsewhere, the bourgeois was confronted daily with social danger.

Observers' reports bear witness to the divisions in public opinion and the slackening of morals. There were complaints about prostitution, the display of obscene pictures, the proliferation of taverns, pedlars and street-singers. Whores 'of the very worst sort' ventured even into the Tuileries. One could not go anywhere 'without coming across a drunkard'. Although begging was forbidden, one could witness 'scenes revolting to humanity'. In squares, on the boulevards, at the Louvre and at theatre shows, one would encounter beggars displaying 'their festering wounds' and 'women huddled against the walls with infants at their breast'. Children were left to their own devices and lived in

---

[14] In order to track down 'malevolence', the *sections* issued passes (*cartes de sûreté*) in different colours to residents and non-residents. J. C. Goeury's study is based on a detailed examination of these documents ('Evolution démographique et sociale du faubourg Saint-Germain', in M. Reinhard, ed., *Contributions à l'histoire démographique de la Révolution française*, 2nd series, 1965, p. 25).

the streets; schoolteachers – who were scarce and underpaid – were unable to look after more than a small fraction of them.

According to an estimate of 14 Germinal, about a tenth of the inhabitants were assisted indigents, concentrated especially in the oldest *faubourgs*, including Saint-Antoine. In this mass of 70,000 individuals, the Convention distinguished between 'invalid citizens without resources and incapable of working' and fit and lazy individuals, 'useless souls for the republican effort and social activity'. This population reacted dangerously to the uncertainty of food supplies. Women in particular would rush to food distributions 'screaming and howling like wild beasts'. The winter of 1793 was hard on the poor, who fought over the scanty deliveries of bread, clogs, firewood and coal. A tiny glass of brandy would sell for four sous. By four in the morning, the national guard, organized by *section*, would be on patrol in the capital, which suffered especially from the shortage of meat. 'The people are tired of losing their sleep and working hours having to wait outside the butchers' shops.' Butchers cut up their meat at night and preferred to serve 'their regular customers'. War was declared on dogs and cats, which were slaughtered.

The second *maximum*, which had been in force since 12 October, made life difficult for the housewives whenever a commodity became scarce. When the price-lists were made public, in early Germinal, there were complaints 'against a law that prices commodities too high for the *sans-culottes* and favours tradesmen'. Day labourers with families to support 'no longer had enough to eat' on their three francs a day. Discontent focused once again on shopkeepers, then on the revolutionary government – convenient scapegoats who bore all the weight of popular resentment. The collective mentality did not distinguish minor events from nearly insoluble difficulties, the vagaries of the weather from lack of good will. Every conceivable pretext was used to attack the regime, which was indiscriminately subjected to conflicting pressures from moderates and extremists. The female population reproved every measure that undermined their traditional way of life. Women publicly deplored the closing of churches and, in the Halles quarter, demanded to hear mass at Saint-Eustache. Fights broke out when officials tried to force women to wear cockades and Phrygian caps. Thus, even patriotic women – of whom there were many – played into the hands of the counter-revolution. *Sans-culotte* opinion itself was not unanimous; its divisions facilitated the *montagnard* counter-offensive.

Persistence of the democratic movement

Despite the 14 Frimaire decree, the Commune and its mayor enjoyed considerable authority, extending from taxation to control of *biens nationaux*, the police and food supplies. There were few wage-earners in the ranks of the 144 members of the Conseil Général, chosen by the *sections* from among the most active citizens. Most were young and from the petty bourgeoisie. They included entrepreneurs, shopkeepers and artisans who espoused, not without reluctance, the views of the *agent national* Chaumette, and of Hébert. The Conseil was a fairly representative cross-section of the *sectionnaire* authorities.

Between the *comités civils*, whose tasks were purely administrative, and the *comités révolutionnaires*, a certain difference in recruitment was perceptible from September onwards; the former being drawn from a more affluent social stratum than the latter, whose members received an allowance of five *livres* a day and included a greater proportion of independent artisans. As for the workers, who formed the militant rank and file, they were to be found in the *sociétés sectionnaires*, where they took over from the *enragés*, adopted the same slogans and assumed supervisory powers that directly rivalled those of the official authorities. Although the problem of food supplies and the saltpetre-collection campaign* dominated *section* proceedings more than did political issues, moderates increasingly took part, questioning the Terror and government action. A 'new breed' of recruits, who fanned the flames by their indiscriminate and incessant criticism, disconcerted true patriots.

These rivalries also worried the *montagnards*. The Convention had already abolished women's *sociétés* on 9 Brumaire (30 October) and, on the 19th, Robespierre attacked the *sociétés sectionnaires*. The Jacobins refused to affiliate them to their club and made them purge their ranks. Saint-Just denounced the ambitious men and rhetors who wormed their way into the *sociétés*. The government, in an attempt to discipline a popular movement that threatened its unity, forbade the *sociétés* from joining forces. 'Popular sovereignty demands governmental unity. It is therefore against factions; every faction is thus a violation of the people's sovereignty.'

Hébert and his friends were held responsible for that violation. At the Cordelier club and the War Ministry they seemed to be in absolute

---

* See below, p. 143. [Trans.]

control. They spoke at the Jacobin club and the *Père Duchesne* was read in the armies and the provinces. The economic situation worked in favour of the *hébertistes* by providing them with a vast female following. Together with Chaumette, they also appeared to be in the forefront of dechristianization. 'Down with the clergy and bigots!' the people shouted with them. Robespierre, once again, warded off the danger. On 1 Frimaire (21 November), he called for freedom of worship for all faiths and accused 'foreign agents' of manoeuvring behind the scenes.

Plots

An indignant public made no distinction between the plots that were being denounced in quick succession. The 'foreign plot', in which refugees participated, provoked a fit of xenophobia fuelled by the speeches of Jacobin leaders and compounded by a hatred of capitalists. Perrégaux, Pereira, Proli and Guzman represented international banking. They had links with *montagnard* representatives, including Chabot, married to the sister of the Frey brothers, who were of Austrian origin. All the conspirators concealed their dealings behind an aggressive show of civic-mindedness.

The Compagnie des Indes affair helped to unmask them. The forged decree of liquidation compromised Fabre d'Eglantine and Delaunay, friends of Danton, who was tarnished by the scandal. These intrigues, revealed by Chabot and Basire on 24 Brumaire (14 November), coincided with those of the Baron de Batz, a royalist and currency speculator. Three days later, the 'government Committees' decided to arrest the most compromised plotters. On 1 Frimaire (21 November), at the Jacobin club, Robespierre used against them the same arguments he had used during the king's trial. Unconsciously perhaps, they had linked their cause to that of the Coalition powers, and unquestionably 'disgraced [that] of the French people'. Because of a few 'corrupt' individuals, comprising both 'indulgents' and extremists, the entire Assembly was in danger of coming under suspicion. The 'foreign plot' – real or imagined – triggered off the campaign against the factions.

The inquiry into the conduct of the former General Dillon, a regular patron of disreputable taverns, had brought to light his ties with Desmoulins and Danton. Robespierre defended them, but many Jacobins had doubts about their trustworthiness because they avoided the club and spoke out in the Convention and the *Vieux Cordelier* against dechristianizers and terrorists, thus encouraging the moderate opposition. In the midst of war and in the depths of winter, the 'coactive force' was in danger of slackening. 'Those who want to tear down the scaffolds are those who are afraid they might be forced to go on them', observed Saint-Just; Robespierre, attacked in Desmoulins's newspaper, rebuked him for his inconsistency: 'I loved you once because I thought you were a republican; I still love you, as it were, despite myself; but beware of a jealous love, an angry love that will not forgive you if you dare go further.'

Since early Nivôse, the 'great' Committee was determined to act. Its policy of even-handed repression was proving ineffective; the blows exchanged between moderates and extremists ricocheted on the government. The Jacobins, who had expelled Camille Desmoulins, were no less attentive to *hébertiste* propaganda and debates at the Cordelier club, where, in protest against the arrest of Vincent and Ronsin – who commanded the 'revolutionary army' – the Declaration of Rights had been covered with a black veil. The *sections* once again expressed their resolved to reinforce economic constraints and the Terror. The *Père Duchesne* savagely denounced the indulgent 'clique' and those who starved the people. There was a danger of a new *journée*. At the Convention and the Jacobin club, Robespierre, speaking for all his colleagues, explained his policy. His reports of 5 Nivôse (25 December) and 17 Pluviôse (5 February) responded to the moderate and extremist threats by reasserting the absolute necessity of maintaining the revolutionary government. Some of the *sans-culottes* agreed with him out of a refusal to compromise the spring offensive at the borders.

Attempts have been made to reduce these far-reaching movements to 'team rivalries'. Such interpretations grossly underestimate the deeper motives and social significance of these movements and give undue weight to verbal excesses and journalistic hyperbole. The *dantonistes* and *hébertistes* did not constitute parties, but represented forces. Public opinion was divided as to the direct impact of a long-lasting Revolution on the lives and property of every citizen. 'Some pretend [the Revolution] is over, and that one must grant an amnesty to all scoundrels...others say it has not proved equal to the task.' Moderatism and popular protest were not confined to the actions of a handful of men, but involved radically hostile masses. The government's intention was only to overawe these masses by striking down those who had sealed their own fate.

The liquidation of the factions

'When a free government is established, it must preserve itself by every fair means: it can legitimately resort to considerable force; it must destroy whatever stands in the way of public prosperity.' The more immediate danger seemed to come from the *hébertistes*, who launched a frontal attack on the government of 'beguilers', 'the broken legs, the worn-out men of the Revolution'. By wildly denouncing corrupt representatives, greedy merchants and fanaticism, they rallied the discontented, the ambitious and the wretched. Their only programme was the guillotine. 'Strike! Strike! Let the revolutionary axe rest only when there are no more traitors and schemers.' The demagogy of the *Père Duchesne* irritated and shocked most of the bourgeoisie. Collot d'Herbois attempted to reconcile Cordeliers and Jacobins, 'two good republican families who must never cease to love each other'. There were further calls to insurrection. Hanriot, commander of the Paris national guard, spoke out against the agents of anarchy. The Cordelier tumult served as an excuse for the Committee of Public Safety to strangle the popular movement.

The Convention had already decided on 16 Ventôse (6 March 1794) to start a preliminary investigation into those who were provoking anxiety about food supplies. On the 23rd, after hearing Saint-Just's report, the Assembly declared the alarmists to be 'traitors to the homeland', along with all those who had encouraged 'by whatever means...the plan to corrupt citizens and subvert authority and public opinion', or who 'had attempted to upset the system of revolutionary government'. Hébert, Vincent and Momoro were arrested at night, together with Ronsin and Mazuel – officers of the 'revolutionary army' – lesser-known militants and 'foreign agents'. Finally, on the 26th, Amar, speaking for the Committees in unison, attacked 'corrupt' representatives. A decree of accusation was voted on 28 Ventôse (18 March) against Delaunay d'Angers, Julien de Toulouse, Chabot and Fabre d'Eglantine.

The political trials that followed gave rise to odd *amalgames*.* The trial of the Cordelier leaders opened on 1 Germinal (21 March). In the dock of the Revolutionary Tribunal sat twenty defendants nine of whom had no connection with the *sectionnaire* vanguard. Proli, Dubuisson, Pereira, Desfieux and the banker Conrad de Kock (who

---

* See below, p. 209. [Trans.]

had invited Hébert and Ronsin to his pleasure parties) – all of whom had been wanted or arrested since Brumair – sat next to Anacharsis Cloots, 'the atheists' pope', and humble commissioners who did not understand what had befallen them. After 'a mock trial', they were executed on 4 Germinal (24 March).

The personal plight of the defendants affected all the *sans-culottes*, who were stunned by the event. Indeed, so involved were the *sans-culottes* with the accused that they could not believe in their guilt. However, there were only a few cases of protest. The *sections* behaved with a cautious restraint that reassured the government and, beginning on 25 Ventôse, they filed past the bar of the Assembly to proclaim their loyalty. On the 29th it was the turn of the Commune 'in a body', the tribunals and the *département*. Only an unusually full attendance at the *sociétés populaires* testified to the general unease. Discouragement and anxiety took the place of patriotic exaltation.

One week passed before Danton was arrested. Neither he nor his friends sought to forestall the attack though they had been given warning. When, on the morning of 11 Germinal, the Convention learned of the measure, which had been decided on the previous day by the two 'great' Committees in joint session, it went into 'a turmoil the like of which had not been seen in a long time'. Robespierre struck the first blows against the 'rotten idol'. But there were few enough culprits for the Assembly not to feel directly attacked. It applauded Robespierre, then heard Saint-Just in utter silence. 'May all those who were criminals perish...May their accomplices denounce themselves by siding with the felons.' No one was brave enough to do so. The decree of accusation against Desmoulins, Danton, Philippeaux, Delacroix and Fabre d'Eglantine was applauded. Guzman, the Freys, the Abbé d'Espagnac (an army contractor), General Westermann and Hérault de Séchelles were added to the list. The trial was stormy. Danton was forbidden to speak by special decree. It even seems that the Committee of Public Safety had planned to arrest the president and the public prosecutor.[15] All the defendants were guillotined on 16 Germinal (5 April 1794). The feeling of helplessness and confusion increased in the Assembly and among the Parisian public, which had watched in silence.

A final trial, that of General Dillon, enabled the authorities, on 18

---

[15] Unpublished note of 13 Germinal: 'Write to Hanriot and have him issue instructions not to arrest the president and public prosecutor of the Revolutionary Tribunal. Get four members' signatures for this.' (Archives Nationales, AF II 22, folder 174, p. 3.)

Germinal, to charge Simond, a representative from the Bas-Rhin who had been detained for several months in the Luxembourg gaol, with participating in a plot to free his fellow inmates and bring down the government. The accused perished on 24 Germinal (13 April) with Chaumette and the widows of Hébert and Camille Desmoulins.

'An incredible number of gaping onlookers' gathered to watch these executions in the Place de la Révolution, which served as a meeting place. 'Did you go to see Hébert yesterday?' people would ask, and the answer would be affirmative. The 'Père Duchesne' was reproached for his cowardice when he went through the 'little window'. He was cruelly made fun of for his pipe and stoves.★ 'I found ordinary people cheerful,' observed an informant, reassuring himself by reassuring the authorities – who were not taken in. Vadier, of the Committee of General Security, inveighed against Danton, scoffing at his 'hideous face'. The representatives on mission issued one appeasing proclamation after another. The burning of *hébertiste* newspapers and the arrest of *hébertistes* in Le Mans, Sedan and Le Havre proved, however, that the provinces were 'contaminated'.

Such were the dramatic events of Ventôse. Their historical significance clearly lies in the government's determination no longer to accept restraints, and in its exclusive vision of the State as the embodiment of Jacobin ideals. Mallet du Pan described this new situation with perspicacity. Previously, 'the aspiring factions had toppled the ruling factions with the aid of popular force'. Now, it was 'the ruling faction that, in fifteen days, struck down two opposing factions whose intentions it feared. It struck them down without the people's assistance, without mob agitation, legally, in due form.' Thus did he describe the reality of dictatorship. The government which, in principle, belonged to the people, deprived itself of their help. Instead of protecting them, it became oppressive. The war effort and the problem of food supplies were no longer regarded by public opinion as a sufficient justification for such a brutal discrepancy between theory and practice, which Saint-Just had so feared: 'The revolutionary government must bear down on itself, not on the people.' The Jacobin dictatorship, by strengthening itself, doomed the Revolution.

★ The 'Père Duchesne', a character borrowed by Hébert from popular theatre, was a pipe-smoking stove merchant. A song sung by the crowd at Hébert's execution accused him of having tried to reduce France to ashes by heating his stoves. [Trans.]

4

The national army and military society

The military history of the Revolution has long been confined to accounts of battles, army organization and tactics. While the essential contribution of the Year II to these areas has been recognized by military historians, they have rarely emphasized troop morale, which historians writing from a civilian point of view have attributed to national spirit and revolutionary ideology. The troops in the two World Wars and fighters in the Resistance have been compared to the troops of the Revolution and their energy has been variously interpreted in terms of territorial defence, patriotism or democratic uprisings against reactionary forces. Was the Revolution a national war or a class war? To pose such a question is to separate arbitrarily issues that are, in fact, concomitant.

In recent years, an agreement has emerged on the need for both a quantitative and a qualitative approach to the mass of hitherto unstudied sources – with some researchers contributing their specialized knowledge of the period, and others their expertise in statistical methods. The first task undertaken was a census of soldiers and a classification by age as well as by geographical and social origins. The earliest results enable us to qualify certain previous hasty assertions. It would seem that the *sans-culotte* army was made up of categories similar to the civilian society it reflected, and that there was no fundamental opposition between volunteers and troops of the line.

We are beginning to study in depth both the modification in behaviour that resulted from the Jacobin dictatorship and the military power that the dictatorship organized and exploited. Refusal to enlist (*insoumission*), desertion and insubordination, for which there is an increasing amount of evidence, reveal hostile trends and the difficulties of the revolutionary government. The soldiers of the Revolution, by their collective outlook and individual attitudes, are fascinating to the sociologist. The study of panic in the ranks promises to be particularly exciting.

But the war machine of the Year II had other features, which are also being studied. With its fighters and retinue of parasites, this machine occupied what turns out to be an unbearably exaggerated position within the republican State. The army became an autonomous society with its own rigid structures and a feeling of superiority. To what extent did the spirit of Valmy and of the *levée en masse* live on in the army of Fleurus?

The army of the Revolution was, like the government, a continuous creation. The great levies were not integrated according to a pre-established plan, as in modern general mobilizations. The influx of requisitioned men upset the structures of the line. Innovation became a necessity in an archaic system that adapted itself while preserving some of its tradition – hence its twofold appearance. As an instrument of national defence, the army was subject to rules and hierarchy. As a means for revolutionary action, it was democratic and Jacobin. The enthusiasm that informed it was the counterpart to that of the great popular *journées*. The people's army exalted heroism and exuded an infectious civic spirit. Citizens turned soldiers mingled with soldiers turned citizens. The soldiers, who felt close to civilian society emotionally and out of a sense of common dangers, were influenced by it, set themselves up as censors like the clubs, and denounced their officers as aristocrats.

The intake of *sans-culottes* infused drive, spontaneity and initiative into the troops, but fostered a rebelliousness that undermined discipline. The Committee of Public Safety re-established discipline and imposed it at every level by resorting to punishment. But strict obedience to orders did not imply unconditional devotion to superiors, on whom civilian authorities kept a watchful eye. *Esprit de corps* developed among individuals regardless of rank. Equality of material conditions cemented their moral solidarity, which, however, was not present everywhere and did not always endure.

One must dispel a twofold legend: Hugo's epic of 'magnificent tramps' rushing to victory, and the myth of pure patriotic exaltation, unwavering and unblemished. With difficulty perhaps, the 'indivisible' Republic did supply the soldiers of the Year II with their basic needs, before Thermidor much more so than after. A number of public messages from soldiers expressed their nationalist feeling, their allegiance to the Convention, and their genuine faith in the future of the Republic. But their private correspondence shows that they were not oblivious to 'paltry details': pay, promotion and glory. As the war went on, some grew tired of it, while others made it their profession and a means of social advancement. Victories strengthened these attitudes, by bringing immediate satisfaction to ambitious men, adding to old soldiers' memories, and fuelling the enthusiasm of the young. The army, united in Jacobinism, helped it to outlive the Revolution in the minds of the people.

REVOLUTIONARY WAR AND TRADITIONAL WARS

The war weighed on the Revolution, and the Revolution transformed the war. Hence this conflict lost its resemblance to previous ones and anticipated modern confrontations. This *rebellion* against foreign powers was national, and the tactics it borrowed from traditional armed rebellions were here transcended by the number and spiritual strength of the French people. In its guise as a psychological war, it became a vehicle for political and social propaganda and was used by the French to educate their foreign brothers. But the liberator was also an occupying force. Revolutionary principles were introduced by coercion, provoking individual acts of resistance and national reactions. To hasten victory, the Revolution – identified with the Republic – resorted to terrorist measures in its armies and conquests. It instilled fear in the European counter-revolution, which understood too late the sacred character of this crusade for liberty.

The crusade for liberty

'If the army retreats, the entire French people must rise and be its rearguard.' The war became revolutionary through the spirit that gradually determined the methods used. The conduct of the war was in the hands of both civilian and military authorities. The great Jacobin spokesmen preached intransigence and rigour. So long as the Coalition was inside the borders, all efforts were directed to expelling it. 'The French people do not make peace with an enemy that is occupying their territory.' Negotiating in these conditions would be tantamount to 'renouncing one's independence'. Robespierre proposed capital punishment for those who involved themselves in such schemes.

Indeed, regardless of the turn of events on the battlefield and individual interests, public opinion remained unanimous. The army, the entrepreneurial class and the mass of *sans-culottes* refused to slacken the war effort. They demanded that the fighting should continue 'against kings...until their total destruction'. This determination was manifest down to the smallest village. It was not enough to drive back the adversary; he had to be exterminated. The war would therefore be total. 'One must wage all-out war or go home' and accept the downfall of the Republic.

The 'great' Committee contemplated invading Britain. In April 1793, the *Père Duchesne* had already invited 'one hundred thousand determined chaps' to set forth. Agents were sent to Ireland and Scotland. The Channel Islands, then the Isle of Wight, were considered as a possible staging post for a military landing. At the end of Pluviôse, Billaud-Varenne and Ruamps planned the expedition in great secrecy, but it was abandoned because of the unfavourable winds. Carnot and Prieur de la Côte-d'Or simultaneously organized their spring offensive. The troops that were holding down the enemy in the north around Dunkirk and Le Quesnoy launched limited actions, winning at Honschoote on 8 September and Wattignies on the 16th; in the east, Kellermann liberated Savoy, and Hoche freed Landau on 29 December; Dagobert warded off Spanish attacks on the Pyrenees. The difficulties encountered in halting the invasion gave rise to new imperatives: coordination of operations, troop cohesion, a vibrant civic spirit and strict subordination of the military to civilian authority. 'The master plans appropriate to the national spirit...can belong' only to the people's delegates.[1]

The Constitution abolished the commander-in-chief, replacing him by the Committee of Public Safety, which, after 14 Frimaire, informed the generals of its new role: 'The time of disobedience is over.' The Committee laid down rules of conduct for the representatives on mission to the armies. It was hoped that people would set aside their own feelings when faced with the magnitude of the common task; that trust, solidarity and friendship would unite overseers, commanders and soldiers, who would be treated as citizens; that morale would be kept high by an implacable justice that would be exercised against everyone. In a national army, equality guaranteed discipline.

The majority of 'missionaries' acted soberly and humanely in difficult conditions. Rare indeed were those who thought of themselves as military leaders and were blinded by their vanity. Most acted as

---

[1] Circular from the Committee of Public Safety to the generals-in-chief, quoted in P. Mautouchet, *Le Gouvernement révolutionnaire*, p. 244.

observers, censors and organizers, in sharp contrast to their easy-going temperament. Their administrative experience and legal training had beneficial consequences. Without the representatives, the government would have been unable to impose its authority; thanks to them, this authority was more bearable, hence more effective. The representatives dismissed timorous and incompetent generals, named their interim successors, and devoted equal attention to troop provisioning and promotion. They knew how to hand out rewards and kindle the imagination; their orders testify to their exuberant activity. Their proclamations stand up to those of Bonaparte and of Napoleon. 'All that the French Republic receives from its enemies and sends them back is lead.' Not all representatives matched Saint-Just, but the troops were grateful for their presence and rarely criticized their behaviour.

Representatives set the example by sleeping in tents and leading the columns into action. Several, including Chasles, were wounded. Often they directed operations with the generals; but relations were not always cordial because the generals, experienced army men with their own ideas about warfare, were bewildered by the practice of revolutionary struggle. As in the days of the royal army, the generals surrounded themselves with a coterie of aides-de-camp and were partial to the line. They were criticized for undertaking risky operations and held responsible for useless bloodshed. Some generals were punished as an example. The others yielded slowly and unwillingly. Paris seemed a long way off to them. By special courier even in the summer months, communications to Paris took two days from the northern border and four days from the eastern one. The generals' reluctance was noted in the most distant areas and in the Vendée.

The lessons of the Vendée

'Actually, we fail to understand how these Gentlemen wage war', the representatives observed of the *vendéens* in late September 1793. Their tactics had changed considerably, from massive engagements to guerrilla war. Taking advantage of natural shelters and of the undergrowth, the *vendéens* conducted night-time raids on outposts and convoys. Quick to assemble and as quick to disperse, they were soldiers without ceasing to be peasants. The harvest and seeding would bring them back to their fields. They had only a rudimentary military training and asked, not for pay, but for the clothing, weapons and food they captured. After a victory, they were allowed to loot briefly.

The *vendéens* were sustained by fanaticism, but their lack of discipline dismayed both their leaders and the experienced soldiers who commanded them. They were excellent marksmen and sturdy walkers, marching tirelessly and causing panic by their elusiveness. They saved ammunition and used their cannon cautiously, treating them like precious objects. These strong points were stressed in order to conceal the Vendée's real weaknesses: disagreement among the generals, the large numbers of adventurers and foreign deserters, and the retinue of women and children.

In Saumur, the Council of generals and republican representatives that was directing the struggle against the rebels copied their mobility and exploited their organizational shortcomings. To a certain extent, the Catholic armies resembled the young recruits who were being pitted against them. Why wage a tactician's war when conventional tactics only resulted in failure? The well-trained Mainz army was sent into battle on its own. Conscript battalions were assembled in camps and trained to go on patrol and advance as skirmish contingents. Following their raid into Brittany, which faltered outside Granville, the *vendéens* were driven from Le Mans, crushed at Savenay on 5 Nivôse (23 December 1793), and pushed back to the south of the Loire. They were contained in Les Mauges and the Marais by an almost unbroken line of defence.

The methods of Turreau and his 'infernal columns' can be understood in the context of the 'petite Vendée'. From January to early May 1794, his forces criss-crossed the hideout with the aim of exterminating the rebels. Just like the enemy, 'whose fury is tremendous', Turreau and his men turned the country into a desert wherever they went, destroyed crops, tore down châteaux used as shelters and belfries that served as look-out posts, and evacuated to the periphery the terrorized populations still faithful to the Vendée.

In military operations, the Vendée was always treated separately. The Committee of Public Safety took the full measure of its importance by the number of troops it diverted from the borders. But the Committee also learned some lessons from the Vendée. Fragmentation of authority fostered both lasting jealousies and irresponsibility among the commanders. The use of detachments was harmful to army unity, since each group kept to its habits and retained a certain initiative. Solidarity was confined to the company, and obedience to captains. The high command was ignored. In small-scale fighting on other fronts, guerrilla tactics were increasingly adopted. They were used in Savoy and in the Pyrenees, as well as for approaches and on defensive positions in the north and east. They were also used, more than has been realized, in the major war theatres.

The tactics of the Year II simultaneously took into account revolutionary drive, the terrain and individual initiative. Frontal mass attacks were improved. The 1794 campaign was worked out in great detail according to a vast plan centred on the northern region. Numbers were an asset, but not the only one. The all-out offensive symbolized the will to win.

Carnot, an officer in the Engineers, still believed in the use of retrenchments as a tactical base; however, the instructions for which he secured approval on 14 Pluviôse (2 February) attest to his change of attitude: 'Always use massive troop strength and be on the offensive; maintain a strict but not punctilious discipline in the armies; always keep troops on the alert without exhausting them; join battle with bayonets in all circumstances and keep pursuing the enemy until his complete destruction.' It was also expected that shoulder-to-shoulder formations would embolden the attackers.

Tactics – advancing in columns preceded by skirmishers, or deploying lines – were determined by topography and objectives. Assaults with blades were imposed by the circumstances and were not as common as a superficial study would suggest. Once a shot was fired, a gun would have to be reloaded – an impossible operation in hand-to-hand combat. Success depended on skilful diversions and on the increasing role of cavalry and field artillery. Thus science and organization conferred a new strength on the national army. The Revolution foreshadowed modern warfare, while the Coalition powers clung to tradition.

The spirit of the Coalition

'The fury that grips the French has made this a campaign of extermination; it is a war to the death.' Mallet du Pan advised the European Coalition to resort to unified command and to the means of its adversaries. It poured vast amounts of men and money into the campaign without sacrificing its bureaucratic habits copied from the Prussians. The officers were noblemen and the troops mercenaries recruited by lottery, as there were no longer enough volunteers. Discipline was not relaxed and corporal punishments were maintained. The sovereigns waged an outmoded warfare, refusing to recognize the new aspects of the struggle. They pursued their particular objectives

and spurned the help of royalists inside France. The Committee of
Public Safety took advantage of their discord and blindness; the Polish
rising, however, came too late to be of any real help.[2]

The diplomacy of the Coalition complacently followed its routine – a
mode of behaviour confirmed by foreign ambassadors' dispatches.
Only the counter-revolutionary propaganda, which the Coalition
treated with great reservations, acted both on civilian populations and
on the armies. Coalition agents attributed to the French people a
succession of sanguinary schemes. Nobles, priests and bourgeois were
to perish at the hands of the patriots. Scare tactics were used abroad
against the Republic; all Frenchmen were depicted as barbarians. The
decree forbidding the French army to give quarter to the British and
Hanoverians justified these utterances, and the certainty of the
revolutionary government's imminent collapse reassured foreign
countries.

England, which partially financed its allies' effort, was governed by
mediocrities. Pitt and Grenville displayed tenacity, not clairvoyance.
They were quite unprepared for military operations, but their naval
forces were still considerable. The men in charge of the fleet, Pitt's
brother Lord Chatham and the Duke of Richmond, were lazy incompetents who failed to make good use of the naval forces. Sailors were
still recruited through voluntary enlistments and press-gangs who
rounded up idlers and drunkards in ports. Poor training and nourishment
undermined discipline. Diminishing rum rations could cause trouble.
Moreover, Britain had little confidence in its Dutch and Spanish allies,
and the economic blockade against France alienated the neutral
countries from the Coalition.

Despite a clear-cut superiority due to the number and fire-power
of its ships, the British fleet was unable to impose its total supremacy.
It had kept to its traditional construction methods and to line combat
tactics, pitting each ship against an enemy vessel. But the navy generally
avoided battle and wore out its crew and equipment in interminable
cruises from the Atlantic to the Mediterranean, without any noteworthy
successes. French corsairs, which were faster and more autonomous,
inflicted heavy losses on the enemy's merchant fleet and fought a
profitable campaign in the West Indies. In 1794, Britain's total export
tonnage decreased, and the share of neutral countries in its trade

[2] The Polish rising broke out in March 1794 under the impulse of a group of radicals
described as 'Jacobins'. On 28 June, they organized a vast popular demonstration, which
was followed by Kosciusko's entry into Warsaw.

increased. The Bank of England felt the effects; unemployment and high grain prices triggered off popular unrest. Thus the resistance to change of the Coalition powers contributed to their defeat. They refused to face the evidence and enlist their people's support for their war by modifying social structures. The Jacobin Republic's outstanding effort and the fighting ardour of its troops consequently had the unforeseen effect of revealing to the subject masses the power that lay in their hands.

THE 'LEVÉE EN MASSE' AND ITS OFFICERS

The Committee of Public Safety scored its victories in the autumn of 1793 with line regiments, volunteers and the troops levied in February. But the volunteers of 1792, who had enlisted for only one campaign, now wanted a discharge. In the army of the Pyrenees, well over half the troops asked for permanent leave. The first battalion of the Seine-et-Oise refused to stay a day longer in Nantes. With the onset of winter, the first contingents of the *levée en masse* were enrolled, bringing total strength up to nearly 900,000 men. However, there were great difficulties and the effects of the levy were slow in coming.

To hasten the implementation of the 23 August decree, the Convention sent out across the country eighteen *montagnard* representatives to be assisted by the delegates of the primary assemblies, who met in Paris in August. The abolition of recruitment by proxy, which had enabled wealthy conscripts to stay at home, marked the end of ' 500-*livres* heroes' and was widely applauded.[3] Military duty, equal for everyone, became the supreme form of patriotic devotion.

A year later, the dangers faced by the homeland provoked the same popular upsurge in the threatened regions. At the end of August the tocsin sounded at Wissemburg and thousands of peasants carrying food gathered at the forges in Bitche. The *district* of Sedan provided 1,700 young men in a few days. In Clermont-Ferrand, between 800 and 900 day-labourers, who had assembled to hire out their services to farms, decided to march against the rebels in Lyons. Makeshift camps to accommodate Parisian conscripts were set up between the capital and the northern border. However, enthusiasm was not universal. It was a bad season for recruitment: when threshing was over, it was time to think about autumn labours, followed by sowing. In the Hérault,

---

[3] So called because of the sum they demanded as bounty.

the grape harvest kept agricultural workers in the vineyards, and disturbances broke out. Representatives wielded the guillotine to convince recalcitrants. It was also permanently displayed in Toulouse, where it impressed 'dandies and coxcombs', accused of talking their friends into shirking their duty. Coupé de l' Oise suggested that they should have their hair cropped as a token of infamy before being sent to their units.

It was soon apparent that it was no use hastening departures, as weapons and equipment were lacking. In Rocroi, the *district* left one thousand requisitioned men encamped in tents for ten days before deciding to send them home – a serious but justified measure that compromised further requisitioning. In the Brie and the Beauce, this new levy on the labour force was deplored. Farmers were worried about neglected land and forecast smaller harvests. Would it not be possible to exempt peasants who owned at least one plough? The representatives granted provisional agricultural deferments, which were extended; on 6 Pluviôse (25 January), the Committee of Public Safety authorized them, and they soon reached considerable proportions. On the 29th, Gillet noted that battalions in the army of the Ardennes were melting away. In one of them, five out of six recruits had disappeared, taken away by their parents. Leave was cancelled on 13 Ventôse, but soldiers were in no hurry to return; many of them still straggling back in mid-Germinal when the offensive got under way.

The requisitioning of horses followed a similar pattern. The 23 August decree requisitioned all 'saddle-horses...to build up cavalry corps' and unused draught-horses to draw artillery and food trains. Although a new representative was appointed in every military region to supervise this task, results were uneven. A special levy was decreed on 7 October. Countrymen held on to their best animals and handed over tired and diseased horses. In the Midi, the operation was not complete until the end of winter. As it turned out there were not enough paddocks and the grooms were negligent: the wastage was considerable.

Consequently, the organization of the cavalry suffered. The units that had mounts lacked horsemen, and vice versa. Recruits themselves chose to serve in the cavalry, not out of any real ability, but to be spared marches; a great number of men proved to have no experience of horses whatever. Since a corps of mounted gendarmes existed to ensure the protection of convoys, it was decided to send them off to battle and replace them in their duties by insufficiently trained men. The artillery, which required special training, also had difficulty with recruitment.

The results of the *levée en masse* are hard to evaluate, but fall within a possible range of 300,000 to 400,000 men. In some places, each age group was requisitioned in turn; in others, the seven groups were all called up at once. The figures varied from one locality to another simply according to the recruits' year of birth, and from one region to another according to the representatives' determination and the circumstances. Local studies all suggest a levy of between one-eighth and one-third of the active population. Near the borders the proportion of recruits was higher. In the *département* of the Vosges there were 25,000. By the end of Germinal a total of twenty-three battalions had been raised in the Nord, fourteen in the Seine-Inférieure, thirteen in the Pas-de-Calais and the Manche, ten in the Calvados, and five in the Eure and the Orne. The central regions provided smaller contingents. However, some localities picked at random show figures comparable to those of World War I: 300 soldiers at Barr out of 700 householders, 100 out of 300 at Taverny, 120 out of 280 at Castel-Sograt (Lot-et-Garonne). The tiniest villages and innumerable families thus found themselves directly caught up in the war, whose setbacks and victories became those of the entire nation.

Officers: promotion

All of the *Montagne* and the Jacobins agreed with Carnot that the fate of the homeland depended on officers' patriotism. 'Soldiers, we come to avenge you by giving you chiefs who will lead you to victory. We have resolved to seek, reward and promote merit.' In this way Saint-Just conveyed the views of the 'great' Committee to the army of the Rhine. The decree of 21 February 1793 had attempted to unify promotion in the line and among volunteers. Infantrymen were supposed to elect their corporals in each company by absolute majority. Up to brigadier level, one-third of the ranks were filled according to seniority and two-thirds were chosen from the ranks just below. The high command was appointed by the government. This system – which the Coalition powers scoffed at – generated great disappointment and put battalions under the command of ignorant officers 'who spent all their time revelling and whoring'.

In 1793 the line included a number of veterans of the campaigns of the *ancien régime*. Nearly 70 per cent had come up from the ranks and enjoyed the advantages of seniority. They competed with volunteers and were promoted more rapidly than the young recruits from the national guard. Contrary to a widespread view, the guard had a number of trained officers who had fought before 1789. They combined military expertise with a good education and a high degree of patriotism. Although the double source of army recruitment was taken into account, promotion varied according to unit. The calculation of seniority on the basis of age and length of service led to older junior officers. This did not escape the representatives' attention: Pflieger noted that cavalry NCOs were 'routine-minded, arrogant and stubborn'. For Gillet, promotion was not just a reward, but a 'duty of which one had to show oneself worthy'. He recommended that it should be based only on time served by the officer in his arm and rank.

The *levée en masse* required a rapid increase in the number of officers. Old procedures were retained, but the greater intake led to a proportionate increase in the number of young officers. Merit, valour and civic spirit were singled out. In battalions and squadrons, smooth-cheeked captains and old soldiers nurtured a common ideal, setting aside their diversity of origin.

There were still nobles among the officers, but of low lineage. The people demanded their exclusion and Hassenfratz had made the same request several times at the Jacobin club. In July 1793 a great staff purge was carried out. Some regiments in the northern army expelled noble officers in September. But they were hard to replace. Those who had proved their courage and dedication were kept on. At the end of Germinal there were still a great number of nobles in the cavalry and the army of the Alps, despite soldiers' opposition. They were reproached less for their noble rank than for their incompetence and opinions. Their arrogance and lack of civic spirit were considered intolerable.

To improve recruitment and develop the revolutionary spirit, plans were made to introduce military training in schools. Little boys played soldiers. Companies were formed spontaneously, such as the one at Colmar called Enfants de la Patrie. Children went on manoeuvres with wooden muskets and were treated to stirring accounts of heroic deeds. On 13 Prairial (1 June 1794) the Convention created the 'pupils of Mars': adolescents aged sixteen and seventeen, six from each *district*, assembled in Paris for intensive training. This breeding-ground was to be drawn on later.

Corps commanders had above all to guard against ambition. 'Better to lose a battle than the homeland.' But there was a shortage of educated and republican general officers. Garnier de Saintes wrote from Le Mans on 7 Frimaire (27 November): 'Three-quarters of them fight the way the nobles' lackeys used to serve their masters.' Lequinio went further on 8 Ventôse (26 February): 'Our generals [in the Vendée] imagined themselves to be the Republic's farmers and tried to extend their lease.' The Committee nearly always approved the representatives' proposals regarding major-generals. It kept on Canclaux, Grouchy, and many others who were nobles, as well as patriotic veterans. But the Committee chose young men of undisputed authority as army commanders. These prestigious promotions were memorable: Hoche, Marceau and Bonaparte became commanders-in-chief at twenty-four; Jourdan was only thirty-two in 1793, and Pichegru thirty-three. Ney and Gérard fought under the orders of Bernadotte, 'brigadier' at thirty in June 1794. When they later became marshals of the Empire, they recalled, not without emotion, their comradeship-in-arms in the days of the 'indivisible' Republic.

Amalgamation and brigading[4]

'A united Republic requires a united army. The homeland has only one heart and you do not want its children to share it out with the sword.' Saint-Just wanted to make a standard practice of amalgamation. The enforcement of the law of 21 February 1793, left in the hands of the representatives until the following winter, produced a variety of results. Sometimes conscripts were used to fill out individual units already in existence by mixing volunteers and troops of the line. In other cases, line battalions and volunteer battalions were set up side by side, each keeping its regional character and its officers.

The *levée en masse* could only increase the disorder and confusion. Generals encouraged the formation of irregular forces, some of which had no more than thirty men, although their chiefs demanded a battalion commander's pay. Newcomers objected to the variety of uniforms and the sumptuousness of those worn by staff officers. It was hard to distinguish ranks, specialized corps and civilian services. Brigading, as decreed on 2 Frimaire (22 November 1793), entailed the creation of 'half-brigades' consisting of one line battalion and two of requisitioned men; the remaining recruits were to be distributed among existing units. This practice led to a confusion of terms.

The government and the Military Committee spent the months of Nivôse and Ventôse preparing legislation that instituted the 'new army', which later served as a model for the army of the Directory. An attempt was made to stabilize troop strength, standardize pay,

---

[4] See above, pp. 41 (note 12), 59 and 81.

uniforms, promotion and accounting, and distribute men evenly among
the three arms. The infantry – the largest arm – was divided into
battalions of 800 soldiers and officers, including old and new formations,
which were 'amalgamated' according to the customary procedure. The
strength of the half-brigade was brought up to 2,400 men. The cavalry
and artillery remained divided into regiments. A spectacular effort was
made to increase army mobility. Light units were set apart from line
and garrison units. All the irregular forces were absorbed into battalions
of chasseurs, dragoons and hussars; the cavalry's strength was increased
to 86,000. The mounted artillery, as distinct from the siege artillery,
was capable of transporting ordnance rapidly in the midst of battle,
and comprised nine highly trained regiments.

The tactical advantages of these arrangements were obvious, and the
organizational rigour displayed was no less so. The system aimed at
tying soldiers to their company. Each half-brigade and regiment was
given a number. Up to the higher ranks, men could benefit from
promotion in the arm to which they had been assigned. Acquired
seniority was easier to calculate. The decree of 12 Ventôse (2 March
1794) laid down remarkably precise guidelines for uniforms: 'The
republican soldier's dress is characterized only by simplicity and
convenience.' Gone were plumes and variegated colours; the 'national
colours' were adopted 'in every army rank'. Officers were entitled only
to choose a cloth of different quality. Units and stripes had to be
recognizable at first sight. Even civilian services were given a special
uniform.

To implement this sweeping reform, the Convention, on 17 Pluviôse
(5 February), assigned seven representatives to the fourteen armies. The
representatives made slow progress, and were hindered by the
widespread practice of detaching units as well as by resistance from
soldiers and officers determined to maintain local recruitment. Southerners drafted into units from the Moselle asked to be returned to their
old corps. When they were refused permission, they rejoined
clandestinely. These *passe-volants* ('flying fugitives') were the bane of
the quartermasters who were responsible for troop statistics, which thus
remained inaccurate. In addition, the grenadiers had to be integrated
into the infantry and their old uniforms dyed blue. Finally, Gillet
reported that he had fourteen battalions of conscripts in the army of
the Ardennes but did not know what to do with them.

As for the navy, Jeanbon Saint-André, on his return from a long
mission to Brest, presented his findings to the Convention on 12

Pluviôse (31 January 1794). After the treason of Toulon, 'work was stagnating in the ports and malevolence was paralysing every arm'. Royalist officers were imprisoned. Seamen, who were anglophobes by 'vocation' and unruly by nature, displayed their patriotism, and agreed to instruct novices. Every vessel was turned into a sailing school. Discipline was re-established. The officer corps and civilian administration of the navy were brought up to full strength. Bonuses were awarded to shipyard workers. Lighthouses were built at Penmarch and Groix, and new ships of the line were constructed with requisitioned hardwood and rigging. Thanks to the experience of engineers like Forfait and to revolutionary zeal, the number of frigates launched at Brest, Lorient, Rochefort and reconquered Toulon was three times greater than that of the British frigates chartered in the same period.

French frigates gave effective protection to grain convoys. During one such operation, from 9 to 13 Prairial (28 May – 1 June), Villaret-Joyeuse kept Howe at bay. The odyssey of the *Vengeur* was followed with wild enthusiasm throughout the country. The *sociétés populaires* launched subscriptions to contribute to the development of the nation's naval forces. Old corvettes were bought to be fitted out for privateering. Over 1,200 sailors from Saint-Malo served on privateers and from Germinal increased their bounty of captured vessels, thus guaranteeing them comfortable profits. Conscripts were levied to swell the naval ranks, but they did not always turn up.

By early spring, the patriots' determination had ensured that the coastlines and borders were properly garrisoned. The enlistment of young recruits hastened their training. Tension decreased between troops of the line and 'volunteers'. Although brigading was never fully put into practice in the Vendée, there was a growing sense of comradeship-in-arms. It would be wrong, however, to think that the military force was created at a stroke, and by the people's will alone. The revolutionary government organized and encouraged the army, providing it with an officer corps suited to its character. But even the Terror did not prevent men from deserting their posts or refusing to serve.

Wastage: 'insoumis' and deserters

The size and compulsory nature of the levies led to a sharp rise in the number of renegades. But actually there was little change in their average percentage or geographical distribution. One should not confuse the *insoumis*, who refuses to carry out a national duty, with the deserter, who abandons the army. The first commits a civil offence, the second a military one compounded by theft, since the soldier takes his uniform and weapons with him. Moreover, peasants made a clear distinction between the two.

Rural France protected the *insoumis*, who belonged to his community and took refuge not far from it. Smallholders were more inclined than rich farmers to keep back their sons or servants. When the search was called off the *insoumis* would go back to work in the fields with the connivance of notables. Mothers and fiancées encouraged such disobedience with sentimental arguments. Should all those who shirked their duty be regarded as cowards? To decrease their numbers, they were treated as suspects, but very few were turned in. Some representatives, such as Réal in the Alps on the eve of Thermidor, successfully used the age-old practice of billeting soldiers with the families of defaulters until their return.

Fear of the unknown and lack of national spirit, rather than subversive attitudes, were responsible for resistance to military duty. *Insoumission* was lower in the border areas – where there was an awareness of the common danger – and higher in the fertile plains in the north and in Normandy, the mountains of the Auvergne, the Pyrenees and the south-east. There was an undoubted correlation between *insoumission* and the strength of revolutionary feeling. Towns were less affected than rural areas, regions along much-travelled routes less than isolated zones. Refusal to serve therefore expressed a political choice. Whatever its motives, it served the counter-revolution. It seems impossible to assess it quantitatively, since it remained hidden.

On the contrary, deserters, who had actually enlisted, were easier to spot. Brigading increased their numbers. They were reported everywhere, from the army of Italy to that of the Côtes de La Rochelle. In Germinal, 1,200 conscripts fled as one near Tours; others did so at Rennes and Saint-Sever. Individual departures were uncommon or went unnoticed. NCOs rarely took part, even in collective escapes. Desertion was described as conspiracy because there were organizers, who would entice away young men, often from the same region as themselves, by playing on their disappointment and boredom and by taking advantage of the incessant movements of convoys and troops. Many ringleaders were arrested, but the gendarmerie could hardly be omnipresent. Military tribunals showed leniency by pronouncing prison sentences. The accused pleaded concern about their families, the need to feed their children and to repair their houses – sincere or naïve excuses that fooled no one.

Civilian populations feared deserters, whom they regarded as aliens. They were armed and indulged in looting and assassination. Clustered in small bands, they hid in woods and abandoned chapels. The Calvados was reported to be one of their hideouts, but there were many others – in the Lozère and the Ariège, for example – where they mingled with *émigrés* and priests. Generally speaking, they contributed to a feeling of insecurity in the countryside. The *agent national* of Montdidier, a stop-over for many deserters from the northern army, ordered frequent watches in the communities of his *district*. On the edge of the Vendée, deserters were summarily executed as an example. Some runaways went back to their units and tried to explain their absence; they were accepted, because troop strength was dwindling.

Invalids and 'malingerers'

Military hospitals served not only to take in the sick and wounded, but also as a meeting-place for scattered comrades and compatriots, granting them a temporary respite from combat duty. This pattern developed thanks to the improper granting of sick leave by commanding officers and to the negligence of medical officers. Attempts have been made to evaluate the number of soldiers who lost their nerve, but hospital administration is complex and its archives for this period are scanty.

The critical state of hospitals was denounced everywhere. When heavy fighting occurred, they were rapidly filled to overcrowding, and their importance was calculated on the basis of their capacity. Staff and equipment were in short supply. Sometimes there was only one syringe for several hundred patients, one chamber-pot for three beds, and one commode for an entire ward. Lack of space led to the wounded being put with patients suffering from scabies and venereal disease. On 3 Ventôse (21 February), the Convention allowed the hospitals to keep their traditional system of administration and provisioning through private suppliers. But the legislature raised the salary of doctors and apothecaries, who were to be recruited under the supervision of a Health Commission. Stationary hospitals – in many cases both civilian and military – were given a different status from that of travelling hospitals, which accompanied the armies. Contagious patients were assembled in special camps.

The reform produced beneficial results. By the summer of 1794, the wounded, of whom there were many in the war zones, were receiving adequate accommodation and care. Less food was being wasted, and complaints on the subject decreased. The representatives nevertheless complained about the number of invalids. The hot and humid season was responsible for dysentery and other contagious diseases; spoiled food caused typhus and scurvy; boredom and inaction bred homesickness. Marcel Reinhard has described this feeling, which could lead to death. It helps to explain soldiers' attempts to escape their duty. Some inflicted injuries on themselves – for instance by cutting off their right index finger, needed to press the trigger – while other simulated madness. An even greater number gave themselves away by frequent short stays in hospitals; such stays accounted for as many as half of the admissions in regions bordering on the Vendée.

Not all units were equally affected, but those who were far from home sometimes saw one-third of their men disappear. Along the Moselle, certain companies were reduced to twenty men. Evacuees would not be heard from for several months and a fair number never rejoined. Camp and army organization suffered as a result. In his section, the good soldier, more often than not assigned to guard and patrol duty, paid for the bad one. Discontent increased when convalescents were allowed to finish recovering at home. The supply corps, which had only inaccurate statistics to work with, accused officers of negligence. As with desertion, the army was worried by the high incidence of illness – whether real or faked.

ECONOMIC MOBILIZATION

The decree on the *levée en masse* did not just concern the fighting forces, but also channelled the entire national production towards the army. The country, having been suitably conditioned, was turned into a gigantic military warehouse, and civilians became army suppliers. Demand – now stretched to the limit – revived, guided and regulated private enterprise without modifying its traditional structures. The government tackled the most urgent needs. Its chief priorities were to feed, equip and arm soldiers. Having first resorted to expedients, the government now introduced them on a large scale. The supply corps had lost momentum by clinging to tradition: the government revolutionized it. Finally, the authorities had to contend with the changes in traditional manufacturing and with nascent industrial capitalism. The *émigrés'* manufacturing concerns had stopped production. Others, more numerous, were in the hands of the underground reaction, which the government set out to curb first by the lure of profit, then by the persuasive force of the Terror.

State control was a means, not an end. National factories such as the *ancien régime* had known were built on a larger scale, in particular for gunpowder production, but the State carefully avoided a total nationalization of industry. Workers were given the same status as requisitioned soldiers and subjected to strict discipline as well as wage controls. These soldiers on the home front nevertheless held on to the work habits that they had inherited from the guilds.

The war commissioners

The nation at war also had to recruit a wide variety of military personnel. In an army that was constantly on the move, the supply corps was obliged to follow suit. The conduct of the war depended as much on efficient provisioning as on troop mobility. The routine machinery of camps and stores was not entirely abandoned, but more itinerant equipment and personnel were deployed. Non-combatant services were expanded to meet increased troop strength. Under the orders of chief ordnance officers, who had the rank of general, the war commissioners inspected the troops in an attempt to evaluate and satisfy their needs with the help of quartermasters, billeting officers, paymasters and submissive contractors to whom they gave preferential treatment.

Little attention has been paid to the commissioners, who were saddled with specific tasks and heavy responsibilities; and yet they had a deep knowledge of soldiers' moral and physical hardship. Their relationships with commanding officers and civilian officials were clearly defined and very close. The commissioners exercised benevolent or strict control over officers, who had often, like themselves, come up from the ranks; but, judging by the few complaints that have survived in the records, this authority was accepted and respected. Civilian officials reacted differently.

Requisitions continued in anarchic fashion until the beginning of the Year II; later, the Food Commission organized provisioning zones for each army – a measure demanded by the representatives on mission as a means of safeguarding their prerogatives. The decision was taken on 7 Nivôse (14 January) but was enforced slowly; news of it took one month to reach Bayonne. The *districts* reacted violently, because the measure reduced allocations for civilians. Food commissioners had a difficult time, particularly in war zones, where the arrival of reinforcements continually disrupted the balance: 'Under the reign of Equality, we must take special care of the soldier.' One could agree with that statement without necessarily resigning oneself to dying of hunger. There were limits to the resources available. The municipalities close to the Vendée and the borders as well as those that lined the highways complained bitterly. Women lurked about bivouacs, army bakeries and army butcher shops. As soon as soldiers ran out of supplies, they reciprocated by criticizing country folk for their subversive egoism.

Basically food had to be fairly plentiful if troops were to perform long marches on foot. Travelling in a rigorous climate, they felt the effects of fatigue before entering battle. Their diet was confined to bread, meat (usually made into soup), wine, and brandy – for which the troops made insistent demands. Double rations were a much-welcomed bonus. The daily ration included 24 ounces (734 grams) of *pain de munition*, made of wheat and rye, half a pound of meat and two ounces of dry vegetables. Soldiers on the march would get an extra four ounces of bread. Each company was supposed to set up its field kitchen every morning before ten and every evening before five. Delays in distribution and distances between bivouacs prevented the troops on campaign from adhering to this schedule. Although they did not suffer from malnutrition, they were fed irregularly. Battles, seasons and convoys resulted in alternate bouts of fasting and feasting.

The requisitions carried out in each region by the supply corps – which paid for goods at prices set by the *maximum* – were deemed sufficient for ordinary provisioning. The paymasters-general had considerable funds available. The paymaster of the northern army – 140,000 strong in September 1793 – reckoned his expenses to be sixty-two million *livres-assignat* a month. In case of emergency, the representatives could decrease rations or order extra requisitions above the official price, even if that meant seeking the approval of the Committee of Public Safety. The representatives made sure that military stores remained adequately stocked.

Provisioning for horses posed similar problems. Their daily requirements were ten pounds of forage, five pounds of straw and half a bushel of oats or bran. Their needs were met by army contractors.

Contractors and transactions

The traditional practice of invitation to tender continued under the Terror. Only finance companies had sufficient capital to enter the market. The Abbé d'Espagnac, Choiseau, and Lanchère are among the better-known entrepreneurs in the field.[5] They signed contracts with the State for the provision and transport of supplies, which they undertook to deliver after negotiating quantities, norms and prices. Contractors undoubtedly took risks, since they had to wait to get their money back. They also had to act quickly to protect themselves against price rises. They used subcontractors and a network of brokers who snapped up goods with a minimum outlay. Contractors skimped on quantity and quality, securing the connivance of members of the Contracts Committee and the officials responsible for uniforms, who received a *nivet* (bribe). Dubois-Crancé exposed these practices, which were common knowledge. But suppliers were needed, and for them only profit counted.

The volume of business was indeed enormous. Contracts would involve the immediate supply of thousands of horses, many of which would on inspection prove to be defective. Many old or glandered horses were slaughtered. Scandals were covered up, and responsibility attributed to small fry and stable-boys. It took the Terror and the cartage inspection service to frighten corrupt officials. Choiseau was condemned to death and executed on 2 Ventôse (20 February 1794), followed by d'Espagnac, who died with Danton on 14 Germinal, while Lanchère, who was imprisoned, survived Thermidor. The Military Transport Commission, created in Ventôse, launched a programme for the construction of carts and caissons; it hired wagoners and horses by the day. But complaints did not cease. Poor roads hampered travel; war prisoners were employed to repair them. Carters deserted, went into hiding, or refused to leave their homes. Nevertheless, the Committee of Public Safety rejected schemes to bring these vital services under State control.

Arrangements for the supply of kit and camping gear were handled until August 1793 by five officials attached to the War Ministry. They signed contracts, supervised deliveries and stores and imported goods

---

[5] A. Mathiez conducted some interesting research on these contractors (see, for instance, 'Un fournisseur aux armées sous la Terreur: Choiseau', *AHRF*, 1924, p. 401). But he was unable to use Piorry's report of 28 Germinal, which contains a summary description of the activities of the *administrations de l'habillement* (departments responsible for military clothing supplies) (*Archives parlementaires*, vol. 87, pp. 682ff.).

to make up for the shortfall in domestic production, which remained in the hands of private industry. The latter employed a host of small workshops in both textile and leather manufacture. Even the small cobbler set aside a few hours of his time for the army. Acting through tenderers, who would advance workers' wages, the State set unit prices and collected finished goods. In Paris, the *sections* provided raw materials and employed women to make uniforms. But women were constantly railing against 'monopolizers', who assigned tasks and fixed wages. Despite the purge and arrest of the culprits, hostility continued. The authorities' control was considered to be too strict and 'capitalist' influence too great.

Provincial *districts* sometimes set up what could be called 'national workshops', notably for the manufacture of shoes in tanning centres. But the troops often lacked warm clothes, good boots and tents. It was only with difficulty that the national army acquired its uniformly 'prestigious' appearance.

War industries and scientists

'It is not enough to have men...Arms, arms and supplies! This is the cry of need.' Barère's distress signal, sent out on 23 August 1793, echoed throughout the Year II. It concerned war industries that were not adapted to the needs of a vast army. The requisitioning of hunting-guns, the repair of old muskets and the manufacture of pikes all testified to patriotic ardour; but preparation for great offensives demanded other means. The Committee of Public Safety, with direct responsibility for such planning, had to exercise an even greater measure of State control. It put private firms under contract and established national manufactures under its own management. Prieur de la Côte-d'Or and the representatives sent to the foundries assumed an enormous task, as one can judge from their orders, instructions and circulars.

Without uprooting traditional structures, they bent them to meet the new requirements. A fully fledged armaments ministry was set up on 13 Pluviôse (1 February) in the form of a Special Commission for Weapons and Gunpowder, with responsibility for heavy industry and cannon, musket and munitions production. The decree of 12 Germinal (1 April) reinforced this central authority by bringing the mining administration under its control. The Commission was headed by Benezech with the assistance of Capon – the former, like Carnot and Prieur, an officer of the Engineers and a graduate of the Ecole de

Mézières. Its departments did not just implement decisions, but were equipped with research units and could count on renowned designers and technical experts. Among the specialists consulted were Monge, the founder of descriptive geometry, member of the Royal Academy of Sciences; the chemist Fourcroy, famous for his analyses of blood and milk; the doctor Berthollet, who, as early as 1785, had carried out research on textile bleaching and dyeing; the mathematician Vander-monde; Hassenfratz, who had served as Lavoisier's assistant; and even Chaptal, despite his dealings with federalists in the Hérault. The central figure was the well-known chemist Guyton-Morveau, an encyclopaedic mind, a jurisconsult and naturalist. Others too participated in the common task: the physicist Périer, who ran one of France's largest metal works at Chaillot; the chemist Darcet and his student Pelletier; Dufourny de Villiers, engineer and physicist, who succeeded Lavoisier as manager of the State gunpowder manufacture. Nevertheless, these distinguished names represented only a minority in the constellation of scientists who were France's pride, for, despite their stature, they had had to give proof of their loyalty and civic spirit.

Besides traditional armaments, the Committee of Public Safety wanted to develop secret weapons. Experiments were carried out first at La Fère, then on the old estate of Meudon, under the close supervision of Prieur, whose initial concern was to increase ordnance range and the effectiveness of explosives. Hydrogen-filled balloons were also manufactured at Meudon. Generals displayed little enthusiasm for the scheme, but the test flight, delayed until Germinal, seemed conclusive. The balloon, named *L'Entreprenant*, flew over the battleground at Fleurus and disconcerted the enemy. As for signalling, Lakanal supported the schemes of Chappe, who set up his first line of communication between Paris and the northern border. The war stimulated scientific research, which could then be applied to various fields.

French industry had depended on imported raw materials: it formerly obtained steel from Sweden, Britain and Germany; copper from Spain and Britain; part of its saltpetre requirements from India; and sulphur from Italy. It now had to rely on domestic resources, which were inventoried. Church bells provided bronze for cannon. After 23 July 1793, only one bell was allowed in each parish and all the others were removed to the foundries. The Gauthier process, developed in Nivôse and put into general use by Fourcroy, eliminated the excess tin that caused brittleness.

Cast iron production led to increased mining of coal — which replaced wood — and to requisitioning of forges and their workers. The 'solid' casting of cannon, as practised by Montalembert at Ruelle, came into widespread use, as did the manufacture of steel by cementation. All the same, the armed forces suffered greatly from the loss of their cannon, and regarded every capture of an enemy gun as a victory. Low wages in the metal industry also kept productivity down. In the anchor factory at Guérigny, the daily wage in Frimaire did not exceed twenty-five sous, and Noël Pointe suggested doubling this 'to stimulate zeal and courage'.

Armaments factory workers were no better paid. Actually, the young workers, who otherwise would have been sent to war, felt that their lives were spared by these exemptions and therefore kept silent. Moreover, daily pay varied according to qualifications. Considerable differentials — compounded by the common practice of piece-work rates — developed between borers, lock-makers and fitters. However, the persistence of a dual economy contributed to a climate of protest. If workers in the private sector enjoyed relative freedom, those in the State-run manufactures were subjected to long working days, from six in the morning to eight in the evening. Public holidays disappeared; negligence and idleness were punished. But it was hard to keep watch over scattered workshops.

The larger workshops were used only to assemble parts manufactured elsewhere. This pre-industrial mode of production involved no real division of labour. A lock-maker would make the whole lock on a musket, and a carpenter the whole butt. The 5,000 workers employed by the Paris factory should thus be regarded as artisans. This helps to explain why the outbreaks of unrest in the early spring were motivated by professional concerns, and were only incidentally political in character.

The capital was the great arsenal of the Republic, but the provinces make a key contribution to arms production. Muskets were manufactured not just in Saint-Etienne, Tulle and Moulins, but in a dozen new plants set up in abandoned churches and convents; swords and bayonets were made in Klingenthal and Thiers: cannon in Strasburg, Allevard and Le Creusot. Although the target set by the Committee of Public Safety was not met, output did reach the gratifying level of 240,000 muskets a year and 7,000 cannon.

National solidarity

To ensure an adequate supply of ammunition, a nation-wide campaign was launched for the collection of saltpetre, which was three-quarters of the contents of black gunpowder. The decree ordering the *levée en masse* had invited the entire population to join in: cellar floors were scrubbed to the accompaniment of songs, municipalities and *sociétés populaires* engaged in productive competition with the encouragement of representatives on mission, and 'revolutionary courses' were given at the Natural History Museum in Paris to young people who in turn acted as instructors. More than 6,000 hastily equipped workshops were inspected by Chaptal, Jacotot and Descroizilles. A tax on the rich covered initial expenses, as the *districts* paid producers twenty-four sous a pound. From Ventôse onwards, monthly production exceeded one million pounds, nine times the previous level. This display of civilian patriotism and enthusiasm had a great impact on collective attitudes. The campaign provided a spectacular proof of rural participation in the war effort. There were other, more localized efforts, such as the burning of marc, brushwood and horse chestnuts – in which children eagerly took part – to produce much-needed potash, and the extraction of soda from sea-salt. Artisans even designed cardboard armour, artificial limbs for the wounded, and carriages for invalids. Gifts received by the *sociétés populaires* were earmarked for a battalion or hero, for example the first soldier to enter Valenciennes. At Champlitte (Haute-Savoie), the blue curtains on the walls of the court room were made into officers' uniforms. Guimberteau, the representative in Tours, wrote on 10 Pluviôse: 'All I had to say to the friends of freedom was "Our brave defenders need shoes" and people everywhere took their shoes off.'

Soldiers made similar gestures, such as sacrificing their meat ration to a country town or volunteering as farm hands. In Messidor, the authorities even set up companies of agricultural workers whom municipalities could employ at harvest time. The communities also looked after conscripts' land by seeding and gathering crops for their families, who had been repeatedly promised assistance by the Convention after their fighting men had petitioned: 'I was about to shed my blood...when I learned that my wife, who used to live on my wages, is now obliged to beg for her bread.' Collot d'Herbois, on 12 Pluviôse (31 January), explained the difficulties that stood in the way of such relief, and the precautions that it demanded. Widows, wives, parents and children all had a right to the nation's gratitude. But they had to submit their claims, and expenditure had to be evenly distributed. The decree of the 21st (9 February) laid down the procedure by fixing a scale for compensation and listing the formalities required to obtain it. The wounded and invalid were not forgotten. The troops applauded this measure, 'which brings France back to the principles of equality by putting right the unfair distribution of wealth'. To keep up patriotic fervour, a share of *émigré* property was set aside for the troops. The representative Thirion even suggested handing over the properties of the *vendéen* rebels to the soldiers who had defeated them.

Foreigners faced the evidence: 'Any attempt to detach the soldier from the cause of the Convention would be fruitless. Nowhere else could he find what he finds in France: liberty, pecuniary benefits and rapid promotion, subsistence, relief of all sorts, and impunity for every excess.'[6] This observer, who was extremely well informed on France's military situation, duly noted its political aspect. The participation of troops in the revolutionary movement explained their enthusiasm and endurance: 'Despite their poor organization and their mediocre commanders, and despite their inexperience and indiscipline, they are holding their own against the best armies in Europe.' What a magnificent compliment! Nevertheless, the writer perceived the limits of sustained action: 'Such resistance is unnatural and must necessarily wear itself out by virtue of the very principles that sustain it.'

MILITARY SOCIETY

'The more soldiers there are in a State, the weaker the nation becomes.' Robespierre, who agreed with the Abbé Raynal's observation, always feared a dictatorship of generals. The citizen army remained faithful to the Republic, but its ethos changed. The requirements of the war had uprooted many human beings, cutting them off from their families and native soil. The majority, led on by their patriotism, adapted themselves to unusual conditions that others refused to accept. They had an ideal to defend and reasons for fighting. At first, the *sans-culottes* settled into an environment that they considered to be the fruit of their own efforts. Then, little by little, the war acted upon individuals by exposing them to emergencies and dangers to which they reacted as soldiers. Duty, discipline and *esprit de corps* shaped their outlook.

[6] Published in A. Rufer, 'Notions sur ce qui se passe en France, 1794', *AHRF*, 1963, p. 231.

This change stemmed from man's deepest instincts: fear, guile, material interest and the appetite for pleasure. It is therefore difficult to say when it began, but it did coincide with the reorganization of the army, and gained impetus with the victorious offensive of 1794 and the wave of conquests. Military society, with its rigid pattern and its hierarchy, differed from civilian society, and restrained the citizen. By seeking rank and honours, officers unwittingly promoted this military ethos, which affected soldiers to a lesser degree. Were not soldiers 'potential generals'? The circles close to the fighting forces also felt involved. Non-combatant services, pensioners and invalids belonged to the same society, whose population was well in excess of one million. The military condition was regarded as a profession. Revolutionary feeling weakened as self-interest was pursued in the name of the homeland. The army of Thermidor was already displaying the symptoms of Brumaire.

The soldier's mentality

The collective consciousness of civilian and military societies was determined by similar motivations but expressed different attitudes. Like the Revolution and the Terror, the national army was intended to be provisional; it was to be dissolved when the enemies of the Republic – who actually justified the army's existence – had been exterminated. The decree on the *levée en masse* called for battalion banners to display the words 'The French people rise up against the tyrants.' Above all, the soldier had to remain a citizen and hence to participate in political life. Soldiers did not fail to do so. The Convention, the *Montagne* and the Jacobins were the idols of the troops, who amply availed themselves of their right to petition. They applauded the 31 May *journée*, unanimously grieved over Marat's assassination, and endorsed the Constitution. In the towns, garrisons and detachments attended the meetings of the *sociétés populaires* and public festivals.

Doppet proposed creating a propaganda committee in each army. The *Bulletin* and special newspapers were widely distributed. In Germinal, the War Minister reported that, in one year, he had spent 450,000 francs on subscriptions, of which 118,000 were for the *Père Duchesne*. Some representatives reprinted several issues of this periodical, 'which did the soldiers a lot of good'. Carnot launched *La Soirée du camp* for the troops, who also received the Committee of Public Safety's major reports. All the same, Jacobinism spread unevenly among the battalions, some of which were lukewarm, others fervent, depending on the authority and sway of the propagandists. Within units, soldiers criticized opinions, collectively denounced comrades, and banded together to resist outside pressures. The military ethos also gave moral sustenance, especially to the weak. In particular, the company, where intimacy prevailed, came to replace the family. Soldiers gave each other news from home, shared their joys and disappointments as well as danger, fatigue and hardship. Together they faced up to arbitrary power. Comradeship served a twofold purpose: resistance and obedience. Moreover, junior officers set an example by their dedication. They carried their own haversacks, ate the same rations as their men, and assimilated themselves totally into the community under their command. The importance of their obscure role can never be overstated. Amalgamation, far from weakening cohesion, extended it to the half-brigade which, by a slow osmosis, acquired a personality of its own. Its commanders, elected by their troops, proved to be humane and supporters of the Republic. Under one flag, the adventure continued.

Nevertheless, young rural recruits had difficulty adapting. Their departure was sometimes traumatic. Their low degree of sociability and the high rate of mortality among young recruits affected their enthusiasm. Royalist and religious propaganda influenced them in Brittany and in Savoy, where they refused to fight against the Sardinians. Those who were short of essentials at home could not accept temporary hardship, for they felt the army owed them subsistence. They also suffered in the camps from their ignorance and from the constant taunting, but became hardened through combat. In the northern army, where they represented half of the troop strength, they put up a good fight and earned praise from the representatives.

Even when their revolutionary faith waned, the troops drew their energy from xenophobia. Coalition agents stressed – indeed exaggerated – this apolitical side of patriotism: 'The armies are neither royalist, nor republican – they are French: they are fighting without difference of opinion against foreigners because they are foreigners, and because the armies assume them to be united against France far more than against anarchy.' But xenophobia, fostered by the government, was compounded by a desire for revenge. Austrians and *vendéens* 'cut off hands and tongues', torturing and massacring patriots. Soldiers replied in kind to the barbarity of 'tyrants' satellites', whom they held responsible for their present condition and, more directly, for their comrades' deaths. Troops returned blow for blow. One dragoon cut down eight enemies, as in a 'western', and was stabbed in the back with a bayonet. Scattered fighting ended in hand to hand combat and sabre duels where deception and force triumphed. Such engagements were far more frequent than the great battles that have gone down in history.

Retaliation led to plunder, which was not just an 'occupational disease', and differed from marauding for food. Soldiers helped themselves to the vanquished foes' watches, money, crosses and epaulettes as rewards and trophies. Each man would claim his share of booty as his due, before carrying out the systematic destruction ordered in enemy country. On the other hand, robbers who attacked patriots and rebels indiscriminately in the Vendée were severely punished. A gendarme laden with women's clothing was 'executed on the spot'. Soldiers were supposed to protect civilians, not attack them. Siblot denounced at the Convention the 'hideous' act committed at Imbleville (Seine-Inférieure) by drunken hussars who had raped the priest's maid. Nevertheless, merrymaking was tolerated as a form of amusement, when it did not degenerate into brawling.

The armies of the Revolution were both slandered and extolled uncritically. Soldiers often shouted 'Run for your lives!', and 'cowardly battalions fled at the first shot'. But panics, though frequent, were limited and virtually disappeared with brigading and the great offensives. Conscripts wanted to fight and those in the camps asked to rejoin the units engaged in daily combat. Their youth, their contempt for danger, and their taste for gallantry increased their courage tenfold — a courage displayed first in long marches on foot and in the interminable wait associated with approaches. Some men on the look-out in marshlands with water up to their waists refused to be relieved. Reports concentrated on individual acts that were used for propaganda. Léonard Bourdon compiled a collection (*Recueil*) of such examples. Who does not remember Bara and Viala? They encouraged the legend of a cohort of children mingling with the troops, and tales of women in disguise. The army did admit a small number of women but refused to expose them to danger.[7]

Actually, soldiers and officers, young and old, served with equal

---

[7] See R. Brice, *Les Femmes et les armées de la Révolution et de l'Empire*. In the Year II, there were only one or two women in each battalion, where they were employed as *vivandières*. They remained in the camps.

distinction. Rather than surrender, some wounded men shot their brains out; others preferred to be shot to death rather than shout 'Long live the king!'. In the name of the Republic, others sacrificed themselves to save their weapons or their comrades. It was a point of honour not to be captured by the enemy, and to pass up deserved rewards. Generals' letters are filled with accounts of this vicarious glory – a glory that excused acts of indiscipline.

Discipline and military tribunals

Both conscripts and troops of the line had difficulty accepting the constraints of hierarchy and passive obedience. They liked discussion – southerners and winegrowers in particular. The unequal imposition of sanctions roused their sense of justice. Why should officers be merely placed under arrest while soldiers were put in prison? At first, it was thought that civic spirit would stem the tide of rebelliousness, but acts of insubordination increased until the winter of 1793. On 22 Nivôse (11 January 1794), the War Committee emphasized the need for firmness and severity: 'Respect for the law and military discipline are the first duties and the true signs of citizen-soldiers.' Obedience became an imperative and submission a virtue.

Of the tribunals created in each army on 12 May 1793, only five or six were operating – and poorly at that. The authorities classified offences according to their nature and seriousness. Treason by generals and corrupt practices by army contractors concerned the Revolutionary Tribunal. Acts of negligence and laziness were dealt with by disciplinary committees. Police officers curbed petty offences. As for criminal courts, they tried cowards, knaves and 'disorganizers', who were considered counter-revolutionaries. Prosecutors and juries were maintained, but procedure was streamlined. Out of a concern for fairness, both officers and soldiers were associated with the judicial process at every level; the military penal code was later revised in the same spirit. The machinery of justice aimed at impressiveness, even in its dress, so as to fire the imagination.

The decree on military justice adopted on 3 Pluviôse (22 January) was immediately enforced, as prisons had to be relieved of overcrowding. The representatives went about the task, even setting up courts-martial. 'Discipline has never been so strict in any French army', the Austrian general Mack observed in March. Actually, although punishments were merciless for rebels and traitors, they were light for inconsiderate remarks such as those of a Parisian gunner who 'would have been quite sorry to be a republican'. All in all, one-third of cases tried led to acquittal. Soldiers were treated more leniently than officers.

Nevertheless, generals were not sent to the guillotine if they had suffered a set-back. Carnot declared that 'a reverse is not a crime when one has done everything to deserve victory'. Some generals were even congratulated in defeat. The government, which had appointed them, no longer doubted their worth. They carried out its orders, which they wanted in writing – a procedure that resulted in a degree of passivity. Collective petitions were forbidden in December 1793, so that it is harder to assess the feelings of troops during the following period. But soldiers did not remain insensitive to the Germinal purges and the banning of the *Père Duchesne*. Hoche's disgrace served as a warning.[8] In any case, generals wrote shorter and more respectful dispatches, apparently avoiding political references: prudence prevailed.

With its solid structure and unity of purpose, the army was able to make efficient use of numerical strength. The army of the Year II, which had created the half-brigades, maintained them until the summer, when it began counting by divisions. These new tactical units grouped under a single staff some 8,000 to 9,000 men of every branch, and enjoyed a certain freedom of manoeuvre at the general strategic level. Rapid movements and dogged assaults brought victory. The patriotic impulse and the spirit of the Revolution – insidiously undermined by inaction in the camps – were revived on the battlefield. However, the magnitude and success of the operations led to a slackening of discipline. On the northern border, 'knaves reappeared' in Messidor.

The spirit of conquest

The Coalition powers, provisionally reunited thanks to British gold, had concentrated their forces between the North Sea and Luxemburg. Rivalries proved their undoing. Victory at Fleurus on 8 Messidor (26 June) reopened Belgium to the French.[9] One month later Jourdan

[8] Despite his successes in Alsace, Hoche was denounced by Saint-Just immediately after he had married a young girl from Thionville. Hoche was imprisoned in the Carmes gaol from 22 Germinal to 17 Thermidor Year II.
[9] It was a conventional battle. The French troops formed a semicircle to the north of Charleroi, with the Sambre behind them. Had they been repulsed, their defeat would have been catastrophic.

marched into Liège and Pichegru into Antwerp. In the Pyrenees, Dugommier invaded Catalonia and Moncey entered Biscay. The Italian border had already been crossed. The Republic's only set-backs were at sea and in the colonies. Everywhere else it 'fed off conquests', and really was able to feed its armies.

Carnot was aware of the limits of the war effort. 'If we had to start again next year, we should die of hunger and exhaustion.' He exhorted representatives and generals to 'settle down for good' in enemy territory. 'What matters to us is to fix with our triumphant armies the boundaries of the Republic; to assign it such borders as to ensure its splendour and greatness.' The aim was no longer to free the inhabitants, but to use their resources. The inhabitants resisted. The Spanish, egged on by the clergy, did not conceal their hostility. 'Peasants migrated in droves, so as to flee the presence of these good apostles of fraternity.' Hostages were imprisoned, churches closed, and submissive administrations set up.

Belgium had to pay a levy of sixty million francs in specie. Works of art and precious metals were seized. 'This time', wrote Cambon, 'our entry bears not the slightest resemblance to that of Dumoriez... we are being sent in rather than welcomed.' The same treatment was meted out to the Palatinate. Representatives proved insatiable: 'To defeat the enemy and live at his expense is to beat him twice.' Only a small fraction – barely one-fifth – of the levies reached the Treasury. The greater part was used for the upkeep of the occupying troops, who revelled in their affluence. Although they remained on the alert, they still felt relatively safe in the face of a disarmed population. Soldiers' letters bear witness to their satisfaction and self-interested motives. If ideology no longer paid, conquest seemed profitable, and represented the essential war aim for the combatants and the government.

But some men felt that they had been away from home too long and wanted to return. False grants of leave were forged by soldiers serving in the army of the western Pyrenees. The season prompted countrymen to go back to their agricultural tasks. Soldiers of rural origin were convinced by the evidence of their numbers that they bore an unfair share of the war effort. 'It is always the same ones who wage war and endure its hardships.' Their animosity extended to all non-combatants. The term 'shirker' began to be applied to 'fops in the bureaucracy', armaments factory workers, men exempted because of their speciality – tanners in particular, and sons of prosperous bourgeois who, having been baptized 'surgeons' and 'apothecaries' after an ill-defined course of study, crowded the hospitals.

Victory encouraged desertion but also favoured ambition. The price paid for victory was steep — more than was admitted and less than was claimed. Each camp concealed its losses and overestimated those of the enemy. Although difficult to calculate, fatal casualties do not seem to have exceeded one-fifth of the number of fighting men.

It has been pointed out that losses were proportionately heavier among officers who, by leading attacks, constituted choice targets. On the other hand, there was a surplus of officers in unengaged units. However, generally speaking, the increase in vacancies was slow, and competition for epaulettes became stiffer.

The mercenary spirit

After the first seven classes of the *levée en masse* had been enrolled, troop strength stabilized in the new military structures. The army, which provided clothing and nourishment, offered a daily pay that increased with rank. Young conscripts, who were soon hardened by action, found in military life the lure of adventure and worldly benefits. Despite its dangers, this profession was as good as any other. It was also a refuge. Austrian deserters, 'more than suspect' Belgians and Liégeois, and disbanded soldiers from the Parisian 'revolutionary army' asked to be integrated into the regular forces. How many were apprehensive about the return of peace, which would cast them back into their misery?

One derives the disagreeable impression, in Messidor, that soldiers clung to the army and intended to live off it. They had become increasingly concerned about bonuses and billets and were always asking for more. Officers who delivered mail claimed tips for delivering money orders. Captains cheated on their service records, falsifying enlistment dates and length of service. A disease spread: 'promotionitis'. Gillet, the son of a petty bourgeois, sub-lieutenant in the army of the Alps, wanted, like many others, to make a career in the army and to cease being supported by his father. A clever and resourceful young man, he became a war commissioner thanks to his good education.

The ability to read and write was made a prerequisite for moving up the ranks, first in the artillery, on 19 Pluviôse, then in the rest of the armed forces on the 27th (15 February). 'Talent had made a come-back' — and none too soon. The army of the Moselle, among others, had between fifteen and eighteen field officers 'who were unfit to be corporals'. The half-brigades were teeming with ignorant NCOs, while a number of Alsatians who spoke only German and had compatriots under their command were debarred from promotion. Courage and civic virtue no longer sufficed to ensure a good career. The NCOs whose hopes were quashed took to advocating desertion, or sought to circumvent the law with the connivance of the administrative boards. To reassure officers, the Convention modified the rules for promotion on 1 Thermidor (19 July), granting equal weight to bravery, seniority and choice. The Assembly did not order the enrolment of new recruits; the same men continued to fight – disregarding equality.

The war machine developed and launched in the Year II formed a socio-economic complex that was slowly drained of revolutionary meaning. The *montagnards* had guarded against 'the ambition of an enterprising leader springing forth from the line'. But there was another danger, inherent in the *montagnards*' methodical cast of mind and in the dimensions of 'this edifice of monstrous might'. The citizen disappeared and was replaced by a serial number. The national army, founded under pressure from the *sans-culottes*, had inherited from its origins the will to defeat the international aristocracy and preserve the benefits acquired through the Revolution. In that respect, the army remained at one with civilian society. But it was now preoccupied with specific problems that took on a professional character. It was 'a thriving industry without unemployment'. Thus, although Mathiez stressed the impact of that change, he refused to admit that it paved the way to Thermidor.

5

The Terror in the provinces

Unity or diversity?

The workings of revolutionary government and the enforcement of the Terror in the provinces represent too vast a phenomenon for so brief a period. Historians of the last century, from Thiers to Michelet and Taine, dwelling on memories that went back to their childhood, passed harsh judgement on the political and repressive aspects of the regime of 1793. Socialism, having discovered the social dimensions of the Jacobin inheritance, laid claim to it. The electoral contests of the Third Republic revived at the local level old disputes that were thought to have been forgotten. At the turn of this century, such disputes were still publicly referred to in towns and villages. Local authors who dabbled in history condemned – in the name of order, morality and religion – the excesses of the Year II that others extolled. The opposing sides indulged in an equal measure of exaggeration that spoiled their otherwise useful monographs, which were rejected later in the name of scientific objectivity.

These studies must be rescued from oblivion. They bear witness both to the revolutionary years they describe and to the period in which they were written – a period that is imperceptibly becoming alien to us. These monographs also reproduce texts, the originals of which were subsequently destroyed through ignorance, fires and wars; in this respect, they are our last authentic resource. Moreover, these studies enable us to reconstruct the process by which the past was appropriated by a later age with different social characteristics. Between 1870 and 1914, several thousand studies on the Revolution filled journals and periodicals. Their abundance was testimony of their importance in the historiography of the First Republic and in the political clashes of the late nineteenth century.

Furthermore, these monographs improved as their tone became that of dispassionate scholarship. In the more rational context of the *district*, the small town took on its true dimension with respect to its rural environment. The complexity of economic and social relationships requires structural analyses in which quantification does not eliminate the human factor. Recent studies have given us the names of influential local figures and investigated their antecedents and family ties. Agrarian questions and the history of attitudes are among the topics being explored nationally. Studies that were once scattered and partial are being combined and made coherent by the work of conferences, and this activity has led to a revival of local history, which alone can provide the vast materials required for an understanding of rural France.

It was not until the middle of this century that the peasant masses ceased to be the symbolic property of the Revolution. Georges Lefebvre, who discovered their autonomy, devoted twenty years to the painstaking search for documents and to writing *Les Paysans du Nord*. Others have made similar studies of western France, the Auvergne and the Languedoc. Thus, when seen 'from below', the peasantry no longer seems an undifferentiated mass. Its tensions are reflected in political attitudes that can be traced down to the very recent past. But how far back do those attitudes go?

Maurice Agulhon's recent study locates their roots in the collective traditions of Provençal life, suggesting a causal link between sociability and the number of clubs in the Midi.[1] Such incursions into the Revolution's past and future demonstrate the artificial character of chronological divisions and the danger of confining the analysis of peasant behaviour to the Terror. Nowadays, peasant behaviour tends to be examined in a longer chronological perspective, and is thus seen to have evolved at its own pace – not the pace of contemporary Parisians and even less that of our times. One of Richard Cobb's conclusions thus assumes its full significance: 'The Terror at village level is as complex as life itself.' It was the cause and justification of reactions, choices and fantasies of all kinds. Was it inefficient because it lacked rigour, or because that rigour, which was capable of massive exterminations, suddenly appeared to be a monstrosity?

Moreover, the *montagnards* remained convinced that they would succeed in rallying a portion of the peasantry. The end of dechristianization, the disbanding of the revolutionary armies, and the Ventôse decrees formed part of that campaign of seduction. But, with the

[1] M. Agulhon, *La Sociabilité méridionale: confréries et associations dans la vie collective en Provence orientale à la fin du XVIIIe siècle*, Aix, 1966, 2 vols.

aggravation of peasant hostility as the war went on, it was doubtful whether that campaign could have had any chance of success.

The army and the capital depended on the provinces, which supplied both men and food. No sooner had the provinces recovered from the federalist tremor than they revealed an underlying complex of hopes, antagonisms and habits that threatened to frustrate all attempts at centralization. How could disorder and unpredictable deviations from official policy in the provinces be tolerated? The government was faced with the crucial problem of its own authority – with the need to impose throughout the country an authority founded on the government's unchallengeable legitimacy and on its revolutionary methods. Public safety demanded obedience; but it remained to be determined who, at the local level, would have the power to command citizens.

The decree of 14 Frimaire (4 December) did not merely state principles; it gave detailed guidelines for its own implementation and it assigned responsibilities. The old wheels of government survived under new labels, but the prevailing impression was one of a far-reaching change that manifested itself in relations between individuals and between institutions. 'Precision, speed and revolutionary movement – these are the standards against which all your actions must be measured.' It was also this haste that disconcerted country folk, who had difficulty adjusting to rapid change and needed time to reflect – a habit that was now out of fashion.

'The laws are revolutionary; those who enforce them are not.' Having observed the backwardness of attitudes compared to social change, Saint-Just and Robespierre voiced the need to 'anger' the patriots and goad them into action. There were a good number of genuine republicans in the provinces, but few zealots. Rural communities followed home-grown leaders; they gave a hearing to outsiders but went on 'acting as they pleased'. Passivity was a mask. In rural areas and neighbouring towns, everyone tried to reconcile his personal convictions with self-interest. The peasant, who was wily by nature, played games with the Republic.

TOWN AND COUNTRY

The revolutionary government, which required unity of action, speed and efficiency, first challenged natural conditions. With its hills and plains, its obstacles and open horizons, the landscape shaped human habits and favoured isolation or communication. Ideas and news travelled along easy or difficult routes – always the same, always slow. Chabot reckoned that news from Paris took months to reach the Tarn. News spread faster along the main roads, in coaching inns, and at fairs and markets; it was delayed and distorted on poorly marked paths. The world of the Jacobin Republic submitted to these contingencies, which accounted both for its diversity and for the tendency of certain communities to withdraw. In the age of the horse, the wagon and the stage-coach, rural France was slow in passing on reports from Paris.

Turbulent zones and untroubled regions

The Terror did not have the same impact in every province or, within a region, in every locality. It spared certain places and bore down on others. The turbulent zones were predictable.

Firstly the borders, where the remaining inhabitants were subjected to both military and civilian authority. Their existence and livelihood depended on the successes of French troops, whom they supported at the cost of compromising themselves in the eyes of the enemy. Traditional trafficking and smuggling were indulged in only by a few hardened individuals, who were easier to track down in the north and in Alsace than in Piedmont or in the Pyrenees. Repression slowed their activity, and they were dealt with harshly. The great panic of the Bas-Rhin sent a mass of workers and their families fleeing into the Empire. J. B. Lacoste suggested guillotining a quarter of those who remained, sparing the patriots, and expelling the useless surplus.

Summary executions were equally numerous on the borders of rebellious zones. There was a fear of defectors and their acts of treachery. The ebb and flow of fighting covered up these infiltrations, which dangerously undermined the morale of soldiers and patriots. Collective massacres were carried out. Saliceti ordered the shooting of 200 Toulonnais in a single batch. In Lyons and its environs, suspects were rounded up. The 'special commissions' pronounced nearly 2,000 death sentences in six months – four times the number in Paris during the same period. In the Vendée, both camps were gripped by such a thirst for revenge that the actual number of executions remains unknown. Lequinio even contemplated doing away with all the inhabitants of the reconquered regions to make way for patriotic settlers.

Isolated rebellions claimed relatively fewer victims. Geography had an unforeseen influence: *bocages*, secluded valleys and arid peaks that protected hostile groups were transformed into revolutionary fronts. The Lozère, the Ariège, the Landes, and the Norman *bocage* were the scene of such tensions. By their armed intervention, the authorities became more oppressive. Suspicion did not disappear when hostilities had ceased. The contaminated zones remained 'under surveillance'.

Coasts were subjected to similar treatment. As they were vulnerable and open to invasion, they were provided with defences; military strength was increased in the ports and along the Channel. The local inhabitants were instinctively suspicious of the comings and goings of foreigners. They knew about smugglers and clandestine landings and rightly assumed that there was collusion in their very midst. Jacobin feeling fed on this apprehension. Public opinion was more actively pro-revolutionary in the coastal zones than in the neighbouring hinterland.

For one part of the Côtes-du-Nord, according to L. Dubreuil, the Revolution meant only the abolition of the feudal regime, requisitioning, conscription and inflation. Similarly, the inhabitants of the Pays d'Auge were described on the eve of the Terror as 'exceedingly unconcerned about the Revolution. [They] follow it less out of self-interest than out of curiosity...They are tired of the excessive price rises on all foodstuffs, and even more so of the scarcity and poor quality of bread...They await developments and yearn for the return of order and peace.'[2]

These attitudes also prevailed in rural areas of central and south-west France in the absence of agitation by local or outside elements. In this respect, the role of native rabble-rousers was more effective than that of armed contingents. The proximity of Paris did not frighten the counter-revolution. Around Meaux, Nemours, Rambouillet and Châtillon-sur-Seine, life was peaceful and uneventful. Social harmony was locally upset by groups of non-peasant wage-earners – weavers of Le Mans, miners of the Nièvre, the Allier and the Puy-de-Dôme, and workers of the Dordogne forges – who were not integrated into community life and reacted to it in the same way as the urban *sans-culottes*.

[2] Notes of an 'observateur du pouvoir exécutif' in Lower Normandy, published by J. M. Lévy, *AHRF*, 1963, p. 225.

Regionalism and community spirit

Regionalism and community spirit, two enduring features of pre-1789 rural France, survived the Revolution but were transformed by it. The new administrative divisions respected the old provincial boundaries, and decentralization encouraged federalism – a term that has been misinterpreted since it corresponds more accurately to an autonomist reaction of the *départements* against both Parisian centralism and a revived communalism. Did the popular movement not long for such a federalist-style liberation, which could have formed the basis for direct democracy?

Furthermore, distinctions were abolished between cities, towns and villages. The only officially surviving units were the communes, now vested with equal rights regardless of their former privileges. Because of their size, however, they created a hierarchy of needs and forces that the country-dwelling majority did not accept. Only one-fifth of the population lived in urban communities of more than 2,000 inhabitants. When dearth struck, these towns wielded the coercive force of the Terror against their traditional suppliers. Old grievances were voiced anew. For the peasant, those who did not cultivate the land were, by definition, loafers. Why come to their rescue?

Above all, why obey town-dwellers who monopolized public office and unscrupulously laid their hands on nationalized properties in rural communities? Paul Bois has pointed out the political consequences of this 'bourgeois spoliation' for the west and the Vendée rebellion. Elsewhere, the inequality of natural resources between fertile regions and their barren neighbours, or between cereal-growing areas and woodlands, pitted Auvergnats of the mountains against Auvergnats of the Limagnes (plains), and Beaucerons against Percherons.[3] Interdependent economies now became rivals. Another aspect of this antagonism was the fear of shortages – a genuine obsession among the poorer peasants, who became revolutionaries if they were not so already. At the local level, peasant reactions meshed with those of urban *sans-culottes*. Demands for bare necessities were backed up by political accusations against egoists and hoarders.

But 'patriotic' towns called the tune, and strengthened their position through the Terror. Reciprocal suspicion between townsmen and countrymen turned into radical opposition, with 'starvers' on one side

---

[3] See C. Lucas, 'Auvergnats et Foréziens pendant la mission du Conventionnel Javogues', in *Gilbert Romme et son temps*, Paris, 1965, p. 129.

and 'empty stomachs' on the other. The peasantry was condemned *en bloc* and accused of criminal deeds such as poisoning its wheat. In the name of Jacobinism, insurrections in restive rural zones were dealt with ruthlessly. The Chouannerie★ was a reaction to this blindness. The *sans-culottes* incited their local officials and the national guard to move against the countryside, and repression acquired a spiteful character. There was widespread looting, and farms abandoned by their inhabitants were burned.

The interests of town and country were incompatible because of price controls on foodstuffs. Village communities accepted the priority of army requisitioning as a basic patriotic sacrifice. They gave up their surplus and sometimes a share of their vital supplies for the cause of national defence, but they could not commit themselves beyond that. Wealthy farmers felt bound by local ties of solidarity; by protecting their stocks, they wanted to assure the provisioning of their clientele. Requisitions earmarked for Paris or the big towns were unpopular, and those for neighbouring towns even more so. Thus, during the winter of 1793, there were many instances of dearth on a small scale amid relative abundance.

The community spirit was influenced by economic constraints. The claims of the rich to the commons and restrictions on usage rights provoked uprisings by poorer peasants avid for land. The rural poor had numerical superiority; they were often armed and they were encouraged by Jacobin authorities. They carried out sporadic, ephemeral actions and later accepted dependent status in order to survive. Payments in kind kept agricultural day-labourers submissive, as bread became scarcer and more expensive. The peasant movement gradually placed itself in the hands of its notables and imitated their attitudes. The indigent rural masses were very malleable, and lacked the protection of a category of small independent producers such as those of the Nivernais, where cattle-fatteners profited from inflation.

Generally speaking, the peasant who worked a small plot and lived off family-run mixed farming was constantly suffering from lack of money, so that he derived no benefits from the Revolution. The *maximum* affected him like an injustice. He had trouble saving enough to pay his expenses. Taxation, more conspicuous than under the *ancien régime*, seemed heavier to him. He resisted tax collection and refused to pay levies in kind, objecting to a practice that deprived him without

★ Counter-revolutionary rising in western France, similar to the Vendée. [Trans.]

compensation. The insatiable and oppressive revolutionary government appeared to him to have taken the place of the former seigneurs.

The weight of habit

The life of the humble is made up of constant hardship and sacrifices that take their toll on collective attitudes. 'Misfortunes are looked upon with indifference; they have been accepted in advance.' Observers agreed on this rural apathy in the face of national danger. '[Country-dwellers] have been disfigured by the long practice of servitude.' The population of the Auvergne mountains was not just 'phlegmatic by nature' but also 'crassly ignorant'. Moreover, rural folk preferred their dialects and patois to French, even if they could speak the national language.

The community organization possessed a framework and traditions that could not be eliminated by decree. In the *district* of Thiers, these age-old influences were strengthened by the existence of powerful patriarchal communities (*communautés taisibles*) in which undivided family estates were exploited under the authority of the eldest member. These units perpetuated an attachment to king and religion, whereas southern customs and fraternities encouraged Jacobinism in the urbanized villages of Provence. In 1793, the parish priest and the propertied bourgeois still acted as guides, administrators and spokesmen for a loyal population. The inhabitants of Saint-Polgues remained well-disposed towards their former seigneur, for 'he had been honest and kindly to the poor'. Near Nemours, the physiocrat Du Pont advised and took care of the population, and managed his estate of the Bois des Fossés in peace. As he subscribed to newspapers, he would be asked to give the news from Paris.

Details of legislation concerning persons and property circulated even less than political news. Chaudron-Rousseau noted that the *districts* of Prades and Céret had been unaware of the Convention's activity for the previous fifteen months. The Cantal was no better informed. 'How can one love the Revolution? Malevolent individuals invariably propagate all manner of humbug.' People believed the slightest rumours, whatever the tidings, from soothsayers' prophecies of doom to predictions of imaginary victories. On the strength of a rumour heard at a fair, a churchwarden of Uzerche, three of whose sons were fighting on the border, led a campaign in favour of the Duke of York. Pitt was equated with the Devil; prayers were said for the destruction of 'the new Carthage'.

Peasant naïvety bordered on recklessness. With the proceeds of the sale of its ecclesiastical estates, the community of Chevannes – at the very height of the Terror – ordered a statue of St Sulpice for its church. Women remained more faithful than men to ancestral practices, and preserved them in the home. Grace was said before every meal even in patriotic households. The master made the sign of the cross over the bread before cutting it. Children would go to bed only after the ritual prayers, which would also be said for the homeland. Edifying tales and diabolic legends would be told at evening gatherings. Thanks to mothers, religious feeling continued to permeate the gestures of every-day life.

Religion and fanaticism

'The people are fond of their bells.' Bells were the memory of days. They measured time for the worker and announced joys and calamities. Like the local church, they were a common patrimony that consecrated the existence of a village before symbolizing worship. Each parish was allowed to keep one bell.

Tolerance was displayed towards the intimate belief of the uneducated peasantry in a divine power and their expectation of an eternal happiness that would make up for earthly worries. The peasant, who was exposed to the caprices of Heaven, needed such solace more than the town-dweller did. This deep conviction was transmitted from generation to generation along with life itself. Religious faith and patriotic faith were not mutually exclusive a priori. The priest of Saint-Sever in Toulouse claimed the right, in the name of Liberty, to believe in both God and the Republic.

Where did superstition begin? It could apply only to visible customs, such as the recourse to sacraments and the outer forms of worship as practised by the priest. The Jacobins considered these habits as a factor of social sclerosis. The *sans-culotte*, who enjoyed playing the free-thinker, considered himself above 'mummery', although he did not prevent women indulging in it. After 18 September 1793, priests who continued to hold services were often tolerated, but, asked the patriots, why pay them a stipend? Priests were not forgiven for being useless, and for observing celibacy. The political attitudes of some priests convinced public opinion that they sympathized with non-jurors and their congregations. After having been indiscriminately branded as fanatics, they became public enemies, agitators and a danger to the homeland. 'The Republic such as we want it cannot exist with these monsters.'[4]

By supporting rural areas in their opposition to measures of public safety, priests proved their accusers right. Through them the dogma of revolution was gradually being attacked. Atheism spread in the towns. The anti-religious struggle merged with the revolutionary struggle to become anti-Christian. In the terrorist's bible, it now took pride of place.

OF INSTITUTIONS AND MEN

The Committee of Public Safety expected that the revolutionary government would be functioning in the whole of France by the end of Nivôse – an assumption that credited institutions and men with magic power and underestimated the forces of resistance. By proclaiming its optimism, the Convention wanted to stimulate local authorities and convince them to act simultaneously. But were there enough determined personnel available? The almost general shortfall in Jacobin recruitment posed serious problems for representatives on mission.

The 'missionaries' of the regime

On 9 Nivôse (29 December), the Assembly delegated to the provinces fifty-eight of its members, whom it invested with unlimited powers. The legislature chose men who were familiar with the areas and populations to which they were assigned. Some were already on the spot; others had supervised levies and requisitions in the same regions. With six exceptions, each envoy was made responsible for two *départements*, that is, one million hectares to travel across, 400,000 to 500,000 inhabitants to keep under surveillance, and some 800 communes to purge, distributed among a dozen *districts*.

These missions required extensive travelling, which the winter made difficult. Therefore, although forbidden to do so by the 14 Frimaire decree, the representatives used scores of agents. Fouché made extensive use of them in the Nièvre. Agents were recommended by the *sociétés populaires* and, within a narrow scope of action, were delegated very

---

[4] Letter from Lanot, 23 Nivôse Year II, quoted in A. Aulard, *Histoire du culte de la Raison*, p. 383.

specific powers that flattered their vanity. Whether locals or emissaries from the capital, they hastened to justify their reputation as ultra-revolutionaries. As they were convinced that right was on their side, they brutalized public opinion, carried out ruthless searches and arrests, and quashed sentences.[5] The countryside experienced the Terror through their excesses.

The representatives intended to coordinate their agents' operations from the towns. The representative would arrive surrounded by local police, call out the national guard or a military detachment, and assemble the *société populaire* to announce his intentions. No one was to remain unaware of his presence. This ceremonial was repeated everywhere, with variants that depended on temperament. Intimidation worked: Carrier's arrival in Rennes made the moderates flee. When faced with unforeseen difficulties, representatives sometimes acted high-handedly and their agents even more so. Perhaps involuntarily, they over-enforced general measures and were more revolutionary than the government.

No mission required so much initiative, for none was so complex. It concerned both things and individuals, both institutions and public opinion. On its success depended that of the Jacobin regime. One of the first tasks was to purge local authorities. 'Summon the people as a *société populaire*; call public officials before it, and question them on their conduct; let the people's verdict dictate your own.' The representatives adopted this procedure, which had been suggested by the Committee of Public Safety. The *scrutin épuratoire*, in which everyone submitted spontaneously to public criticism, represented a more democratic form of expression than election. The results were uneven: in some places, the *scrutin* was a mere formality, in others, a stiff examination. Instead of the usual questionnaire, Dubois-Crancé put this simple question: 'What have you done to be hanged if the counter-revolution were to arrive?' Until Germinal, this periodic 'skimming' worked in favour of the intermediate social categories and followed a by now familiar pattern. Artisans and shopkeepers replaced lawyers, for whom office jobs were nevertheless set aside. Continuity of services was preserved by keeping on administrators who had not acted unworthily. Wholesale purges were rare.

The new local governments were not very difficult to organize since

[5] See C. Lucas, 'J. M. Lapalus', *AHRF*, 1968, p. 489. Lapalus, an agent of Javogues, issued more than 300 arrest warrants against priests and Lyonnais rebels. He was condemned to death and executed on 23 Germinal.

offices were remunerated. Most of the abolished *procureurs-syndics* were kept on as *agents nationaux*. The existing *comités de surveillance* perpetuated themselves. When vacancies came to be filled, the *sociétés*, which proposed candidates, did their best 'to reward patriotism and talent, while entrusting the interests of the Republic to experienced hands'. Such candidates were easy to find in the towns, but in the countryside municipal officers had to be pressed into service. They accepted their additional responsibilities and the national allowance of five francs a day without devoting their time to the *comités révolution-naires*. Since the new posts were effectively at the discretion of the representatives, the latter were courted assiduously. They allowed themselves to be taken advantage of and incurred the reproaches of the *départements'* own representatives. Thus Massieu was denounced by Harmand in the Meuse for having 'handed over revolutionary powers to supporters of Pitt and Coburg...These are the creatures who manipulated, accompanied and pestered you!'

But representatives were undeterred by this relentless calumny. They knew they had the backing of the 'great' Committee and they abided by its decisions. 'Pronounce, and we shall execute. We do not fear responsibility, but we are afraid of lacking prudence.' Their activity was indeed considerable. They submitted decrees to the Committee for approval by the armful. Locally, their orders had force of law, and those who suspended them were liable to ten years in irons. It would therefore be hard to judge the impact of the Revolution in the provinces without consulting the collections of these decrees, which reveal the republican faith that guided their authors. Often local authorities took decisions without consulting representatives. Thus the situation varied from region to region and within each one.

Local authorities

The determination of local authorities depended on the presence of representatives and energetic patriots, for public opinion was never 'unanimous and clear-cut'. Nowhere did it fully accept revolutionary government. The Jacobin minority, striving to assert its pre-eminence, was subjected to constant pressure. It felt spied upon and hounded; it rarely acted with composure, and more often overplayed than under-played its hand.

The Jacobins themselves lacked cohesion. *Sans-culotte* militants and purchasers of *biens nationaux* did not share a common social provenance.

The latter group, which was revolutionary out of self-interest, practised opportunism. They kept up appearances but only committed themselves half-way. But, here and there, obscure rabble-rousers managed to whip up popular feeling. Jumel in Tulle, Vassant in Sedan, the Gerbois brothers in Amboise, Goullin in Nantes and Lepetit in Saumur all enjoyed a following. One could also surmise the presence of such figures in certain rural towns whose political attitudes contrasted sharply with the surrounding apathy. During the winter of 1793 the influence of these men grew; they were the 'pillars' of the 'constituent bodies'.

The *agents nationaux*, who represented the revolutionary regime in the *districts* and municipalities, 'were assigned no limits other than laws'. They did not take part in the deliberations of local administrative bodies, but ordered and supervised the implementation of decrees, 'denouncing negligence and breaches of the law'. The *agents* were depended on to fire the zeal of local officials, but many were themselves tepid. In Romorantin, the *agent* was none other than a canon of the cathedral; several others, including the *agent* in Thonon, admitted their lack of competence. Their difficult and thankless task embodied a double threat that inspired them with caution: punishment from above and repudiation from below. They adopted the attitudes of the former *procureurs-syndics*, confining themselves to recording the removal of bells, the sale of *émigré* property, and the abjuration of priests. Their brief and optimistic reports, sent every ten days, are disappointing.

Municipal council proceedings are no less so. The larger the locality, the more substantial the deliberations, those of the big towns being the most interesting. However, apart from the problem of food supplies, which was their overriding concern and sometimes inspired original schemes, most assemblies strove to demonstrate their civic spirit by methods common to all localities. It was important to show oneself 'equal to the situation'. The standard fare would consist of planting a liberty tree, inaugurating a temple of Reason, and organizing civic festivals. Town clerks reinforced this impression of uniformity. The greater their legal experience, the more laconic and impersonal the proceedings become – with nothing in them for the historian.

For various reasons, the countryside was even less prolix. In the smallest communes, elected officials barely outnumbered electors. A commune of 800 inhabitants comprised some 150 national guards and 20 town officers and notables. The partly illiterate administrators sometimes entrusted the management of municipal affairs to the seigneurs' stewards, who were the leading exploiters of land in the community. The *société populaire* of Sées demanded their exclusion from public office, but they stayed on throughout the Terror in many places, such as Gonesse, Villers-le-Bel, Acquigny, Beuzeville and Lauzun. A priest administered the commune of Réchésy without interruption from 1775 to his arrest on 9 Thermidor.[6] In a good number of villages the same officers were kept on from 1792 to 1795.

Everyday business followed its uneventful course. Officials went about their duties unhurriedly. The impoverished and less affluent patriots who put in 'a huge effort day and night' for the *levée en masse* did not receive the compensation that had been asked for them. They confined themselves strictly to implementing basic decrees, carrying out requisitions, and collecting taxes. In Grézolles, it was only after Thermidor that relief was distributed to the families of volunteers.

A different situation obtained when municipalities and *comités révolutionnaires* were composed of the same men. The mayor of Issy-les-Moulineaux also presided over the *comité* and the *société populaire*. These men were not content with administering, but indulged in surveillance and punishment, exercising arbitrary and uncontrolled power. While sparing their protégés, they put their personal enemies in gaol. Priests worked their way into positions of power in the Creuse, and bourgeois imposed their will on *sans-culottes*. In Mende, there were complaints about domination by wealthy landowners. The *district* of Benfeld was run by former 'agents of the Necklace cardinal [the Prince de Rohan]'. Abuses seem to have been more common in small towns than in large ones, where the law was more rigidly observed. All accounts agree as to the degree of loyalty of local officials. The most one could expect was one genuine patriot out of every six, the others being 'unconcerned individuals and aristocrats'.

True patriots stood out by their constant desire to serve the Republic, as the government had officially invited the *sociétés populaires* to do: 'You shall be our most powerful auxiliaries'. The *sociétés* swore oaths, such as 'to exterminate whoever would advocate the monarchy directly or indirectly, and to denounce those who...would vilify or destroy the nation's representatives'. Poor and rich alike took the oath. Since 1789, hatred of the aristocracy had inspired the collective consciousness of rural France, which was, however, loath to resort to needless violence.

---

[6] See C. Bairet, 'Histoire de la paroisse de Réchésy', *Bulletin de la Société Belfortaine d'Emulation*, 1964–5, no. 65, p. 99.

The *sociétés* did not all adhere to the same political line. Moreover, there is disagreement as to their number. Aulard's figure of one thousand can apply only to those that were formally affiliated with the Jacobin club. In fact, *sociétés* were created spontaneously, or at the instigation of representatives, in nearly every municipality from October 1793 onwards. In the six south-eastern *départements* alone, there were over a thousand; the list stopped growing after Germinal.

During the winter, most of the population attended the *sociétés*. In medium-sized towns, the turn-out was relatively heavier than in big towns. Members identified themselves by wearing cockades; militants pinned a badge with the words 'true *sans-culotte*' on their coats. In rural areas, women were less assiduous participants. Sometimes, where they had not formed their own *société*, a special gallery was set aside for them. At the beginning of the Year II, the *sociétés* laid down rules of order after a fashion, but they were not observed: the 'shrines of Liberty' remained noisy and discussions remained impassioned. Meetings were held in churches, where patriotic inscriptions replaced holy pictures: there was much singing. The activities of the *sociétés* ranged from recreation to propaganda and civic instruction.

Fraternal feelings, disinterestedness and patriotism guided their action. Newer *sociétés* displayed much goodwill and a genuine enthusiasm, but had little means. They were supported by the *chef-lieu*, which helped them to gather saltpetre, collect gifts, draft messages and recruit horsemen, who were always 'Jacobins'. Thus was accredited the idea that the revolutionary movement was spreading to the countryside. 'No one listens to anybody who is not a Jacobin, because it is known that the Jacobins have done their utmost for liberty.' This elusive state of affairs did not obtain in Noyon: laws are obeyed out of love for one's homeland or out of fear, an observer remarked, 'but the latter sentiments are unknown'.

Forms of protest

The more oppressive the Jacobin dictatorship became, the more it had to contend with various types of opposition at the local level. The most unexpected resulted from administrative communalism: each locality wanted to run its own affairs and settle its own quarrels. Local opinion resented unsolicited intervention. Rather than submit to it, communities observed a rule of silence. This conspiracy was not punished; however, it gave a misleading picture of the Republic to the government.

In demanding obedience, the government was primarily concerned about the 'active minority', which – unknown to the authorities – was moving down the path towards democracy, like the Parisian *sans-culottes*. There were few activists, and most of them were in the towns. In Bordeaux, Tallien denounced the brother of his colleague Ysabeau, 'who indulged in this excess'. Activists were described as disciples of Marat, then of Hébert; they were flattered by these titles, bestowed by *les Messieurs*. If only through the press, they received a broad inspiration rather than specific orders from the capital. Most activists were aware of being at the forefront of the Revolution. They put forward summary but constructive proposals, which they were able to adapt to the wishes of their fellow citizens. They spoke out against both government centralism and the 'bad rich'. One can trace their activities from 10 August 1792 onwards. This continuity and the fervour of their convictions gave the activists a strength that they communicated to the Jacobin *sociétés*, which endorsed their schemes for a national monopoly on foodstuffs, a levy on high incomes, and taxes on servants and bachelors. These projects were abandoned along with their authors when the latter refused to submit to the government.

Other 'extremists' took their place. Even in small towns the appearance of 'patriots for the nonce' was reported. Collot d'Herbois denounced them at the Jacobin club after the elimination of the *enragés*. Maure, in the Seine-et-Marne, recognized in the new breed 'an infinity of *émigrés* from Paris, legal practitioners, men of finance and agents of the *ancien régime* who are flooding the country and campaigning for their election to the next legislature'. They streamed into Montpellier from all over the Languedoc. In Blois, Garnier de Saintes destroyed 'this oppressive faction led by an evil and hypocritical priest'. In Saint-Malo, renamed Port-Malo, 'bad citizens thought they could intimidate good citizens by taking the lead in denouncing them'.

Such were the standard tactics of the federalists. Rather than stubbornly clinging to a doctrinal opposition doomed to failure, they imitated the methods of 'Père Duchesne' and tried to merge with the ultra-revolutionaries. The artificial and sudden character of their reversal misled urban opinion, which knew little of their origins. Their resolutely negative attitude consisted of getting rid of patriots and voicing ceaseless recriminations. In Pluviôse, Tallien ordered the arrest in Bordeaux of one of those federalists who 'with no other means than rhetoric and blanket condemnation, spoil everything and influence weak men'. These elements were spotted too late in some small towns where they did harm. 'You know as I do', wrote Legendre, on mission in the Cher, 'that a good number of hypocrites have marched under the banner of those who support the Revolution. They have acted out of self-interest, vanity and cowardice.'

The great coalition of absentees also served the designs of these opponents. A majority, composed not only of enemies of the regime, resigned itself to an unavoidable situation and refused to take sides, leaving the way open for bolder men. It is at the local level that one must appreciate individual behaviour. The urban artisan, a good *sans-culotte*, could not devote all his time to militant action. His professional and family obligations brought him back home; pleasure-seeking took him to the cabaret. As Richard Cobb humorously observed: 'Billiards and women had the final say.' Agricultural work had the same effect on countrymen, who spent their spare time trimming vines in late winter and ploughing and sowing in the spring. The *décadi* would be spent at home or visiting neighbours and only on occasion at the *société populaire*. The 'revolutionary armies' had already lost their power of persuasion.

The 'political' armies

The 'revolutionary armies' were one of the most original creations of the *sans-culotte* movement and the anarchic Terror. All too often, only the Parisian army is mentioned, whereas such armies were raised spontaneously in the provinces. Far from the capital, in the centre and south-west, they were born of local initiatives. The *sociétés populaires*, *comités révolutionnaires* and *sections* were more often responsible for them than were the representatives.

There were fifty-seven armies with a total strength of 30,000 men, of whom 6,000 belonged to the Parisian army.[7] But elsewhere the number of soldiers ranged from 50 to 1,000. They were a mixed lot: townsmen and countrymen; *employés*, workers and unemployed men; respectable folk and bandits, who, along with their common-law crimes, passed into legend. However, even the Marat Company in Nantes, which had a reputation for ferocity, was composed of shopkeepers and modest artisans.

In fact, in order not to compete with ordinary levies, the 'revolutionary armies' had to pick family men of reasonable age; such men

[7] See above, p. 96.

did not hold extreme views, but were attracted by the high pay, the uniform and a more flexible discipline than that of the regular army. Indeed, there soldiers intended to remain civilians. Their officers agreed to this, even though most of them had belonged to the royal army, the gendarmerie or the national guard. The prospect of rapid promotion was attractive; but the men's civic virtue was vouched for: both officers and soldiers were democratically chosen and had to undergo the *scrutin épuratoire*.

These popular forces were subordinated to local authorities, none of whom, however, was legally put in charge; the civilian commissioners who accompanied the armies wielded discretionary powers. Chosen from among the most ardent revolutionaries, they behaved like gang leaders, acting in turn as 'apostles', policemen and judges. They represented the Jacobin Republic, which was judged by their conduct. A few men were enough to frighten a village. Their sudden appearance, determined attitude and military trappings caught the imagination. They demanded immediate obedience and then disappeared promising to return – which they seldom did. This itinerant Terror radiated outwards from the towns, and was enforced intermittently in one-third of the country from September to late December 1793.

The Parisian army participated on a larger scale and with the backing of the Committee of Public Safety. Its commander, Ronsin, displayed considerable organizational talent. Together with the civilian and war commissioners, he succeeded in maintaining the cohesion and *esprit de corps* of the various units. The nucleus of the army was composed of the 'active minority' of *sans-culottes*; hence the troops were older and more politicized than the staff. Government orders were transmitted by the officers to the detachments, which operated not only around the capital, but also in Lyons and the Vendée.

As propagandists and executive agents of the Revolution, the armies took advantage of their mission to spread *sans-culotte* ideas in the countryside wherever they happened to stay. The *sociétés populaires* were used as a power base by the armies, who controlled them from the gallery. Cooperation between the armies and Jacobin agents worked against the moderates. The armies' egalitarian sermons pitted the poor against the rich. 'Egoism is winning against humanity; the Terror must win against egoism.'[8] The armies meddled in local disputes, fostering intrigues and demagogy.

[8] The *société populaire* of Lisieux to General Vialle, 26 Nivôse Year II, quoted in R. Cobb, *Les Armées révolutionnaires* (6), p. 66, note 130.

By their blunders and exactions, the 'revolutionary armies' contributed to the alienation of the rural populace from the government, giving them fresh reasons to complain against the urban *sans-culottes*. Parisians became aware of their own isolation. Instead of strengthening national unity, the 'political' armies aggravated the conflict between town and country. The peasant masses countered the armies' puny numerical strength with collective resistance and a solidarity of interests.

REVOLUTIONARY ACTION

'The countryside must be brought to heel because it is fonder of the *ancien régime* than one thinks.' With vehemence, Saint-Just called for pitiless rigour against the enemies of the Republic and 'whoever does nothing for it'. 'One must rule by the sword those who cannot be ruled by justice.' This outlook inspired the terrorist, who committed himself totally to action in order to achieve success. The struggle against aristocracy, religion and egoism became indistinguishable from social democracy. Marchand, a member of the committee of the Paris *département*, who had been sent on mission to collect food supplies, crudely expressed this aggressive mentality:

Tomorrow at noon at the latest we will be in your area. We will deposit most of our vermin at the louse-ridden château of Chantilly and, in the presence of the guillotine birds who live inside it, we will pierce the air with the cries of Liberty that make them shudder with fear and horror. Most likely we will also pierce a cask of wine there.[9]

The language of this injunction belonged to the realm of folklore. Such style was commonly used, as much by the most peaceful agents as by the most violent: all were obliged to do so because of their function and the hostile environment. Rural resistance proceeded from the counter-revolution, turning economic offences into political crimes.

Policing food provisioning

In the supply zone for Paris, which extended from Orléans to Beauvais and from the Champagne to Le Havre, the 'revolutionary army' played a thankless but beneficial role. It ensured that wheat was collected from the producer, transported and delivered to bonded warehouses. Small

[9] Letter to the municipality of Chantilly, 4 October 1793, quoted in Adrian Sée, 'Clémence et Marchand: trois mois sous la Terreur en Seine-et-Oise' (**170**).

detachments travelled up and down the region getting municipalities to act and enforcing price controls. Others escorted wagons and barges. The poor classes in large rural towns looked forward to their arrival: 'Come, O *sans-culottes*! Come, O champions of good principles... Come, O Jacobins! You are our only hope.' Triumphal arches were raised and garnished tables laid out in their honour.

Local authorities consisting of farmers and landowners, 'those caterpillars of the Republic', often set an example of fraud. Rather than produce not very profitable corn, they cut down on cereal acreage. Rather than hand over grain at fixed prices, they hid their reserves. 'When it was pointed out to them that such practices were harmful to the armies, they replied that they didn't give a damn so long as they were able to eat as much bread as they wanted.' Ill will was a general phenomenon.

To subjugate 'the farming and mercantile aristocracy', soldiers and control commissioners carried out domiciliary visits by night. Terrified villagers jolted out of their sleep would reveal their caches. Millers were harassed by inspectors checking the calibre of their sieves and the quality of their bolted flour. Commissioners also supervised bread-baking. They devoted their attention to all commodities of primary necessity, including firewood, and were relied upon to hasten military requisitions and the provisioning of markets.

Wine and meat aroused particular concern. Innkeepers disregarded price controls on wine, cheated over quality, and served vile concoctions. The *sans-culottes* turned into excisemen, demanding to be shown bond notes for wine duties. The winegrowers, a rebellious and undisciplined lot by temperament, outsmarted the commissioners, who were unable to assess their production. Nor could the exact quantity of livestock be determined. As a big consumer of meat, the Parisian resented restrictions, spurning proposals for civic days of fasting. The contradictory practices of free sale of livestock and price-fixing of retailed meat were responsible for this dearth, which was also blamed on speculation by breeders and butchers and on excessive requisitioning of oxen for the armies – a practice that, in addition, disrupted ploughing.

These complex and almost insoluble problems yielded neither to the most ardent zeal nor to denunciations. The 'political' armies and the representatives just about controlled the major routes and basic products, but 'secondary' commodities and local circuits eluded their vigilance.

Milk and vegetable produce would be carried by hand over long distances to reach the highest bidder. Cheese was made instead of butter, which was too perishable. Peasant women were waylaid by their customers before reaching the market and picked clean. A few citizens thus enjoyed the food of some twenty others. Retailers did not hesitate to scour the farms. Eggs and pork meat were made into preserves. Sea- and river-fishermen disposed of their catch as they pleased. Trafficking and clandestine slaughter flourished. Could all those involved be treated as suspects?

Similarly, how was one to punish the corrupt practices of commissioners and paid carriers, some of whom levied their 'tithe' and distributed supplies to family and friends? Their greed exposed them to attack, as the population took its revenge on them for its humiliations and fears. These agents were collectively accused of 'shady collusion' in order to discredit the controlled economy, which could not have been established without the concerted efforts and the determination of the *sans-culottes*. Despite its inadequacies, the provisioning of armies and large towns was assured; that of the smaller towns remained precarious wherever their administrations lacked energy and their populations lacked civic spirit.

The struggle against the aristocracy

Repressive action was more limited than is commonly imagined. It can be compared to that of a political gendarmerie. The revolutionary soldier was not an executioner. He delivered arrest warrants, escorted prisoners and kept suspects under surveillance using the police methods of the *ancien régime*. Wherever he went, he was the agent of the representatives and the *comités de surveillance*. Local terrorists, 'his brothers in Revolution', considered him a specialist of the Terror.

The revolutionary soldier's commitment to the Terror was total. The Republic's adversaries were also his own and could be recognized by their status and wealth. These remnants of social groups – former nobles, federalists – were regarded as condemned men; their elimination was a public health measure in which the revolutionary soldiers took part without hesitation. However, their action had no noticeable effect on the total number of arrests.

The tally included rich landowners and merchants implicated in royalist movements – but this distinction does not carry a social connotation. Sometimes, specific orders issued by the 'government

Committees' against certain personalities such as Duval d'Eprémesnil were carried out. Often, *sans-culotte* militants were the unsuspecting instruments of private vendettas, settling of scores and petty ambitions. But they always thought they were serving the cause of the Revolution. In the Midi, as soon as it was realized that the enemies of the Revolution would be systematically punished, the number of its friends increased 'considerably'. Avignon, which completely ignored the law on suspects, was teeming with aristocrats. 'I have seen men there, racked by the voice of conscience, turn pale with dread at my slightest step.' Maignet encountered in the surrounding area the after-effects of Marseillais federalism. On 6 Germinal, 116 counter-revolutionaries were rounded up in Alès. Taillefer took similar action in the Aveyron.

Legally organized punitive missions were carried out on a particularly large scale in rebel areas. The classic example is Lyons. What was the actual role of 'political' soldiers in the shootings? What was that of the *sabreurs* who hunted down survivors? The armies were less feared than local commissioners, but they sat together on the 'special commissions'. Countrymen were durably impressed by the spectacular presence of itinerant tribunals and by 'avenging excursions'.

Another case often mentioned, in the context of the Vendée, is that of the drownings at Nantes 'master-minded' by Carrier. 'I admit to having tolerated and endorsed the measures taken', he was to say later, 'for a civil war can end only by the destruction of one of the two sides.' It is not known for sure who gave the orders to the Marat Company, and yet that mass murder did not lack witnesses. Out of fear and a sort of panic, they kept silent; in the Year III, the most compromised culprits were acquitted in order to increase the chances of settling with Carrier. Except for priests, however, victims were not chosen according to their social category. Noblemen and common folk were treated as equally guilty. Women who helped them and 'fostered fanaticism' were brutalized: among the victims at Nantes, there were almost as many women as men, and the women equalled the men in courage.

The destruction of the signs of feudalism also formed part of the revolutionary struggle. Kings disappeared from card decks and shop signs were republicanized. Old parchments and seigneurial archives were burned until the decree of 8 Pluviôse; coats of arms were effaced but masterpieces 'that are an honour to French genius' were preserved. The Convention rebuked *agents nationaux* who acquiesced in acts of vandalism. In Brumaire, representatives in the Midi prevented the demolition of Roman ruins at Fréjus, Les Arcs and Riez. When it was decided to burn the Coronation carriage, its 'artistic' parts were saved. In Prairial, paintings by Veronese and Rubens belonging to the abbey of Saint-Amand were brought to Paris. Grégoire estimated the treasures of sequestered libraries to be about ten million volumes.

One should therefore refrain from holding the Terror responsible for base acts of all kinds. No government at war has ever failed to take the precaution of muzzling its opponents; every religion has spawned its heretics. In the revolutionary mentality, the non-juror priest was regarded as a public enemy on a par with the aristocrat. Later, the anathema was extended to forms of worship that were still tolerated and to their priests. The anti-clerical struggle acquired the same features as the battle against the aristocracy.

Spontaneous or organized dechristianization?

The anti-religious struggle – a complex phenomenon in its diversity – preceded and went beyond the bounds of the Terror. The offensive was not launched in Paris; in fact, the capital was less affected by it than the provinces, where it received unexpected stimuli. Who, then, were its leaders, what were its manifestations and their true impact? These questions are still unanswered. The mental processes of faith under constraint are impossible to grasp. Even the analysis of tangible facts defies ready-made theories.

The dechristianizing movement had a variety of agents. It was triggered off in the Loiret, the Nièvre and the Nord by representatives on mission who were themselves former churchmen, such as Laplanche, a vicar-general, Fouché, an Oratorian, and Chasles, canon of Chartres Cathedral. Simultaneously, the movement spread to Alsace, the south-west and Brittany. The entire country was affected by it in some form or other. From towns where civilian authority exerted sufficient sway, dechristianization spread to the countryside with the help of soldiers. Battalions of conscripts took part wherever they went; 'political' armies were especially active in isolated regions.

'Revolutionary armies' engaged in collective action. Commissioners and troops banded together to face hostile populations, egging each other on. Their enthusiasm spread from one man to the next with increasing violence. The peasant masses were the helpless spectators of these sudden flare-ups. Fanaticism and superstition, which were inseparable from rural life, forged a mental bond between rich and poor country folk. The Jacobin minorities, soon deprived of outside support, simply recorded the damage, without aggravating it. 'The religious plague' survived: socially, its strength was enormous.

In its public aspects, dechristianization bears the mark of a certain conformity, and one can question whether it was the product of spontaneous forces. It is undeniable that, for the *sans-culotte*, indifference to Catholicism preceded hostility. In the towns, he hardly ever attended services except – atavistically – on high festivals, preferring to spend his time at the tavern. Even in villages, priests repeatedly demanded that taverns should be closed during mass. Jokes about religion circulated along with chapbooks. There were many wisecracks about 'pommaded', 'bastard-making', and 'household-breaking' vicars, as well as 'ill-kept' secrets of the confessional. Emotional factors, rather than theologians' quibbles, shaped the pattern of revolutionary behaviour that emerged in the immediate aftermath of 10 August.

The 'active minority' displayed an unpremeditated unity. The roots of iconoclasm were obscure and its outbursts spectacular. It was compared to a frenzied crusade, its worst effects coinciding with the winter of 1793, economic difficulties and the foreign peril. Thus it was a component – and not the least significant one – of revolutionary and national defence. The distinction made between a legal action encouraged by the civilian government and a series of anarchic outbreaks provoked by military authorities does not stand up to scrutiny. Both varieties of iconoclasm stemmed from the same eagerness to destroy the tokens of a useless and dangerous worship. Was Catholicism not counter-revolutionary? Had it not endorsed 'kingship and tyranny'?

The sequence of events is well known. One ought to emphasize here the destructive intent that guided the protagonists, who wanted to make a clean sweep. Abandoned churches belonged to the communes, and their fate lay with the *sociétés populaires*. The mass of citizens, while having accepted the closure of churches, wanted to spare them. Except in rebel areas, they survived, suffering only superficial damage. However, they were stripped bare with an immoderate zeal that local authorities tried to restrain. The State claimed its share, demanding valuable objects, brass, lead, gates and bells, as it had done when sequestering estates for the nation. Only the surplus was sacrificed in symbolic *autos-da-fé*. Wooden saints, holy images and worthless objects – the 'trinkets of fanaticism' – underwent an ordeal by cleansing fire amid rejoicing by a populace who asserted their support for the Republic. *Agents nationaux* stressed these reversals of opinion: 'The people are vigorously calling for the destruction of prejudice...Confessionals are being turned into sentry-boxes and crosses into liberty trees.' Gold, silver, vermeil and embroidery were sent in from all over the country to the Convention and collected in the Treasury. Municipalities thus displayed their civic spirit and were cited in the *Bulletin de la Convention*. This collection went on until Thermidor.

The revolutionary detachments were reproached for sacrilegious gestures. They mutilated statues and tore down crosses without even pretending to act with popular consent. But their action was directed mainly against individuals – priests and fanatic women – whom they arrested with the agreement of civilian authorities. 'As long as there is one priest left on the soil of the Republic, Liberty will not have won a total victory.' Bo, in the Cantal and the Lot, also persecuted priests: 'I do not think there is a single one left in office.' Dartigoeyte, André Dumont, and Lebon boasted of similar achievements. However, Mathiez rightly points out that Fouché closed few churches in the Nièvre and that Couturier, in the Seine-et-Marne, 'married priests by the dozen who went on celebrating mass'.

In the wholesale imprisonments, no distinction was made between non-juror and juror priests. Those who were willing to resign were given a chance. Many did so, but often under pressure. In numerous districts, full-scale epidemics of resignations were recorded in Germinal, while elsewhere they had already begun in Frimaire. The resignation of Gobel, Bishop of Paris, on 17 Brumaire (7 November) did not create a precedent: the others were isolated cases, motivated by vows extorted under pressure and by genuine patriotic convictions, especially among the young, several of whom immediately enlisted in the army or took a job in a workshop. Others married peasant girls, entered secular life without fuss, and raised families.

These marriages came as no surprise to the population. The newly-weds – some of whom were in fact regularizing their situation – were acclaimed. In late Brumaire, at Etampes, priests who married were granted a communal estate settlement. Out of self-interest or fear, some also entered into 'attractive' unions after having wrestled at length with their consciences. Indeed, how many pretended they had lost their letters of priesthood only to find them afterwards at the right moment! How many priests who had resigned continued, under the protection of their parishioners, to minister clandestinely! Their duplicity perplexed the representatives, who complained about it as early as Ventôse.

The cult of Reason seemed at first to be an effective distraction. It

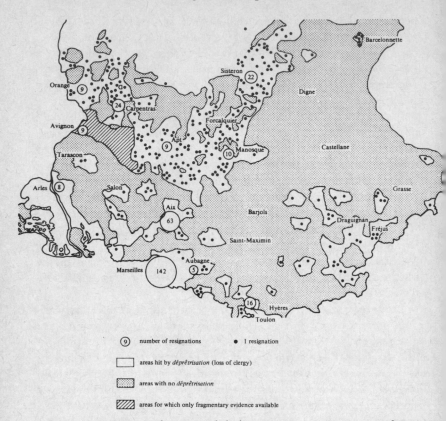

Fig. 5 Resignations of priests and dechristianization in Provence. After
M. Vovelle in M. Reinhard (ed.), *Les Prêtres abdicataires...* (**175**), p. 48

was carefully prepared: in Blois Cathedral, each chapel was consecrated
to a republican virtue. The representatives forced local authorities to
swear that they would tolerate no other form of worship. But there
were excesses almost from the outset, as the population 'let off steam':
Massieu announced that the church in Verdun was 'turning into a vast
Vauxhall Gardens where dance devotees can amuse themselves'. At
Meymac, the *sans-culottes*, led by Jumel, paraded in clerical dress. Their
masquerade irritated the country folk, who started a fight by tearing
off cockades and shouting 'Long live Louis XVIII! Long live religion!
Long live our priests!'

   'How can one slay this incredible hydra?' asked Albitte, one of
the dechristianizing representatives. 'By destroying today's priests?

No, because others would replace them. Instead, one must prove to the
people that there must be none.' This was the opinion of the Committee
of Public Safety, which, by early Nivôse, was advocating leniency
towards 'sincere fanaticism'. At some time around 20 Pluviôse (8
February), it invited the *sociétés populaires* 'to lead back to truth, by
the language of reason, the multitude that has indulged in error'.
Persuasion was to replace coercion. Compared to the number of
imprisonments, there were few executions until Prairial, but they
occurred in scattered places with random violence. These massacres upset
the populace, who regarded them as pointless. Dechristianization
aroused 'an all-encompassing wrath against the new times'.

Towards a new spirit?

The Revolution aimed at changing habits:

> Adieu psautiers et catéchismes,
> Source de bêtise et d'erreurs,
> C'est du bon républicanisme
> Qu'il faut désormais à nos coeurs.
> (Farewell psalters and catechisms,
> Source of foolishness and error;
> Good republicanism is
> What our hearts now require.)

Reason could make no headway against the faith of the humble, which
survived without worship. How, therefore, was one to 're-create the
people that one wants to restore to Liberty'? The Republic needed a
religion without priests — a religion founded on a dogma of civic spirit,
patriotism and virtue, and capable of coexisting with a deism that
permeated Creation and would be deeply felt by everyone.

Robespierre was neither the first nor the only one to put forward
a scheme for national festivals: the idea was the brainchild of the
Federations. The number of celebrations increased from mid-1793
onwards, well before the dechristianizers set to work. The initiative
came from the municipalities and *sociétés populaires*. 'Representatives',
wrote the *société* of Blois on 21 Brumaire, 'if you will hasten to replace
religious festivals by republican festivals, the simple-minded will be
disillusioned and will soon abandon the dens of fanaticism to join us
in our songs.' 'The *sans-culottes* are laughing...the Republic is growing
stronger, and liberty is prospering. All is well and all will be well. (Ca
va et ça ira.)'

The Convention provided pretexts, such as the recapture of Toulon, but in fact each town organized festivals in its own way. Bordeaux celebrated the emancipation of coloured slaves. Municipalities paid homage to Lepeletier, Marat, Chalier and local martyrs, including Bordier and Jourdain at Rouen, where three public ceremonies were held in Frimaire alone. These festivals were a vehicle for Jacobin propaganda in the smaller towns.

Processions took place in the street, as on religious occasions, and with similar features: the hierarchy of authority, symbols, speeches and hymns. But the originality of the new celebrations manifested itself in their details, which were the product of collective inspiration. A balance was struck between civic spirit and imagination, without resorting to vulgarity. When ridiculous roles were proposed, actors shied away from them. Soldiers invited to Armentières refused to cut off a pig's head representing Louis XVI.

These events afforded opportunities for rejoicing and for meetings and so resembled votive festivals and village 'strolls' (*ballades*) without losing their political and social character. The ideological content reflected popular attitudes and patriotic drive. Antiquity did not serve as a model for all these festivals, but hatred against the enemies of the Republic was universally proclaimed. Everywhere too, the unity of the participants was emphasized. 'Spartan' meals brought them together; there was much singing and dancing. The festivals had become a success by the time the government decided to appropriate them. Despite the decree of 18 Floréal (7 May), which codified celebrations, they continued as before, taking place perhaps more frequently though without reaching the prescribed rate of one every ten days. Villages organized festivals when it was realized that the latter were not in competition with Catholic celebrations.

For the same reason, the authorities accepted the popular devotion that surrounded patriotic female saints such as Perrine Dugué in the Mayenne and Marie Martin, 'St Pataude', in the southern part of the Ille-et-Vilaine.* There was an obvious shift from traditional cults to those of revolutionary heroes. The cult spontaneously dedicated to Marat persisted for a long time. Together with the name of Lepeletier

---

* Marie Martin was attacked and killed by the Chouans for having denounced a Royalist hiding-place. She was locally recognized as a 'martyr saint' (St Pataude, or 'St Clumsy', the Chouan word for Republic). Pilgrimages were made to her tomb, in the Forest of Taillay on the borders of the Ille-et-Vilaine and the Loire-Inférieure, at Easter, Whitsun and Midsummer. [Trans.]

and the words 'liberty or death', Marat's name was made a part of the republicanized sign of the cross. It was also used as a name for new-born babies.

A recent study conducted in the Eure confirms the joint use of saints' and republican names.[10] It is hard to tell whether the phenomenon reflected a political attitude or a passing fad, but families did not hesitate to expose their children to ridicule by making obeisance to the new mode. Brutus one can accept, but what about Asparagus or Column-of-Liberty? A Rouennais named Canesson was baptized Montagnard-Sans-Culotte. Fouché called his daughter Nièvre. The new names took some time to spread to the countryside; their proportion never went beyond ten per cent of all births.

Names of months were borrowed from the republican calendar, which transformed the habits of officialdom before becoming part of everyday life. Its use was considered proof of civic spirit. The new calendar was set against the 'old style', which women and old people continued to use for a long time. Workers preferred the seven-day week to the *décade*; the Sunday sabbath was preserved. As for communes whose names were reminders of feudalism, many changed them with embarrassing uniformity: no less than 16 Fraternités, 21 Marats, and 87 Montagnes were recorded. Other localities, for reasons unknown, refused to change their names.

At fairs and in the offices of *notaires*, who persisted in using the old system, sums were still reckoned in *écus* and *pistoles*. Traditional-style clothes were handed down from father to son. Cockades were rarely worn. Fire-backs kept their crowns and forest markers their fleurs-de-lis. *Assignats* were saved sou by sou. Even though country-dwellers had means, money remained very scarce; the rural population lived from hand to mouth on its own produce. Rent payments were minimal in the Year II. In fact, individuals changed their attitudes less out of revolutionary conviction than out of opportunism and necessity. The Revolution had a very superficial influence on the rural mentality.

The number of illiterates did not decline. The establishment of village schools would have transformed the young, who were stirred by accounts of heroic deeds. The Société Populaire des Cultivateurs of Ecully suggested depriving suspects of the right to raise their children. Couthon levied a tax on the rich with the intention of setting up

[10] M. Le Pesant, 'Prénoms révolutionnaires et contre-révolutionnaires dans l'Eure', *Bulletin de la Société des Antiquaires de Normandie*, vol. 58, p. 482.

secondary schools in the Puy-de-Dôme. But the Revolution could not sustain the war effort while financing other, long-term projects. The peasant was abandoned to his routine.

The Convention had no agricultural policy to speak of; it had been left by the Constituent Assembly with a rural code that it patched up as circumstances required. Its Agricultural Committee was flooded with schemes that were quietly shelved. The Food Commission, which was loath to resort to authoritarian regulations, reprimanded municipalities. Inevitably, a contradiction arose between a programme on a national scale and mixed farming designed for family consumption and between the immediate needs of provisioning, financial imperatives, and peasant demands.

Moreover, techniques could be changed only in the long term and by creating an agricultural education system. Isoré, describing on 3 Floréal the results of his experience in the Ile-de-France, advised against precipitous action: 'Farmers' habits, about which economists complain, are rooted in such a way as to prevent their destruction, and perhaps that is as it should be.' The government worried only about the next harvest.

Productivity or property?

It was vital to promote the production of commodities of primary necessity, and above all of cereals. Conscription had dislocated the labour market; military transport had aggravated the shortage of equipment. In its obsession with national defence, the Committee of Public Safety was dangerously sacrificing vital sectors of the economy. By setting aside iron reserves exclusively for weapons manufacture, the government deprived farmers of indispensable tools. One could not go on repairing old ploughs indefinitely. Artisans received quotas of raw materials. Gradually, the war loosened its grip on agriculture, whose needs were now taken into account.

However, yield increases were less a subject of concern than the total volume of crops. Fallowing was limited to one year everywhere. The decline in livestock breeding meant less manure. The soil was cultivated to exhaustion. Fallow land was 'revolutionarily' appropriated and even poor plots were seeded. In Thouars, the *comité révolutionnaire* threatened to treat negligent yeomen-farmers as suspects. A farmer of Varzy was accused of being a 'starver' for having sowed sainfoin. Even in Champagne, old vines were torn up, as were mulberry trees in Provence.

These primitive reactions developed in the spring of 1794 under the impulse of the small peasantry, which represented a majority in rural communities. The poorer peasants thus voiced their hostility against the big agriculturalists, who were attempting to achieve balanced production. While admitting the need to care for the land and to distribute plantings according to soil composition, the representatives advocated a middle course 'between stable and loft'. They were apprehensive about the risks of single-crop farming and did their best not to discourage large landowners, whose surpluses guaranteed the fulfilment of requisitions.

Nevertheless, from its democratic intentions, the Republic took spectacular action in favour of the small peasantry. As early as 10 August, it had invited them to share the spoils of the aristocracy. Similarly, *émigré* property was broken up into small plots and leased out, seigneurial dues not founded on authentic titles were abolished (as was the *domaine congéable* in Brittany),[11] and usurped commons were reclaimed. The *montagnard* laws followed the same principles: on 3 June 1793, *émigré* estates were set aside for the needy; on 10 June, common fields were shared out among peasant heads of households; finally, on 17 July, all seigneurial dues were abolished without compensation. The representatives wanted to help the poor, but they were restrained by the national interest. Free distribution of land would decrease the *assignat*'s collateral, and sales would benefit the rich. Between these two policies the Convention struck a compromise. It announced its generous intentions and carried them out timidly in a few specific instances. Though forewarned of the danger of political disaffection, the Assembly endorsed a policy of social immobility. Established structures were consolidated. A more equitable distribution of property was sacrificed to productivity.

Peasants who worked small plots protested unsuccessfully against the plurality of farm tenure. A farmer, argued the poorer peasants, could live off a tenure whose rent did not exceed 300 francs, so why grant him more? During the Terror, such arguments were put forward with increasing adamance in a spate of petitions. A portion of the peasantry

---

[11] This precarious land concession to a tenant in exchange for cash rent and payments in kind was very unpopular. See L. Dubreuil, *Les Vicissitudes du domaine congéable en basse Bretagne à l'époque de la Révolution*, Rennes, 1915, 2 vols.

regarded communal rights as immutable entitlements that were not to be whittled down by any technological innovation. Jacobins in Paris wanted new landowners to settle on common fields, but the partition of commons had been badly received by the rural population. Wine-producing municipalities in Touraine were totally opposed to it and preferred to 'preserve the entitlement to grazing rights'. To revive patriotic fervour in rural Burgundy, the authorities evoked the memory of seigneurial encroachments: 'If you have any shreds left, it is because these bloodthirsty leeches were unable to extort them from you.'[12]

Agricultural improvements were of little import as only landowners benefited from them, and the abolition of feudal dues also mattered little since they survived in leases. Old contracts, which stipulated dues, remained valid. In new contracts, the value of dues was included in the rent despite a decree of 1 Brumaire (22 October) that forbade such practices. Rents rose sharply – by four francs an acre, according to a farmer in Ebly. Dues in kind and in services allowed lessors to compensate for monetary inflation by indexing their landed income.

The agrarian crisis deepened. Peasant rivalries turned into economic struggles no longer pitting rich against poor in rural communities, but farmers against landowners, employers against wage-earners. In order to put an end to social oppression, it was even suggested that all contracts should be abolished. The nation would replace property-owners and appropriate three-quarters of farming output while the farmer would enjoy the surplus for his own consumption. But sales of nationalized land, by reinforcing existing patterns of ownership and rural attitudes, acted as 'technical brakes': land was purchased instead of livestock, seed and manure.

The sale of nationalized land

The vast number of nationalized Church estates had enabled country-dwellers to quench their thirst for land. In the Sarthe, for example, nearly one-tenth of the *département*'s acreage had been sold off by 1793. The already prosperous bourgeoisie laid its hands on half the area of certain communes. The peasants, who were put at a disadvantage by auctions conducted by *district*, had better luck making joint purchases and sharing out plots. All their savings went into these acquisitions.

Smallholders and share-croppers (*métayers* or *bordiers*) were theo-

---

[12] Quoted in P. de Saint-Jacob, *Les Paysans de la Bourgogne du Nord au dernier siècle de l'Ancien Régime*, Paris, 1960, p. 517.

retically entitled to *émigré* property, which was carved into plots on
3 June 1793 to expedite proceedings. When informed that they would
soon have to leave, occupants ravaged forests, let buildings fall into
decay, and 'devastated lands'. This debasement was ruinous for the
Republic. Yet estimates and divisions were late in coming. 'What is
needed is the total liquidation of farm property,' declared Dolivier, *curé*
of Mauchamp near Etampes. Several *districts* tried to achieve it while
others contented themselves with making a census of existing plots.

Real estate sales – first of urban houses – began in the Rouen area
in mid-October, followed by sales of rural property in late Brumaire.
This timetable was repeated in almost all of France. Successively, *curés'*
patches, parish estates, school and hospital land endowments and the
property of individuals condemned to death were added. In regions
where customary law prevailed, the victims' families tried to safeguard
their patrimony by claiming dowers and did their best to delay
auctions.

The nature of the sales changed; they took on a political character.
Purchasers prided themselves on their act of civic virtue. There were
some Jacobins among them, but not all buyers became Jacobins. The
operation was highly profitable and attracted many investors. Reserve
prices, calculated on the basis of rents at 1790 levels, seemed relatively
low, and knock-down prices were well in excess of them. 'Bidders are
vying with each other to prove that the enemies of the Republic are
incapable of frightening republicans who have sworn to live in
freedom.' The Convention applauded these reports of victory.

'The purpose of dividing up *émigré* property was to extinguish
misery', Couthon recalled on 1 Floréal. The poor hardly benefited from
the measure. The law of 13 September 1793, which allowed them to
acquire small plots in exchange for 500-franc certificates issued by
municipalities, was too vague and came too late; it had little effect and
caused many disappointments. People complained that the beneficiaries
were always the same – 'lawyers, bourgeois and merchants of the
district'. The rich played a less predominant role in these transactions
because many were suspects. But civil servants were more influential:
some served as figureheads by buying land for others or organized
auctions at short notice, while others were denounced for dishonest
practices that went beyond the trading of favours.

Despite these dealings, the number of medium-sized properties rose
and their acreage was increased by adding on adjacent plots. On the
other hand, the leasing system, which delayed payments, proved

catastrophic in the post-Thermidorean inflation. Although they sold better than Church property, *émigré* estates were not as profitable for the State. Families were soon able to recover part of their assets through many transfers. The nation kept the great forests. Rural France remained outwardly unchanged. National land sales, which have been called a 'turning-point' in agricultural and social history, are hard to assess in the short term; they must be analysed in terms of a century.[13]

It is also possible, as Mathiez suggested, that the Jacobin regime regarded the peasantry as sufficiently well-off in comparison to the urban *sans-culottes*: it had enough to eat and profited by the rise in food prices. The government seemed less responsive to the wishes of the agrarian population and less in a hurry to satisfy them; it was mainly concerned with the neediest citizens.

Property as a civic reward

The Republic had a duty to reward its staunchest supporters. On several occasions it had solemnly committed itself to doing so. Saint-Just was still asking the same question in Ventôse: what had been done for the people? The Revolution was their achievement and 'it was time for them to enjoy it'. 'Property, a wife and children are the assets that a lawmaker must use to tie a man to his native soil.'

Soldiers and their families formed the most neglected category. Their claims to national gratitude were obvious and their expectations high, but they received only a pittance. Wounded and invalid soldiers and the widows and children of the fallen were awarded pensions drawn from the Treasury. There was no comprehensive policy, no general allocation plan, and no sense of urgency in the distribution of relief. Since October 1792, the State had been paying off this sacred debt in the same way as it aided victims of natural calamities – at random and with offensive parsimony.

Why not set aside for soldiers the fruits of their conquests? Was enemy property not 'legitimate capture'? Its loss was the price paid by the enemy for his crimes; his property should therefore be the victor's trophy. This was the verdict of the most elementary justice. 'He who has shown himself to be the enemy of his country cannot own property in it.' Why worry about reducing the *assignat*'s collateral when rebellions provided new opportunities for adding to it? Let the

---

[13] See J. Vogt, 'Aspects de la vente des biens nationaux dans la région de Wissembourg', *Revue d'Alsace*, 1960, p. 90.

spoils of the Vendée and Lyons be shared out among patriotic soldiers![14] The commander of the Paris national guard in vain submitted the following request to the Jacobins on 7 Brumaire (28 October): 'Everything the aristocrats lose must be given to patriots. Houses, land, everything must be shared out among the men who defeat those scoundrels.'[15] Reward or booty, the distinction mattered little to the *sans-culottes*; either way, it was a positive measure.

Some harboured the vision of a new society born of the Revolution, a society indebted to the Revolution for its prosperity and hence possessed of 'an interested motive for defending it'. But one had to avoid filling this society with invalids!

The Convention adopted the same hesitant policy towards the indigent. Between January and June 1793, it decided to award relief to the poor, to abandoned children, pregnant girls and the elderly, in a show of the worth of national assistance and the Convention's own humanitarian aims. But these measures were stalled for months. In late Germinal, Delbrel complained of unacceptable delays. Besides, how was one to single out 'the neediest'? Nearly all potential beneficiaries had a roof over their heads or a patch of land. They were not 'without property' and yet could not live off it. To invite them to take part in national land sales, even with subsidies, was to pit them against less deprived citizens. 'If the rich are allowed to compete, there will never be anything left for the poor.'

The only conceivable solution was a free distribution of suspects' property. The wholesale confiscation of their assets was a popular and widespread demand; there was no shortage of arguments in favour of it. Imprisoned suspects had to contribute to the cost of their upkeep and of the war. Therefore, their share would take the form of a levy on their land or income. This tax was to be proportional to their wealth and would be applied like a forced loan; it would be used to 'compensate indigence'. The representatives of the *Plaine* and a good number of *montagnards* did not want to be forced to go beyond that: the Jacobin State was apprehensive about total confiscation.

'The destitute are the mighty of the earth; they have the right to give orders to governments that neglect them.' The demands of the poor were heeded in the *départements*. By late 1793, Desgrouas, in the *district* of Mortagne, was proposing that 'the property of all the egoists who refuse to serve the Revolution' should be confiscated. On 16

[14] See above, p. 144.
[15] Quoted in A. Mathiez, 'Les Décrets de Ventôse...', *AHRF*, 1928, p. 199.

September, Roux-Fazillac wrote from the Dordogne to the Committee of Public Safety with the same advice. 'All these bad citizens would be granted a food allowance and registered in the Grand Livre.'* Despite themselves, they would be given a stake in the Republic's prosperity. Fouché, in the Nièvre, ordered analogous measures on 2 October: 'They shall be allowed only the bare minimum for themselves and their families.' Thus, suspects were increasingly equated with *émigrés*.

Although the Convention did not encourage these initiatives, it could not dodge the issue indefinitely. Suddenly, on 7 Pluviôse (28 January 1794), Couthon presented a clear-cut case for the social merits of confiscation. Robespierre made the same point on the 17th: the homeland had to 'ensure the well-being of each individual', naturally, of the least privileged first of all. But it is to the name of Saint-Just that the Ventôse decrees will remain linked.

The illusory decrees of Ventôse

While Saint-Just 'was already despoiling the rich to shelter and clothe the poor', in Strasburg, and while he was writing the *Institutions républicaines*, he was obsessed by a single thought: 'If you give land to the needy, if you take it away from all the scoundrels, I admit that you have carried out a revolution.' Following Jaurès, Mathiez presented this programme as an innovation. But it was not. All the same, the *robespierristes* had the courage to press for its adoption. Couthon and Robespierre had been bedridden for the previous twenty days and, although they probably agreed with Saint-Just, they were unable to articulate their views on the issue.

These decrees, submitted to the Convention in their absence on 8 and 13 Ventôse, came at a time of acute crisis. It was therefore concluded that the decrees were a political ploy, aptly timed to limit the impact of growing opposition. By promising the poorer peasants a share of national wealth, the addition of their discontent to that of the *sans-culottes* would be avoided. The representatives' reluctance and the amendments to the original bill revealed the disagreement and fears within the Assembly. The scheme was made to appear as an expropriation that had to be kept within limits.

---

* Presumably a reference to the scheme for a national welfare register, the Grand Livre de la Bienfaisance Nationale (not to be confused with the Grand Livre de la Dette Publique), which came into official existence only eight months later, on 22 Floréal (11 May 1794). [Trans.]

To enforce the decree, a list of victims and a list of beneficiaries had to be drawn up. Each list presented difficulties. Which suspects would be involved? It seemed unfair to include them all even when their guilt was in doubt. A selection was required on the basis of the charges brought against them. The Committee of General Security was asked to collate the charges and on 23 Ventôse the 'popular commissions' were asked to rule on them jointly with the Committee of Public Safety, which, in turn, was to assemble the lists of indigents prepared by the communes. Who was to be included? What were the limits of indigence, its yardsticks? The puzzled municipalities awaited detailed guidelines that never arrived.

A great number of *sociétés populaires* hailed the decrees. As soon as the *districts* were informed of them, they carried out confiscations, which took place in some thirty *départements*. Albitte, in the Ain, used part of the revenues for urgent expenses and began distributing the surplus to the poor. Guards were assigned to watch over sealed property in the areas around Mortagne-en-Perche and Fréjus. But the onset of the harvest slowed these operations, which otherwise would have endangered crop yields. Thus the season added unexpected obstacles.

Actually, the principle of free land distribution – a central feature of Saint-Just's reports – was not expressed in the decrees, which instead referred to the principle of compensation. As early as 16 Ventôse, confusion arose. To eliminate pauperism, 500,000 francs were allocated to the Minister of the Interior, Paré, who enjoined government departments to expedite the distribution of relief promised earlier.[16] It is worth pointing out Danton's two interventions: on the 8th, he used stalling tactics to delay the census of prisoners; on the 13th, he suggested that maimed soldiers should benefit from the distribution of 'estates in the environs of Paris and be given livestock in order to activate, under the Convention's very eyes, this colony of patriots who have suffered for the homeland'.[17]

The rapporteur's intentions were unambiguous, and for the *sociétés populaires* it was clear that the decrees provided for a more substantial and profitable gift from the Republic than mere relief. On 10 Germinal, the *société* of Mont-Saint-Vincent (Saône-et-Loire) suggested drawing a distinction between old and invalid persons – to be supported by the proceeds of sales of houses and furniture – and the landless, who would receive plots of land proportionate to the number of their dependents.

[16] A decree of 13 Pluviôse had allocated ten million francs for the same purpose.
[17] Published in *Archives parlementaires*, vol. 86, p. 24.

In areas where there was no landed property to distribute, the poor hoped to receive livestock or cash.

It was expected that the groundwork for these measures at the local level would take about two months. But before it had been completed, the Committee of Public Safety voiced its disapproval of this potentially dangerous policy. The report presented by Barère on 22 Floréal (11 May 1794) on behalf of the Committee outlined an ambitious plan for national relief. To 'eradicate poverty from the countryside', the plan called for the auctioning of suspects' property, which would both finance a national solidarity fund and help fill the Treasury. The report did refer to Saint-Just's project, but the Convention adopted the new scheme with the intention of torpedoing the earlier one.

Although the new scheme still talked about the destitute, they were to receive a few national properties only on an exceptional basis and by way of rewards. As for old people and invalids, they would be put on the welfare rolls of the Grand Livre. 'Terrorist expropriation was forgotten; immediately after Thermidor it was definitively abrogated.'

Could the Ventôse decrees adequately offset the burden of the war and of economic restrictions? A fundamental lack of understanding developed between the *robespierristes*, who dreamt of a more just society, and the rural world, which did not raise its sights beyond its day-to-day concerns. The former aimed too high, the latter too low. The *robespierristes* expected to become landowners through the Revolution so as to assure their family's livelihood and their independence by their own labour. They did not question the notion of property, whether of individuals or of communities – which they intended to preserve. But it was useless to offer land to the handicapped; the destitute would, for the most part, remain poor. 'The good farmer is the one who holds the plough himself; he has not been corrupted by ambition or idleness.' He alone could strengthen the Republic. And the Republic turned a deaf ear to demands for limiting farm tenure and lowering farm rents. Ultimately, the Republic's contribution was more imaginary than real.

6

The end of the Jacobin dictatorship

Was the crisis of confidence a crisis of authority?

The ninth of Thermidor is still judged according to political criteria.
Those who restrict their analysis to the debates in the Assembly regard
the event as a come-back for the losers of 31 May 1793 and as an act
of vengeance for the *girondins*, Danton and Hébert. But how could a
government crisis and a mere change of parliamentary majority have
swept away the Jacobin Republic along with the *robespierristes* without
either the tacit consent or the indifference of public opinion? To answer
this question, the scope of historical investigation has been gradually
broadened, bringing to light the existence of a set of conditions that
encouraged, at a given moment, the disaffection of the masses.

What were the causes and basic motives of this phenomenon?
Although the divergent explanations all contain an element of cogency,
one cannot single out an overriding factor. Aulard suggested dechristianization, Mathiez the Ventôse decrees. But the government's doctrinal
approach to religious and social issues was too abstruse for the
population, who experienced the impact of these issues in the form of
economic restrictions and terrorist repression. One can agree with
George Rudé and Albert Soboul that the announcement of wage
controls in Paris may have influenced the *sections*' behaviour on the
decisive evening.[1] Perhaps this was the last straw. It yet remains to be
seen, however, how the situation reached breaking-point.

Recent studies have failed provide a convincing solution. For their
authors, only the *montagnard* bourgeoisie – and not the interplay of
conflicting forces – was capable of influencing revolutionary action;
hence the pointless discussions on when the Revolution began to 'ebb'.
For Soboul, the starting-point was the Ventôse crisis; Daniel Guérin
dates it back to Frimaire and the codification of the regime. This notion,

---

[1] G. Rudé and A. Soboul, 'Le Maximum des salaires...' (**208**).

which he borrows from Richard Cobb, is borne out by the behaviour of the provinces after the breakup of the 'revolutionary armies': the Ventôse decrees were interpreted as a promise to free prisoners; the abolition of special tribunals, as a sign that there would be fewer executions; the price- and wage-scales of the *maximum général*, as an opportunity to cheat on retail prices. Thus the ebbing of the Revolution was part of the dialectical movement of history and was the only factor that could make the government – which, incidentally, has earned praise for its perspicacity – 'steer to the right'.

This deep and hidden disease slowly contaminated the collective mentality. An examination of political attitudes reveals their fragility. Rural France viewed the events in Paris from afar and through a haze, equating party struggles with a series of vendettas. In fact, the countryside was badly informed. The historian is no better served. Journalists were the first to travesty the facts; later, both victors and cowards constructed their own truth. Thus, we have only fabricated evidence to go on. Nevertheless, the documents, by their variety and contradictions, bear witness to the confusion and to a widespread fatigue. Thermidor resulted, above all, from the unconscious abdication of Jacobinism.

'If one wishes to found a Republic, one must not people it with malcontents.' From the beginning of the Year II, however, their numbers continued to increase not because of events – the 'force of circumstance' – but because of intransigence and human egoism. Peasant France, which had settled into a 'provisional' Revolution, went back to its fields, its parochial concerns and its religion. Apathy, indifference and ambition were denounced everywhere. Patriotism became a profession, and civic spirit an ornament. 'Dread and discouragement have spread even to a portion of the *sans-culottes*. At the first signs of liberation, six-eighths of France... would rise against the Jacobins.'[2] Saint-Just, more than his colleagues of the 'great' Committee, felt this rising tide: 'An unhappy people has no homeland.' By the spring of 1794, a section of public opinion – which on the whole had wanted the Republic – was already afraid of its excesses. After the 'drama' that this section had failed to understand, the sacrifices it had agreed to turned into meaningless vexations.

[2] Mallet du Pan to Sir Trevor [*sic*], 18 February 1794, reproduced in *AHRF*, 1965, p. 469.

Robespierre attracts our attention because of his frequent utterances, but he was not alone. It is too often forgotten that the reinforcement of public authority was decided upon after extensive consultations. The Convention and its committees agreed on the means to establish their dictatorship. Moreover, until early Messidor, victory was in doubt and the constraints imposed by national defence weighed heavily on political developments. While it was apparently hastened by the Germinal executions, the ebbing of the Revolution was a deep-seated response to the craving for life and the appetite for enjoyment that inevitably followed excessive tensions. The Terror made citizens cautious but did not prevent them from thinking. Thermidor came as a liberation.

THE REGIME'S EXCESSES

'Democracy perishes because of two excesses: either the aristocratic character of its rulers, or the people's contempt for the authorities it has itself installed.' Both these features, which stemmed one from the other, were inherent in the artificial structure of the government edifice and its despotic character, a reminiscence of the *ancien régime*. Foreign observers emphasized the fact, and ascribed to the Committee of Public Safety an 'absolute, strong and restrictive' power similar to that of Louis XIV. The Committee was a 'supreme council' dominating an Assembly reduced to '150 registration lackeys'. It was 'Robespierre's chancellery, with Barère as his secretary and ranter, Saint-Just his zealot, Couthon his scoundrel and Collot his proxy at the Jacobin club; the rest do not deserve the honour of being mentioned'.[3] Thanks to royalist propaganda, the existence of a triumvirate became a widespread belief, bringing home with greater vividness the image of a dictatorship crystallized around a handful of men. Excessive centralization substantiated this image.

The new policy and public opinion

Having liquidated the factions, the government withdrew to its Jacobin base and launched a policy favourable to property-owners and detrimental to the workers. Hébert had predicted that 'a single step backwards would be fatal to the Republic'. The Committee of Public

---

[3] Letter from Frossard to Mercy-Argenteau, 14 April 1794, quoted in G. Walter, *Robespierre*, 1961 edn, vol. 2, p. 354.

Safety disregarded the warning and Mallet du Pan, with his usual perspicacity, weighed the consequences of this reversal: revolutionary power would be adjusted to bear down on the extremists and would

forgive the vast herd of bourgeois, royalists, *feuillants* and federalists – who until now have been persecuted to excess... The Committee does not exist outside Paris. By dint of shooting the Revolution's troops, it is reduced to seeking assurances from its victims. It has taken off its mask; its tyranny will be forgiven only so long as it is successful.

Could the Committee wield its tyranny with impunity? Did it possess a sufficiently solid apparatus and a strong enough authority? Police and finances were outside its grasp. The revolutionary government, which had established itself slowly in the provinces, was still not functioning on the eve of Thermidor in the Ardèche, the Var, the Chalosse and the Basque country. How would the representatives on mission, who were implementing the Terror, react to being treated as subordinates? Finally, how would public opinion respond? Moderatism was a matter for concern; confusion in people's minds was reason for apprehension.

Disarray was apparent at the club in the Rue Saint-Honoré, which the *Montagne* had chosen as a forum for announcing the government's intentions. As the officially consecrated dispenser of the 'good word', did it still deserve this special trust? The purge of the club's membership, still incomplete in Messidor, worried observers. Absenteeism increased as accusations of subversive behaviour were made on the merest suspicions. Robespierre the younger, on his return from a long mission, noted this decadence: the club used to look after 'the higher interests of the Republic; today, it is stirred by miserable quarrels between individuals'. *Honnêtes gens* took part in debates, allowing themselves to make fun of 'sensible patriots' for their clumsy language. Was this the 'energy conductor' that the regime wanted?

For the benefit of the Jacobins, it was decided to get rid of the *sociétés sectionnaires*. On 27 Germinal (16 April), the *société* of the Brutus *section* offered itself up in sacrifice to the Convention. The others were slow to follow its example, but their dissolution was expedited: 'It is there that cupidity, discontent with the Revolution, grumbling against the government, and ambition founded on patriotism have a free rein.' With the abolition of the *sociétés*, 'popular power went out of the window'. The Paris *sections*, now reduced to holding their general meetings twice every ten days, would henceforth correspond only with the Jacobins, to whom they presented themselves *en masse* one after the other. The Commune and the other administrative bodies of the capital were revamped.

The Commune was called *robespierriste*. Robespierre presented himself as the defender of the Jacobin order, taking the floor at the Jacobin club to repeat his old ideas about the union of patriots and the crimes of the aristocracy, Pitt and Coburg. He was listened to with respect, but no longer carried conviction. The once-bitten *sans-culottes* were twice shy, while former suspects looked forward to the time when they could once again 'sleep in their beds, go to the opera and enjoy the remnants of their fortune'. Conspirators were seen everywhere; flowers in a woman's hair were read as a rallying-sign. By treating Paris like a fortified town and expelling nobles, foreigners and officers relieved of their duties, the decree of 27 Germinal (16 April) came as a response to public anxiety.

Provisioning difficulties also soured the climate and fuelled popular unrest. While the Commune refused to raise wages, the Halles offered a sorry sight. 'C'est foutu!' (We've had it!), declared a worker in an armaments factory: 'We are worse off than before, because our money won't buy us anything; we're going to die of hunger. We are being fooled by fine words.'[4] Recriminations were rife in all professional groups, despite police repression and arrests. Production dropped and tenderers were subject to delays. As some employers made concessions, demands spread. There was growing disaffection with the Revolution. 'Yesterday [7 Germinal] I was with a true *sans-culotte*', reported an informant: 'As he was listening to a child recite a few articles of the Constitution, he said that he preferred a bottle of wine to all that. What support can the Republic expect from such men?'

Were the provincial Jacobin *sociétés* any more reliable? They were becoming so suspect that representatives hesitated to turn to them for help and blamed them for their own failures. Had the representatives not acted on the advice of the *sociétés*? The latter were now turning into dens of intrigue and were 'doing the Republic the greatest disservice'. Everywhere ill will divided them. In some places, 'the despotism of the rabble' prevailed; in others, the despotism of civil servants and the rich. In Le Mans, the young, claiming to be the followers of 'Père Duchesne', held out against Garnier de Saintes: 'I have never regarded as patriots these fiery and vitriolic schemers who,

---

[4] Quoted in G. Rudé and A. Soboul (**208**).

in their sweeping scorn and vilification, looked on the Convention as a worn-out political institution.' Elsewhere, charity was confused with patriotism. The gift of a few shirts was enough to earn the donor a testimonial to his civic spirit. Moderates cashed in on the situation. In the towns, their supporters ousted ultra-revolutionary outsiders and took firm control of the *sociétés*.

Did these associations still deserve to be called 'popular'? 'In the interior of France, the Terror paralyses all opinions that are not republican and revolutionary.' Participants remained silent out of fear but they also felt that they were wasting their time. Presidents and secretaries monopolized discussions and forbade criticism. The victors pandered to the representatives, who controlled local jobs. Visitors' galleries, once 'vigilant sentinels', were now open to children and supplicants, and turned into asylums and employment agencies. A greedy and humiliated residue of men from the luxury trades and abolished religious orders impatiently awaited rewards for their patriotic zeal.

The reign of the bureaucrats

To meet the requirements of the revolutionary government and of the State-controlled economy, the administrative machinery was stretched to its limits. A smattering of education and a veneer of civic-mindedness were enough to obtain a degree of authority. Thus the authority of the State was broken down into a multitude of individual wills. Under its aegis, a bureaucratic mentality developed behind the whitewood tables. Seals, embossed stationery and the influx of official printed matter all gave State employees a feeling of superiority and a discretionary power that they used and misused by taking decisions, writing and delivering all manner of certificates, and granting their signature as a reward or withholding it as a sanction.

If one takes into account permanent and temporary staff, elections and appointments, how many State employees were there in all? No doubt several hundred thousand in the provinces in all administrative, police and judicial posts, and several tens of thousands in Paris, not counting the *sans-culottes* who attended *section* meetings, for which they were paid forty sous. The offices of the Committee of Public Safety had 418 employees in Prairial, seven times more than in Frimaire, five months earlier. The more numerous employees in the ministries went on to work in the 'executive commissions' created on 12 Germinal (1 April 1794). These new bodies, which gradually came into their own, institutionalized a *de facto* situation, as the Committee already supervised the activities of the ministers. The Committee's centralizing intent was displayed with useless ostentation and, moreover, it had an unforeseen consequence. By reshuffling ministerial departments, the Committee not only disorganized their paperwork, but also created havoc among the employees, who now felt vulnerable. Having been deprived of their accustomed routine, they realized the provisional character of their functions.

The bureaucracy's apprehensiveness coincided with political uncertainties. On what model was it to pattern its behaviour? The immediate future was laden with threats. Local authorities were taken aback – just as the capital was – by the gaoling of their militants. The well-deserved criticisms heaped on a handful of officials rebounded on all of them. Misuse of power was predictable in these difficult times, but it deserved understanding and leniency. Complaints were voiced about arrogance and brutality. The Food Commission reprimanded its agents: 'All republicans are equal, but equality does not preclude consideration and affability; on the contrary, it is by those signs that one recognizes a people of brothers.' Disputes broke out between volunteer and paid administrators, particularly in the ports.

The deluge of 'red tape' also caused irritation. In Floréal, the Committee of Public Safety sent out sixty orders a day, demanding rapid enforcement and requesting excessively complicated surveys at too short notice. The slightest administrative matters were minutely codified. Initiatives were discouraged. Representatives on mission reported carelessness and fatigue everywhere. From Caen and Moulins, they wrote describing this growing weariness and the resurgence of the moderates. To be sure, there were still many patriots, 'but unfortunately it is not they who are the most educated; men of ability are either more indifferent or not entirely trusted. Many of them did not come out early enough in favour of the Revolution.' The time seemed ripe to 'rouse from their sleep all the trustees of public authority'. Actually, it was too late.

The civil servants had erected a rampart between the population and the government. The country was run by a caste of parvenus who confused their own interests with their revolutionary faith. Saint-Just railed against them on 23 Ventôse (13 March):

What do you want, you who are competing for posts to attract attention and have people say of you: Look! it's so-and-so who's speaking, there goes so-and-so! You want to leave your father's profession – perhaps he was an honest craftsman whose middling condition made you a patriot – in order to become an influential figure in the State. You shall perish, you who chase after fortune and seek a well-being distinct from the people's.

Not only did they forget their duties, but they grabbed positions of authority by convincing the *sans-culotterie* of its ignorance. How could bureaucrats in the *assignat* office keep mistresses and fill the taverns on their five francs a day, without taking bribes?[5] After a temporary exclusion from public affairs, legal practitioners and notables replaced shopkeepers and artisans. Men of modest ability went back to their obscurity, their occupations, their families and their fields. Furthermore, summer encouraged absenteeism among country-dwellers, who abandoned the *sociétés populaires* to look after the harvest.

Even the *sociétés* placed themselves in the hands of their officers. 'Now that there are too many bureaucrats and too few citizens, the people are totally absent. It is no longer they who judge the government, it is the coalition of bureaucrats who, by pooling their influence, impose silence on the people.' Since citizens were entrusting their fate to the Republic's employees, 'where then is the polity?' asked Saint-Just. 'Under the pretence of acting in a revolutionary manner as if they were vested with revolutionary power', bureaucrats were taking control of public opinion. One should therefore banish these 'deceitful beings' from the 'temples of Equality, if we still want Liberty to live'.

Conformism and 'tedious' virtue

Elected officials and civil servants, who were supposed to respond to changes in public opinion, interpreted it according to their temperament and interests. *Agents nationaux*, tribunals and *sociétés populaires* praised themselves or shirked their responsibilities in these difficult circumstances. Their public behaviour and private feelings were not always in harmony, even if they were resolutely patriotic. In their written and spoken pronouncements, these men slavishly imitated proven models.

The government provided them with these models through its intensive propaganda, which, although produced by the 'great' Committee rather than by the Jacobins, remained Jacobin all the same. The Committee arranged for subsidized newspapers to be sent out

---

[5] Quoted in M. Eude, *Paris pendant la Terreur*, vol. 6, p. 324.

directly, post-paid. Two thousand *sociétés* in the *chefs-lieux de cantons* received the *Républicain français* free of charge. The smallest communes insisted on receiving the *Bulletin de la Convention*. Barère's report on 'The Crimes of the British' and Robespierre's on 'Religious and Moral Ideas' were printed in 200,000 copies and read out at the *sociétés populaires*, which studied them along with the Declaration of Rights. Thus there developed throughout France a common stock of references that was abundantly drawn upon.

Nevertheless, the *sociétés* avoided naming names. The Convention and its committees, the *Montagne* and the Jacobins were invoked as entities. The collective nature of power did not escape the *sociétés'* writers. Thousands of messages were sent to the Assembly in Germinal to congratulate it on having triumphed over 'the plot'. In composition and inspiration they bear similarities to the *cahiers de doléances* of 1789. Messages reproduced typical expressions of political leaders and arguments used in the largest town in the area. Each *société* copied its neighbour, tried to outdo that neighbour by the choice of superlatives, and attested to its own activities by providing proofs that were nearly always the same everywhere.

This uniform and naïve chorus of praise was something of a prayer, an act of contrition, and an anthology of heroic deeds all in one. The Holy *Montagne* was likened to Jupiter 'in the midst of lightning and thunder'. Unconditional devotion to the Convention was proclaimed. 'Liberty must not perish. It is in your hearts that its incorruptible roots are planted.' The Convention had acted wisely in the past and would certainly do so in the future. May it continue then to 'steer the helm with a firm and steady hand until the ship has docked'. Such statements of approval, read to the Assembly at the beginning of each session, impressed the representatives, who interpreted them as an expression of national unity and a blanket endorsement of their own policy. Moreover, many letters were accompanied by an imposing array of signatures. When only the authors signed, they took care to state that they were speaking for all their fellow citizens. If there was opposition, its existence is hard to prove.

These apparently collective manifestations occurred between Germinal and Thermidor on the occasion of major events. Whether they were intended to voice warm congratulations for decrees and victories, or outrage at the assassination attempts of early Prairial, it was positively touching to hear all present respond with one voice – as if triggered off by a signal – using the same forms and expressing the same concerns. The artificial character of these messages soon became apparent.

Such displays were as tedious as virtue, the latter being the indispensable corrective for the Terror. 'The popular government's mainspring in revolution is both virtue and terror: without virtue, terror is lethal; without terror, virtue is powerless.' Following Montesquieu's definition, Robespierre, on 17 Pluviôse (5 February), defined virtue as being rooted in human dignity and popular sovereignty, 'in the love of one's homeland and of its laws'. The foundations of virtue were both moral and civic; democracy could not exist without it. 'We shall not enjoy liberty and public peace until we have enough morals to adhere to our principles and enough common sense not to give ourselves up to knaves and charlatans!' It took a lofty soul to understand such language. Could virtue substitute for patriotism, dispensing common sense and strength of character?

Camille Desmoulins had already argued that 'in the handling of major affairs, one could depart from the austere rules of morality'. The Jacobins' thinking was no different, but the *sans-culottes* opposed vice to virtue, simplicity of morals and honesty to the corrupting influence of wealth and luxury. Were 'a little cottage too modest to be taxed and a family protected from a bandit's lustfulness' enough to ensure happiness? So Saint-Just promised; but how many would espouse that ideal, even among patriots? The latter were described as pure and virtuous, but virtue lay only in appearances. Its name was used as a shield. It prevented neither robbery, nor violence, nor excesses, and encouraged hypocrisy.

As Richard Cobb observed, virtue was ineffective and seemed tedious. Local authorities singled out for public admiration a handful of spontaneous acts of charity, fleeting instances of abnegation, and charming, childish gestures. With the connivance of civil servants, the Revolution sank deeper into the quagmire. A misleading conformism fed the illusion that the regime was unchallenged. The truth was that the tightening grip of the executive triggered off an almost total reaction of self-defence and revealed the system's inadequacies.

The recall of terrorist representatives

The representatives on mission were the first to be concerned about the new situation. They were upset by the Ventôse crisis. As sincere *montagnards*, their pride was hurt by the lack of consideration shown towards them. Had they perhaps behaved unworthily? Chateauneuf-Randon, attacked for having been a noble, bitterly replied: 'My whole life has shown that I was a man and a citizen before the Revolution, equal to everyone, above nobody, the enemy of courts and prejudice, of the mighty and the rich.' Gaston de l'Ariège took offence at an unfavourable comment: 'Either the representatives enjoy your confidence and you must trust them and them alone, or they do not enjoy it, and you must recall them.'

Indeed they were increasingly recalled and often they resisted by trying to exculpate themselves, publishing accounts of their action, and denouncing one another. Some invoked their poor health as an excuse to obtain sick leave. Others took a host of precautions and refrained from acting even on minor matters without the Committee's stated permission. The Committee's disavowal of twenty-one representatives on 30 Germinal (19 April) completely demoralized their colleagues. By singling out Fouché, Tallien and Carrier – whose excesses in Lyons, Bordeaux and Nantes were condemned by the Committee – the very implementation of the Terror was called into question. Nor did the opposition spare the representatives, who were less and less feared – indeed they were hardly tolerated at all. Dartigoeyte only narrowly avoided being assassinated in the office of the *société* at Auch, and Bo was almost lynched near Aurillac,. Royalist slogans were painted on walls to welcome representatives; the population would deliberately refrain from wearing the tricolour cockade. Representatives were also bombarded with grievances. Prisoners' families denounced informers. It was hard for representatives to know whom to trust: if they were outsiders, they suffered the consequences of local intrigue; if they were locals, they had ties with one of the two camps and would give it preferential treatment. They were surrounded by malevolence and isolated amid a hostile populace. Their attitudes were influenced by these difficulties: 'Nothing is further from severity than harshness; nothing is closer to fright than anger.' Fear made some act with increased rigour and others with excessive weakness. In late Ventôse, for example, Vernerey was criticized for having hastily agreed to release prisoners in the Creuse.

The Committee replaced with its own agents the representatives who thwarted its policy or seemed hesitant. Since the decree of 27 Germinal empowered it to watch over civil servants, the Committee set up its subsequently much-maligned Police Bureau and sent Vialle to the Ain, Demaillot to the Loir-et-Cher, Jullien de Paris to Nantes, and

Pottofeux, Guermeur and others elsewhere, paying them out of its secret funds. Robespierre, Saint-Just and Couthon made it their business to examine their reports, annotate them and request further investigations if needed. As for arrests, which were carried out through the agency of Rousseville, Lejeune and the *comités révolutionnaires*, they were decided on collectively. The minutes unearthed by Arne Ording are in different handwriting and also bear the signatures of Barère, Carnot and Lindet.[6] Even though its work methods were those of the other departments, the Police Bureau was considered 'an instrument of tyranny in the hands of the triumvirs'. It encroached on the sphere of the Committee of General Security, which in turn blamed the Bureau for the 'great' Terror.

THE 'GREAT' TERROR

While attention has been focused on the political and social aspects of the Ventôse crisis, collective attitudes were also affected in a way similar to that of the 'Great Fear' of 1789 — a fact that Georges Lefebvre noted. The announcement of the liquidation of the factions provoked two simultaneous reactions — plot-phobia and a determination to inflict exemplary punishment — that spread throughout France and persisted beyond Thermidor. The representatives, fearing for their own safety, shared these feelings. They accepted the notion that the country's woes resulted from the crimes of the British and of the counter-revolution.

Without doubt, it was very much in the Coalition powers' interest to upset public opinion. The launching of the spring offensive brought them new hope. After breaking through the northern border, they captured Landrecies on 10 Floréal (30 April) and threatened Cambrai. Their spies infiltrated everywhere. The Committee of Public Safety was not unaware of the fact and replied in kind by attempting to separate Scotland and Ireland from London. Despite the sacrifices imposed on the population, the foreign threat, which had been briefly eclipsed, reappeared. Officials became convinced of the existence of a Machiavellian scheme, hatched and financed by foreign powers, to plunge the Republic into civil war, anarchy and bankruptcy as a prelude to the reinstatement of the *ancien régime*. The country therefore had to be purged of its domestic enemies before they massacred patriots. 'May the nation's vengeance run its justly destructive sword over the guilty

---

[6] A. Ording (**193**). A. Soboul (**5**) gives many additional details on the Bureau's activities.

heads of the enemies of the public good; may it strike them all down inexorably.' Those who were vested with even the slightest degree of authority were convinced of this urgent necessity.

However, the psychological explanation is not sufficient. There was another imperative, which Mathiez perhaps over-emphasized but which still deserves attention: the implementation of the Ventôse decrees.[7] To keep the promises made to the indigent, was it not advisable to draw up a precise inventory of the property to be distributed? By identifying suspects, one could establish at the same time the amount of available property. This great social measure seems inseparable from judicial centralization and the reinforcement of the Terror. My impression is based not on any particular decree, but on their sequence and the reasons adduced for them. Local officials, frightened by the increase in the number of prisoners, also made the same assessment.

Prisoners and 'popular commissions'

Gaols were no more expandable than hospitals. By early summer, they were filled to capacity. Three new prisons were opened in Paris in Germinal, and the total of political prisoners rose from 6,300 to 7,500; but in the old gaols, including the Luxembourg, La Force, Bicêtre and the Conciergerie, the number of inmates remained stable. In the provinces, the situation became more dramatic, as the abolition of the 'special commissions' no longer sufficed to clear the prisons to make room for newcomers. In Nantes, Angers and Saumur, between 2,000 and 3,000 prisoners lived in cramped quarters. Mallarmé ordered the simultaneous arrest of 35 inhabitants out of 2,000 in Varennes, and the proportion was higher elsewhere.

Municipalities were confronted with the problem of guarding and feeding detainees. Even the penal colony of Rochefort became hard to police. There was a shortage of wardens and they were totally unreliable. Some twenty turnkeys were on duty in the Luxembourg, where 649 suspects were confined. The prisoners lived together, moved freely within the prison, and shared their cells at night with several other inmates. Sometimes they were asked to provide their own beds. Contacts with the outside were made easy by the practice of having linen sent out to be laundered, and food sent in by the family. But these

[7] See above, p. 188.

supplies were inadequate and the representatives in Dax authorized a levy on prisoners' fortunes to provide for their upkeep. Many suspects stayed at home under the surveillance of guards whom they paid themselves. The number of detainees represented a permanent danger that was aggravated by their concentration.

Mass escapes were feared, as well as uprisings supported by relatives – such as those who marshalled their forces at Alès. Rival clans emerged. Patriots, who were incarcerated in their turn, were segregated. Even if the latter were detained only briefly, they plotted vengeance. In Carcassonne, the many releases that took place stirred up hatreds. Moreover, former members of the Constituent Assembly who thought they had been forgotten, such as Goupil de Préfeln, Du Pont de Nemours and the Comtes de Durfort and de Lauraguais, were brought out of their retirement. With a few precautions, a high proportion of suspects managed to live through the Terror unscathed. Several of them – and not the least prominent – were known to the authorities, barely concealed their whereabouts, and were arrested very late.

Moreover, the Committee of General Security, which had received reports of blatant abuses, had little faith in the *comités révolutionnaires*. As early as 17 Nivôse, it had asked the *districts* to investigate the legitimacy of arrests and the manner in which they were being carried out. The replies were late in coming and evasive, as in a large number of cases presumption of guilt was a sufficient motive for arrests. The officials responsible were neither scrupulous nor imaginative. The registers, many of which disappeared after Thermidor, used the same expressions; suspects were always asked the same questions: How had they behaved on the *grandes journées*? What company did they keep? What proofs could they show of civic conduct? Letters and papers gathered during searches were interpreted by incompetents.

On 8 Ventôse (26 February), Saint-Just had already envisaged a general review of the status of prisoners: 'The Terror has filled the goals, but the guilty are not being punished.' Since 'the Revolution's aim is the triumph of the innocent', errors had to be set right, and misguided citizens had to be distinguished from the people's true enemies, who would be exterminated. So great was the expectation that releases would be expedited that, within two months, 40,000 cases were submitted to the Committee of General Security. But of the six 'popular commissions' that were to have been set up before 15 Floréal (4 May 1794), only two had been created – and these not without reluctance – by the end of the month. The others never saw the light of day. Commission members, who were paid at the same rate as judges on the Revolutionary Tribunal, conducted the selection of prisoners on the basis of actual evidence and recorded their decisions in log-books. The final decision was up to the two 'great' Committees, which, for six weeks, seemed to overlook these lists and approved the first ones only in early Thermidor.

No one, however, disputed the urgent need for such a measure. *Sociétés populaires* called for it in the provinces and offered to appoint local commissions. The transfer of prisoners to the capital was somewhat more complicated than sending documents. Maignet, in Avignon, declared that he could not pay for the transfers. After the Bédoin incident, in which decrees were trampled on and public authority held up to ridicule,[8] the Convention, on 21 Floréal (10 May), created a 'popular commission' at Orange along lines that were soon copied by the Paris Tribunal. The commission passed several hundred sentences and was still operating on 9 Thermidor. For their part, Saint-Just and Le Bas maintained and widened the powers of the Arras Tribunal – set up by Lebon – which survived until 22 Messidor (10 July). There too, the aim was to frighten the counter-revolution and to reassure 'the Republic's faithful and unshakeable friends'.

Plots and assassination attempts

The Jacobin militants, described as *hébertistes*, were constantly exposed to the danger of being disavowed: they complained or remained silent. The moderates' audacity knew no bounds; they schemed everywhere. Gatherings were reported near Chimay and worrying disturbances in Nancy, where Levasseur de la Sarthe had twenty 'accomplices of Lafayette' arrested. In the Pyrénées-Orientales, Chaudron-Roussau discovered a pro-Spanish plot involving 150 persons. Pinet and Cavaignac exposed another one in the Landes.

The authorities were exasperated not only by rebellions fomented by priests and royalists, but by individual acts. 'A blood-stained dagger is hanging over the heads of the people's representatives. The Jacobins no longer expect anything but assassinations and hemlock.' On 18 Germinal, Legendre and Bourdon de l'Oise had already brought to the

---

[8] The affair ended with 63 executions and the burning of a town of 2,000 inhabitants. Actually, the incident was used as a pretext to liquidate 60 counter-revolutionaries who were not directly involved in the events (P. Vaillandet, *L'Affaire de Bédoin*, Avignon, 1930).

Convention anonymous letters exhorting it to 'blow out the brains of Saint-Just, Robespierre and others' and to lead the population against the Revolutionary Tribunal in massacring its judges. Some did their best to spread these distressing rumours. The club in the Rue Saint-Honoré was alarmed at the news from Coulommiers and regions close to the capital. On the northern border, the imminence of danger overexcited the population.

The Prairial assassination attempts were interpreted as an omen. On the 1st (20 May, Admirat (and not Admiral), a lazy and violent drunkard, tried to kill Robespierre, then shot at Collot d'Herbois and missed. Three days later, Cécile Renault was arrested as she was attempting to break into the Duplays' house.* She was carrying two small knives and made no attempt to conceal her counter-revolutionary sentiments. A search was launched for accomplices, but in vain: probably there were none. Mallet du Pan described these attacks as portents and predicted the 'imminent massacre of a part of the Convention and of all prisoners... You will soon see blood flow on the home front.' This clever ploy alerted the *Plaine* and implicitly accused the *robespierristes*.

Threats and grievances, whether coming from Hébert's supporters or from Danton's, naturally focused on Robespierre. Lecointre even boasted of having planned to kill him in a session of the Convention. Robespierre did not disown his responsibilities: 'The crimes of tyrants and the assassins' sword have made me freer and more fearsome for all the enemies of the people.' But even the people did not treat him leniently and each individual blamed his private woes on Robespierre.

Government employees reacted with considerable emotion to the danger that Robespierre had faced. Through him, they felt threatened. Suggestions were made to the Committee of Public Safety to distribute weapons only to certified patriots, to ban arms sales, and to protect its own members. The Assembly was urged to display vigilance and severity, while calls were issued to continue the 'all-out' struggle.

This climate of anxiety affected both the militants involved in the Terror, who demanded that the Terror should be reinforced, and the 'silent majority', who feared that very escalation. Moreover, the provinces were concerned about the increasing number of war prisoners and foreign deserters, although at Fontainebleau they were preferred to the *sans-culottes* 'because of the low wages they accepted'. A

* Where Robespierre lodged. [Trans.]

particularly strong current of anglophobia led to the decision of 7 Prairial (26 May) that no British prisoners were to be taken – and no Hanoverian ones either. The army, which had some grounds for fearing reciprocal treatment, did not always obey the decree.

Such a violation of the laws of warfare and the ceaseless reminders of implacable vengeance corresponded to emotional attitudes: unreason replaced reason. The government was carried away by this ground swell, which also made itself felt in debates among the Jacobins. The latter were said to have lost their composure; it seems more likely that they realized the futility of their efforts. 'It is not natural that a sort of coalition should rise up against a government dedicated to saving the homeland.' The government already felt doomed. Robespierre admitted on 6 Prairial that he did not believe in 'the need to live'.

The law of 22 Prairial Year II

'A Revolution like ours is not a trial, but a thunderbolt aimed at the wicked.' On 26 Germinal, Saint-Just called down lightning upon the Republic's enemies. All persons 'charged with conspiracy' were now brought before the Revolutionary Tribunal in Paris, which now – after the failure of earlier attempts – had to be adapted to its task. 'For the past two months you have been asking the Committee of Public Safety for a more far-reaching law than the one it is submitting to you today.'

The preparation of the decree was shrouded in the same mystery as the Committee's other bills, all discussion on them remaining secret and off the record. Logically, Saint-Just should have been responsible for drafting the decree, but he was prevented from doing so by his mission to the northern army. A note from Robespierre, countersigned by the members present, recalled him. The Committee believed it was directly threatened, and the political situation was judged to be extremely serious. Saint-Just arrived on 12 Prairial (31 May) and left on the 18th. There is no doubt as to his agreement in principle: we need only refer to his earlier statements. Couthon, who drafted the bill, defended it before the Convention, which voted it – not without misgivings – on 22 Prairial (10 June). The law aimed less at 'punishing' than at 'annihilating' counter-revolutionaries, and was extended to those who sought to 'inspire discouragement, deprave morality, and corrupt the purity and force of principles'. Defence counsel for the accused was abolished. 'Patriotic' jurors would reach a verdict on the basis of material evidence; only if it was lacking would witnesses be heard. As for judges, after recording the identity of the accused, they had no choice other than to pronounce a verdict of not guilty or the death penalty.

These provisions, which simplified procedure, are shocking to us, but they barely affected contemporaries, who saw them as the recognition of a *de facto* situation. The presence of lawyers had become useless and the exclusive reliance on written evidence was already a well-established practice. Indeed, an examination of the Revolutionary Tribunal's records shows that preliminary investigation were often very thorough. Were they not considered sufficient to allow 'popular commissions' to take decisions? Finally, judges could also rule that a case should be withdrawn, thereby recognizing that legal proceedings were pointless.

Moreover, through this bill, the Committee of Public Safety expressed its determination to supervise the Terror. 'An attempt has been made to misdirect and precipitate the course of justice.' The Committee of General Security was frustrated at not having been consulted; it was only after a heated discussion that its sphere of action was defined in the decree. In the draft of the bill, the name of the Committee of General Security appears as an addition in Couthon's hand. The Committee pursued its ordinary activities unhindered by the Police Bureau and handled four times as many cases as the Bureau: 1,814 as against 464. One cannot accept Mathiez's assertion that the Committee of General Security deliberately sabotaged the enforcement of the law; all the same, the *robespierristes* and the apparently forgotten Convention were strongly criticized for the decree. The sight of so many empty seats haunted the members of the Assembly, who wondered when their turn would come! Proscription lists circulated. In practice, the legislature lost its right of control over the indictment of its members, who were thus exposed to arbitrary action by the executive. The representatives also regarded the terrorist apparatus as sufficiently repressive. While they renewed the powers of the 'great' Committee, the notion of a personal dictatorship gradually spread. Robespierre was said to harbour such designs. 'I thought I saw in him', wrote D'Yzez, 'a man who truly loved freedom . . . His policies seemed to me to be the least removed from the true path. Now we are faced with a new order of things.'[9]

---

[9] Published in *Revue de France*, vol. 35 (1926), p. 517.

The 'fournées'*

The spate of executions in Messidor was not a direct result of the Prairial decree, which facilitated but did not provoke it. The government had the authority to prevent a new prison massacre. The *amalgames*, which brought together in the same trial prisoners of various origins, were an extension of the methods used in Germinal. Such procedures were attributed to the bureaucracy, and particularly to the Civil Administration, Police and Courts Commission chaired by Robespierre's compatriot Herman, who in fact was merely implementing the Committees' decisions.

The Committee of General Security bears responsibility for the 'trial of the red-shirts', in which the fifty-three accused had been made to wear the smocks reserved for parricides. All had been more or less involved in the Baron de Batz's intrigues. Together with the Finance Committee, the Committee of General Security also brought action against the farmers-general, including Lavoisier, and the members of the former *parlements*. The execution of the 'Virgins of Verdun' was planned by the representative Mallarmé. As for the 'prison plots', they were invoked as a justification for putting together ten *fournées* of prisoners taken from Bicêtre, the Luxembourg, Saint-Lazare and the Carmes.[10] The orders were issued by the Committee of Public Safety; they were signed by Barère, Lindet, Collot, Billaud, Saint-Just and, more infrequently, Robespierre. Fouquier-Tinville, for whom Robespierre had little regard, received a daily report on the behaviour of prisoners and was empowered to bring troublemakers to trial. In the space of one and a half months, 1,376 took place – more than the total for the previous year.

But the victims were rarely chosen at random. The fate of well-known persons was sealed by their counter-revolutionary views. Prisoners from the provinces transferred to Paris for a long-delayed execution knew from the moment of their departure what awaited them. Others, taken to the prisons of the capital like common-law criminals by gendarmes on direct instructions from the Committee of General Security, were condemned in advance. Du Pont de Nemours, for example, harboured no illusions: too many friends of his had already succumbed.

---

* The arrest, trial and execution of suspects in indiscriminate 'batches'; a broader term than *amalgame*, which applied more particularly to mass trials. [Trans.]

10 André Chénier was a victim of one of these *fournées*. It was in the Saint-Lazare gaol that he met Aimée de Coigny, the 'young captive'.

The guillotine, which had been transferred to the Place de la Bastille, then to the tollgate called 'Toppled Throne', functioned daily: it was a nerve-shattering sight, capable of arousing pity. Some would have us believe that the people were saturated with horror and revolted at the spectacle of such abundant bloodshed. Perhaps a few individuals reacted that way, but the majority of Parisian bourgeois made no such references. The onlookers, who were always present in great numbers, recognized and insulted victims, criticizing their behaviour and applauding their execution.

Not only did the Prairial law seem to go unnoticed, but no one objected to the 'great' Terror, with the exception of Robespierre. 'I blame him', said Reubell, 'only for having been too gentle.' Those who have ascribed to him the desire to temper the repression have misinterpreted his position. With his keen political flair, he measured the danger of an exaggerated and anarchic use of violence. Did he not declare at the Jacobin club, on 23 Messidor (11 July): 'One must put an end to the human bloodshed caused by crime'? 'Crime' precisely consisted not in the punishment meted out to the guilty – that was a necessity – but in its excess. Once the desire to punish had been satisfied, punitive action, if continued, might alienate a new portion of public opinion. 'I still find it impossible that this should last, and yet it lasts', observed Casanova.

The balance-sheet of the Terror

The general balance-sheet drawn up by the American historian Donald Greer does not take into account the total number of victims. Greer counted the sentences passed by the Paris Tribunal, the criminal tribunals in the *départements* and the 'special commissions'. His census contains some 17,000 names distributed according to specific geographical areas: 52 per cent in the Vendée, 19 per cent in the south-east, 16 per cent in the capital and 13 per cent in the rest of France. He draws a distinction between zones of turmoil – which constitute a majority – and an insignificant proportion of quiet rural areas. Between *départements*, the contrast becomes more striking. Some were hard hit, like the Loire-Inférieure, the Vendée, the Maine-et-Loire, the Rhône and Paris. In six *départements* no executions were recorded; in 31, there were fewer than 10; in 32, fewer than 100; and only in 18 were there more than 1,000. The number of victims also varied from one *district* to another and not all were sentenced by local tribunals. Of cases tried by the Paris Tribunal, 16 per cent concerned provincials. The well-known examples of Rouen, Tours, Montauban and Lunéville illustrate this overlap. The proportion of persons condemned or decapitated in their place of residence remained low, except in troubled areas. In the *district* of Rouen, only 8 out of 42 were executed by order of the criminal tribunal of the *département*.[11]

The examination of charges leads to similar conclusions. Rebellion and treason were by far the most frequent grounds for execution (78 per cent), followed by federalism (10 per cent), crimes of opinion (9 per cent) and economic crimes (1.25 per cent), which included counterfeiting *assignats*. Artisans, shopkeepers, wage-earners and humble folk made up the largest contingent (31 per cent), concentrated in Lyons, Marseilles and neighbouring small towns. Because of the *vendéens*, peasants are more heavily represented (28 per cent) than the federalist and merchant bourgeoisie. Nobles (8.25 per cent) and priests (6.5 per cent), who would seem to have been relatively spared, actually provided a higher proportion of victims than other social categories. In the most sheltered regions, they were the only victims.

Furthermore, the so-called 'great' Terror is hardly distinguishable from the rest. In June and July 1794, it accounted for 14 per cent of executions, as against 70 per cent from October 1793 to May 1794, and 3.5 per cent before September 1793. Admittedly there was a sharp rise in the monthly average, but the concentration of executions in Paris over-emphasized this late upsurge, which was exploited by the reaction and depicted as a Machiavellian enterprise designed, like the war, to eliminate human surplus. At that very same time the counter-revolutionary thrust of the Terror was intensified: the proportion of victims belonging to the governing classes doubled; that of nobles increased fourfold.

Although premature, this statistical study, based on one-third of executions, still provides a useful approximation. If one adds executions without trial and deaths in prison, a total of 50,000 seems likely, that is 2 per thousand of the population. In addition, half the prisoners were released after Thermidor. Of the very approximate number of suspects, the Terror eliminated a bare tenth. But one has to take account of deportations and prison sentences – whose frequency has been revealed by local studies – to measure the build-up of hatred against the Jacobin Republic.

---

11 Most of the Rouen victims were involved in the Rougemare affair; they had been tried by the Revolutionary Tribunal and executed in Paris in September 1793.

Fig. 6 Distribution of executions by *département*. After D. Greer, *The Incidence of the Terror: A Statistical Interpretation* (**198**)

In the short term, the quickening rate of executions on the eve of Thermidor triggered off a general reaction of fear. The population felt more or less an accomplice to the massacres, and more or less involved. The Terror seemed to have been deflected from its initial aim in order to serve the ambitions of the men in power who personified the dictatorship. It is against them that the malcontents, the cowards, the humiliated and the corrupt marshalled their forces while the masses refused to make new sacrifices.

GENERAL UNEASE

'It is above all against the people's fatigue that we must protect ourselves.' Beffroy and other representatives informed the Committee of Public Safety of the growing disaffection of rural areas. Reality constantly contradicted the Rousseauian myth: representatives no longer discerned the 'infinite wisdom' of the peasants and even doubted whether they were endowed with reason. The very tone of representatives' letters testifies to their bitterness: 'The stupid inhabitants – automatons by temperament – do not seem in the slightest impressed by the prodigies engendered by the Revolution.' Even the national spirit was weakening. In Alsace, it was an insult to be called a Frenchman, and there were fewer patriots in the region of Nice than in nearby Piedmont.

Only the defence of the country justified, for a majority of the population, the pursuit of the revolutionary struggle, but this majority was no longer frightened by the executions in Paris. Those who did not yet dare express their hopes in public were shocked, saddened and morose. They needed recreation to take their minds off the present situation. Chaudron-Rousseau, who recommended such diversion, forced the municipality to pay for 'the violins that made them dance'. A plentiful harvest and military victories, while bringing some real relief, also revived complaints against economic controls and repression. Solidarity played against the Jacobin dictatorship.

The wave of purges

The representatives, whose missions were confirmed in Floréal, lost their cocky self-assurance. They were often forced to go back on their decisions, abandon their assistants, and renege on friendships; they implicitly accused and questioned the perspicacity of the very government whose authority they invoked. The keener they showed themselves to secure the Committee's approval, the more the Committee seemed to disdain them: it failed to consult them and confined itself to acknowledging the receipt of their circulars and, by a banal phrase, to blessing the continuation of their work: 'Keep to the same course; we are relying on you.'

This shifting course – this tottering course – discredited the regime.

The constant turnover of 'liaison men' and their contradictory actions made the Terror less frightening at the local level. Everything became provisional. More than ever, people asked themselves whom to obey. The *scrutins épuratoires* followed one another at such a rate that there was a shortage of candidates. In Brest, by late Floréal, the *société populaire* 'had already regenerated itself three times'. In the regions bordering on the Vendée, where the local administrations were inadequate, the country had 'no resources for training them'. Panics and the persistence of dialects caused greater difficulties in the Maurienne, the Tarentaise and Alsace. Civic spirit could not make up for ignorance. 'It is a shame indeed that men of the least ability are suspect and cannot be put in charge without risk.' This remark did not apply to the Auvergne alone.

Purges took on a demagogic character. Representatives encouraged prevailing currents and swam with the tide. In Le Mans, Garnier de Saintes shamelessly admitted: 'I am going to purge my purges once again, because I was misled by cabals and intrigue.' Generally, representatives imposed a list of names chosen by a select committe. Le Carpentier disbanded 'the *société patriotique* of Saint-Malo in a revolutionary manner so as to improve its membership'; he adopted the same procedure in the Manche and the Côtes-du-Nord. Some made public the names of citizens who dodged taxes, requisitions and levies, while others referred decisions to public debate that degenerated into private disputes. Local terrorists were eliminated. The people had had enough. Representatives entrusted the pursuit of their task to *agents nationaux* who knew that their authority was challenged and preferred to refrain from exercising it.

As soon as the government emissary had left, intrigues resumed with renewed intensity. There were no reliable men left to implement a government policy whose sporadic character had made it ineffective and ultimately counter-productive. In the Meuse, local administrators had been absent without permission for over a month and spent their time denouncing their opponents throughout the region instead of enforcing decrees, which in the Indre and the Cher were not even published. It was by now out of the question to 'oblige the intermediary agents to comply strictly with the wishes of the nation's representatives and the people' or to coerce them through the Terror. The national guard, whose ranks were thinned by conscription, obeyed without enthusiasm, and vacancies for guardians of sealed property – hitherto much sought after – no longer attracted any candiates. People were more concerned with their own activities than with the Revolution.

'How guilty they are, those communes that, having sunk into a lethargic slumber, seem to await the outcome of the clash that is shaking the universe before rousing themselves from their impolitic indifference.'[12] Once the mainspring of revolutionary action had unwound, the 'oppressed' stood aloof.

The crisis of authority and the 'maximum'

The deficiencies of the local authorities worked in favour of the reaction and jeopardized the government. Excessive reorganization had made officials indifferent to their duties. They had no knowledge of public affairs; they failed to answer questionnaires and to draw up lists of indigents – or else larded them with gross mistakes. Their advice was heeded less and less. They no longer represented either the people or the republican State.

The regions of the south were particularly rebellious. In the *district* of Quillan, gendarmes were stoned by inhabitants who disapproved of their assignments; prisoners were freed in the Haute-Loire. Old plundering instincts came to the surface: livestock was stolen from pastures and people helped themselves to their neighbours' fruit; poaching increased. Gleaners and grape-pickers freely indulged in pilfering; national forests were devastated and fallow lands were seized. A sort of agrarian pre-communism loomed up from the depths of time. 'The land belongs to those who cultivate it'; 'its fruits belong to the community'. Near Moulins, a priest called Petitjean preached the sharing of foodstuffs.[13]

Indeed, this distribution was to have taken place within parish limits. Parishes turned in on themselves, resisting intrusion by strangers. Searches were met by systematic obstruction; the population gave evasive answers to even the most innocuous questions. Pinet and Cavaignac observed this attitude among Basques: 'They want the Republic but are still imbued with an inward-looking spirit that makes them want to shelter their area from national measures.' At Montfort-l'Amaury, women undid by night the wheels of carts used to carry grain from the commune.

Unrest took on political connotations. The signs of Jacobin presence were attacked. In Montesquieu (Lot-et-Garonne), the liberty tree was

---

[12] Published in *Archives parlementaires*, vol. 88, p. 77.
[13] See E. Campagnac, 'Un prêtre communiste: le curé Petitjean', *Révolution française*, 1903, p. 425.

torn up and replanted with its roots facing upwards; in the region of
Melun, casks of saltpetre solution were smashed. Speculators invaded
auctions of national estates, bribing peasants to keep the bidding down.
In Prairial and Messidor, such disturbances became rife and created an
impression of insecurity.

Representatives emphasized the spontaneous and sporadic nature of
the outbreaks, and described them as acts of banditry. A few executions
restored order and 'malicious individuals disappeared'. Were these
troubles not being magnified in order to alarm public opinion? In actual
fact, they occurred in what were traditionally rebellious areas, which
in the aftermath of 10 August 1792 and 31 May 1793 had been hotbeds
of federalism and now served as havens for nobles, priests and
moderates expelled from Paris by the decree of 27 Germinal. From
known 'trouble spots' – the Ariège, the Lozère, the Valais and the
Isère – disturbances spread to the reputedly quiet 'flat country'.

The opposition resorted to its customary tactics. On the eve of the
harvest, there were reports announcing the arrival of bandits who would
destroy crops. In the *district* of Tarbes, rumours were circulated that
old persons and children were being indiscriminately massacred in order
to reduce bread consumption. Georges Lefebvre pointed out the effect
of these panics, which drove entire families in the north towards the
Austrians. People tried to protect their own lives and property since
the Republic was no longer capable of doing so. Recent legislation,
which the *sans-culottes* so strongly supported, divided the people instead
of uniting them. The implementation of the *maximum général*, regarded
by poorer peasants as depriving them of the fruits of their labour,
increased their animosity against the towns, which imposed price and
wage controls. A winegrower of the Loiret held the 'Orléans riff-raff'
responsible. The poor, insatiable and menacing town-dweller was now
regarded as a 'starver'.

The *agents nationaux*, who were in charge of drawing up price-scales
in each *district*, rarely managed to complete them before Thermidor.
The lists were full of mistakes and were generally disregarded, except
by a few persons who leafed through them out of curiosity. With the
setting of official prices for requisitioned supplies, producers accepted
the risks of the black market in view of the huge profits involved. 'The
quest for lucre mobilized many people who had never thought of it.'
Butchers became livestock traders. A barter economy developed
between town and country. Sugar was exchanged for butter, and wine
for corn. Suppliers and buyers covered up for each other. The *comités*

révolutionnaires, which were swamped with denunciations, did their best, but police courts proved ineffective in the task of repression that had been entrusted to them.

Among *sans-culottes*, the benefits gained by some stirred envy in others. Their coalition against the peasantry disintegrated, while community spirit was strengthened. Thus the consequences of the *maximum* went deeper than those of the dechristianizers' excesses and capital punishment. All forms of peasant resistance converged against the Revolution.

God or Supreme Being?

The influence of priests on this massive opposition was indisputable yet weaker than official pronouncements would have us believe. Relentless persecution caused priests to be regarded as martyrs or heroes. They gave a human significance to the turmoil in which all believers were caught up. The artificially provoked and brutally conducted dechristianization campaign had swept away the visible signs of worship without affecting rural religiosity.[14] Faith subject to coercion became shrouded in mystery. Believers behaved like conspirators in order to receive the sacraments. 'We have made Reason a sort of Heavenly Queen and we imitate the fury of fanaticism!'[15]

The Committee of Public Safety, which condemned persecutions, sought the support of the *sociétés populaires*: 'The more violent the convulsions of dying fanaticism, the more careful we must be. We must not give it new weapons by substituting violence for instruction...One cannot give orders to consciences.' This position was inspired by tactical considerations that were not shared by local terrorists and representatives. Where the anti-religious struggle continued, disturbances spread. The women of Manosque refused to let their churches be despoiled and the army had to be called in. 'Divine' letters were circulated in the area of Montbrison to bring the faithful back to Catholic worship. Believers became convinced that profaned saints would work new miracles. Despite prohibitions, the Sunday sabbath was observed and pilgrimage sites were visited. People went all the way to the environs of Rambouillet to have their wedding-rings blessed. Even in Paris, religious books fetched 'insane prices'.

[14] See above, p. 179.
[15] Letter from a former dean of the Protestant theological school of Montauban to Robespierre, 16 Floréal Year II.

The apparent success of toleration confirmed Robespierre's assessment. He feared an anti-republican union of juror priests – whose civic spirit had often been appreciated by the population – and non-jurors. Only blind archaic atheists could accuse a traitor and a patriot priest of the same crime and sentence them both to death. The decree of 18 Floréal (7 May) aimed at eradicating, in Robespierre's own words, 'the rightful indignation that had been repressed by the Terror and was silently brewing in every heart'. Robespierre invoked the majesty of Providence: 'Being of beings! On the day when the universe emerged from your all-powerful hands, did it shine in a more pleasant light for you!' As a deist in the Rousseauian mould, Robespierre encountered God throughout creation, without intermediaries or external demonstrations. Since this belief made priests and churches useless, was it not a fatal blow against fanaticism? Let not Robespierre be accused of having promoted a cult when he eliminated all of them by inviting the people to adhere to the universal religion of Nature. Although, in reasserting the immortality of the soul, he did not have Christianity in mind, he did restore to the destitute a hope for happiness.

However, Robespierre irritated atheists and all the dechristianizers. The Convention and the government reacted with unconcealed hostility. Vadier, for example, on 27 Prairial, did his best to magnify the case of an old eccentric, Catherine Théot, and to implicate Robespierre.[16] As for the people, they interpreted the cult of the Supreme Being as the end of the campaign against religion, and publicly went back to their God, their masses and their processions. Rumour had it that the solemn festival of 20 Prairial (8 June) would be followed by the restoration of Easter. Married priests, such as the *curé* of Beaudeau (Hautes-Pyrénées), continued their ministry in the guise of a cult of the homeland.

The population seethed with anger when commissioners attempted to forbid such practices locally. In the Douai region, the Convention and the Jacobins were accused of reneging on their promises. Disappointment triggered off new outbreaks in Prairial. A priest in the Ariège avenged himself by setting fire to a patriot's house. The authorities, who were caught in the cross-fire, avoided taking sides. After all, was it not widely rumoured that the end of the Revolution was near and that altars would be restored?

---

16 Mathiez made a detailed study of this affair (*Contributions à l'histoire religieuse de la Révolution française*, Paris, 1907, pp. 96–142). More recently, Michel Eude (**204**) has shown that in fact Robespierre asked for Théot's sentence to be suspended so as to allow the Police Bureau to conduct a further investigation. Robespierre's move was resented by the Committee of General Security.

The problem of wages

Religious anxiety coincided with the economic anxieties of the Republic's wage-earners. Social order and economic production depended on wage and price stability. Like the *maximum* on foodstuffs, wage controls were enforced only in State-run factories, whose workers – in exchange for pay restrictions – were entitled to distributions of bread at fixed prices. The difficulties of the inter-harvest period led to lower rations. Forge workers in the Dordogne received a soldier's ration of one pound of poor-quality bread a day. Even in towns in cereal-growing areas, there was dearth; it was severe in all of the larger towns. But the condition of workers was not the same everywhere.

The private sector rewarded the best workers with piece-rates. Bonuses for overtime were distributed to shipyard workers. Arms workshops in Paris broadened the wage-scale for specialists. In the provinces, fraud was practised by common consent, for example by paying porters three times for the same assignment. Such methods led to a fivefold increase in transport costs. Moreover, industrial and agricultural workers compared their economic situations. Those employed in workshops in the Allier and the Nièvre were distinctly underprivileged. They were paid on average thirty sous a day, the same sum awarded to the casual unemployed and to refugees from the Vendée. Was it not better to stay at home rather than work for controlled wages? Timber-floating ceased on the Yonne and lumberjacks, who were requisitioned, went into hiding. It seemed preferable by far to hire oneself out for the harvest.

The situation was urgent and there was a shortage of agricultural manpower. Workers took advantage of the situation: those who were available in the region of Cherbourg asked for up to two francs a day with board. Le Carpentier, taken by surprise by the increase, which upset the labour market, called for wage controls; these were decreed on 22 Messidor (10 July). Ignoring the widespread doubling of private-sector wages, the Committee of Public Safety granted ridiculously low increments. Relative to prevailing prices, they were almost starvation wages. Blacksmiths in the arms workshops of Paris, who were paid sixteen francs a day, would have been paid five, and carpenters three francs fifteen sous instead of eight francs. The enforcement of the *maximum* was out of the question; it was a serious enough political mistake to have announced it. Labour unrest threatened to paralyse the arms workshops, the Louvre press and the Gobelins manufactory. The Paris *sans-culottes* in particular voiced their disappointment. There was a widening gap between the government's priorities and the people's rightful demands. Wage-earners had reasons to unite against the employer-State, while price controls on commodities provoked the collective opposition of rural France.

FEAR'S REVENGE

A new drama, greater than that of Ventôse, was in the offing, and would in any case have unfolded before the autumn. The breaking-point had been reached between a resolutely conservative society and its new, artificial structures. From a political, social and human point of view, the terrorist apparatus – despite the underlying principles – had become unbearable. The population and the army resisted as best they could against an overweening authority. Increasingly, the wheels of the machine were spinning without gripping. It was kept in motion by the government's resolve, but came to a halt the moment the government split apart.

Dissension in the government

When Saint-Just returned to the Committee of Public Safety on 10 Messidor (28 June) after twenty days' absence, he sensed the impending break: 'Where are the familiar faces?' Robespierre was absent, and the files from the Police Bureau were delivered to his house. In one month he signed only five times. Robespierre's untypical behaviour was symptomatic of his deep discouragement. Much has been made of divergences on social issues between members of the Committee. The Ventôse decrees, the 'great' Terror and total war may also have generated disagreement. However, the circulars concerning these areas bear several signatures, and the decision to create the four 'forgotten' 'popular commissions' was taken by a majority of the Committee on 4 Thermidor.

On the other hand, insufficient attention has been paid to the personal animosities, hesitations and backbiting that inevitably soured relations. Each member made a preserve out of his speciality, thus paving the way for conflicts of authority. Will we ever know the number of minor decisions whose usefulness was questioned? The cumulative effect of mere glances and tactless gestures could easily wound men who had shared their lives for a whole year, without rest or relaxation. These men, who were equally responsible and equally fastidious, became all the more irritable as they fell prey to fatigue. Eleven men in the same boat – what a challenge! Campaign plans and the choice of generals usually pitted Carnot against Saint-Just; they were exasperated by Barère's tirades in the Assembly, and he was replaced by Couthon. Unity of action – the 'great' Committee's major strength – was dangerously coming apart.

Dissensions had been noticed since late Germinal; they became sharper and more frequent after 22 Prairial. The Committee's quarrels could sometimes be heard from the street, and meetings were shifted to the floor above. The Committee of General Security fanned the flames: Robespierre had only two friends on it, one of whom, Le Bas, was often away on mission to the armies. Vadier and Amar did not conceal their aversion to Robespierre. Rival police forces fuelled the animosity by exposing shady affairs. Nevertheless, the hostility between the two Committees was not strong enough to worry the Convention.

The *Plaine*, which until now had remained loyal to the government, was not to be swayed until it believed itself to be seriously threatened. The recalled terrorists did their best to persuade the *Plaine* of the danger, even resorting to royalist arguments and prophesying the wholesale slaughter of the representatives by which Robespierre would inaugurate his reign. A few members, 'terrorized by the rumours spread by those scoundrels', no longer slept at home. But the centrists' attitude was still shrouded in uncertainty. Even the *Montagne* was disintegrating under the effect of rivalries over missions and personal issues. André Dumont's brother and Thibaudeau's family were arrested. 'A few more days', wrote Fouché to his sister on 30 Messidor, 'and truth and justice will score a resounding victory.' On 5 Thermidor, he added: 'Today perhaps the traitors will be unmasked.'

The plot did exist and the conspirators were impatient. Tallien trembled for his imprisoned mistress, Thérésa Cabarrus. Dubois-Crancé, singled out like Fouché for his excesses at Lyons, had tried in vain to make Robespierre relent. Danton's friends Legendre and Thuriot supported the dissenters. News of the imminent crisis circulated abroad. As early as 23 Messidor, the *Mercure universel*, printed in Belgium, carried the story: 'Bourdon de l'Oise and Tallien are regarded by the Coalition powers as the champions of the faction that is supposed to topple the Committee of Public Safety.'

Who can tell if Robespierre had committed a mindless error, had given up all hope, or was acting out of supreme disdain? Whatever the case, he left a clear field for his opponents by boycotting both the

Convention and the Committee and taking refuge at the Jacobin club, from whose tribune he still had a chance of rallying public support. In eleven meetings he intervened fourteen times to refute slander. Robespierre, who was always frightened of dictatorship and had so easily confounded his Girondin accusers, could not tolerate such charges. 'I am depicted as a tyrant and an oppressor of the nation's representatives', he bitterly observed on 13 Messidor to a chorus of unanimous protest. At the same time he confessed to his misgivings and indecision.

All was not lost for Robespierre, whose position remained solid. He could still count on devoted supporters in the Commune, on Dumas, president of the Revolutionary Tribunal, and on Hanriot, who commanded the national guard. The Jacobin authorities in the provinces still identified Robespierre with the Revolution, whereas public opinion in Paris, which was directly affected by the political crisis, judged him differently. Some praised his moderation and prudence; others called him conservative. The *sans-culottes*, who had not fully recovered from *hébertisme*, remonstrated against scarcities, hoarders and the black market. Isolated acts testified to the persistence of a democratic opposition that concealed itself under unofficial festivals (*fêtes partielles*) – which were banned – and fraternal banquets monopolized by the reaction. On 28 Messidor (16 July), Robespierre applauded the ban on such manifestations: 'Let it be clearly said to the patriots that their unity constitutes their strength, and that their enemies have not yet been defeated.'

The impossible conciliation

It was not just the fate of a few individuals and the outcome of doctrinal conflicts that was at stake. The continuity of revolutionary government and the very future of the Republic were in danger. The members of the Committees of Public Safety and of General Security attempted a reconciliation – undoubtedly in good faith – through the self-appointed mediation of Saint-Just. On 4 Thermidor, they proposed uniting the Police Bureau, as well as the four 'popular commissions', with the Committee of General Security. Robespierre, who had been invited to the discussion, turned up the following morning; Billaud-Varenne and his colleagues assured him of their friendship. Barère informed the Convention of this new-found harmony, which Robespierre, however, sensed as a diversion aimed at buying time for his opponents. He at once prepared his case.

Time was running out and there was deep unease. Robespierre took no heed of this disquiet and discouraged those of his friends, such as Payan and Le Bas, who were planning to organize resistance. Was resistance even conceivable? Would the *sectionnaires* – whom the Committee seemed to harass for its pleasure – respond? The new wage-scales were made public on 5 Thermidor in Paris. The Jacobins enjoyed the support of only a fraction of the patriots, and their weapons were blunted. Fouché and Dubois-Crancé, who had been expelled from the Jacobin club, made common cause with the men they had earlier driven out.

Those who reproached the *robespierristes* for their passivity under-estimated their character and energy. While Maximilien preferred the silence of his study and the rostrum to mingling with crowds, he was not afraid of the masses. As for Augustin, Saint-Just and Le Bas, they had demonstrated their capacity for decision. They were not loath to lead the people and take on responsibilities. But to rise against the Convention – whose indisputable sovereignty they had always proclaimed – would be a negation of their principles. This they could not accept.

As a parliamentarian and genuine democrat, Robespierre took his case before the Convention. Saint-Just seems to have disapproved of this personal approach; he realized its dangers. It is probable that he would have preferred a report to have been read in the name of the Committee of Public Safety. The Assembly would have hesitated to condemn a government whom it had just reinvested with powers, but it would have agreed to vote a decree of accusation against a few members designated by name. Robespierre's solitary undertaking lent credence to the widespread idea that he was planning to install a dictatorship. His behaviour was that of a head of the executive asking for a vote of confidence, not that of a people's representative: 'If no one believes me, then I have no business being here.'

The long speech he inflicted on the Assembly on 8 Thermidor was his political testament. It has not been examined closely enough. Robespierre began by exonerating himself: 'They call me a tyrant. If I were one, they would be grovelling at my feet, and I would be stuffing them with gold.' Why then attach such 'gigantic and ridiculous importance' to a single man? Robespierre went on to denounce 'the agents of general security' – 'a power superior to the Committee itself' – and Treasury employees, 'ex-nobles, *émigrés* perhaps'. It was the small fry, the subordinates, who were doing all the harm. Like

Saint-Just, Robespierre blamed civil servants and the bureaucracy. Because of them, 'we are walking on volcanoes'.

Robespierre avoided personal attacks. 'I want the culprits to clear themselves and I want us to become more reasonable.' In a lofty and impassioned plea, he exhorted the Convention to regain 'its power' and all patriots to set aside their differences. The homeland's safety depended on their unity. The revolutionary government, as guardian of that unity, 'must be protected from every pitfall'. 'If it is destroyed today, there will be no liberty tomorrow.' 'Slacken the reins of the Revolution for one moment, and you shall see military dictatorship take it over.'

This supreme attempt at conciliation has been interpreted as a political speech and an indictment. On the contrary, it was a sermon and a prophecy. It was a call to friendship, honesty, honour and forgiveness for abuse. The representatives who gave Robespierre a long ovation shared his fears, but his enemies did not lay down their weapons. The first round of this imprudently joined battle was inconclusive.

The second round was fought that very evening at the Jacobin club. Robespierre — flanked by the now ever-present Couthon — repeated his arguments before a nervous audience, which he once again won over. Collot d'Herbois and Billaud-Varenne, who had united against Robespierre, were unable to make themselves heard. By driving them away, the audience forced them definitively into the other camp. With such reinforcements, the opposition planned its strategy for the following day, while Saint-Just feverishly worked at the speech that he was determined to deliver. Robespierre, who was aware of his own powerlessness, accepted his fate with resignation: 'I have the experience of the past; I can see the future. What friend of the homeland would want to stay alive at a time when one is no longer allowed to serve it and to defend oppressed innocence?'

The last round

The final act was played out on 9 Thermidor (27 July) and went on into the night. Events unfolded as in a tragic dice game whose tosses took the protagonists — the Convention and its committees, the Commune and its *sections* — by surprise. Everything seemed rigged, even the blunders. The victors, uncertain of their victory until the very end, immediately feared its consequences. The most impassioned of the actors looked back on their gesture as a misdeed. For a number of representatives, the drama of Thermidor was, like the king's trial, a personal ordeal. By condemning men who embodied the Revolution, they repudiated a cause they had themselves served. The violence was excessive – as was the cowardice. The people, in their astonishment at the suddenness of events and at a brutality unusual for politicians, could not keep up with the action on stage.

The Convention opened its session at eleven o'clock, as usual, by reading correspondence and giving audience to petitioners. At about noon, Saint-Just tried to avoid disaster 'out of human respect', but without much conviction. Tallien interrupted him and, by a systematic obstruction countenanced by Collot, who was chairing the session, the only members allowed to speak were the accusers, who shouted denunciations and insults from their seats. The rare objective and spontaneous eyewitness accounts give some idea of the uproar and of the efforts of the accused. Robespierre literally clutched the rostrum, proclaiming his indignation without being able to make himself heard. Saint-Just, who reckoned the game was up, fell silent.

The premeditated plan went off without a hitch. The acquiescent *Plaine* voted in favour of it. First, Hanriot and Lavalette were deposed together with their aides-de-camp, General Boulanger and Dufraisse, to discourage any moves by the Paris national guard; next, Dumas was removed in order to secure control of the Revolutionary Tribunal. A proclamation drafted by Barère reassured the population. Vadier, Bourdon de l'Oise, Tallien and Billaud-Varenne then turned to Robespierre. His trial took less than an hour. The decree ordering the arrest of Robespierre, his brother, Couthon, Saint-Just and Le Bas was issued without a vote, and they were incarcerated in separate prisons. The gatekeeper of the Luxembourg, however, refused to admit the elder Robespierre, who was then taken to the Hôtel de Ville on the Quai des Orfèvres, where he received an enthusiastic welcome and remained until the evening.

The Commune did not fail to react, but it was taken by surprise, and Jacobin assistance proved useless. However, the prisoners were freed and there was hope yet that the *sections* might be roused to action. Payan issued a call to arms. His orders and those of the Convention crossed putting the legion commanders in a quandary. Precious time was lost in oaths and endless discussions. The turbulent Hanriot lacked stature, if not courage and boldness. In the Place de Grève, at about seven in the evening, 3,000 *sectionnaires* with artillery were waiting for a commander.

The troops would have had no trouble besieging the Convention, which resumed its session. A raid on the Tuileries to deliver Hanriot came as proof of the danger to the Assembly. First it succumbed to panic, then it regained its composure, declared the rebel deputies to be outlaws, and tried to rally the *sections*, of which only sixteen had sided with the Commune. While the troops of these *sections*, tired of having nothing to do, dispersed, Barras and Léonard Bourdon led the others to the Hôtel de Ville, which they entered at about half past two in the morning without encountering the slightest resistance.

At the very same moment, Augustin Robespierre jumped out of a first-floor window. He had just heard the news that his brother was wounded in the jaw by a pistol shot, which in all likelihood had been a suicide attempt. Robespierre was carried nearly unconscious to the Convention – where he was turned away – then to the Committee of Public Safety, and finally to the Conciergerie; he was executed on the evening of the 10th, without sentence, in the Place de la Révolution, in the company of twenty-one of his friends. The corpses were thrown into a grave in the Errancis cemetery, located on the former estate of the Duc d'Orléans at Monceau. The slaughter continued for several days, and was directed particularly against the Conseil Général of the Commune. A total of 108 persons paid with their lives for their attachment to principle, their devotion and their trust. Others, like the wife of the carpenter Duplay, committed suicide.

The people of Paris were passive spectators of this repression. But along the Seine, bourgeois neighbourhoods loudly voiced their satisfaction as the convoys of victims were led past. For the young pupils of the Ecole de Mars, who had been suitably indoctrinated, this conspiracy resembled the previous ones. The provinces at first refrained from reacting; later, when local administrations had been purged of Jacobins, they congratulated the Convention. Public order was not disturbed; the country accepted what had happened.

Those who examined only its consequences described 9 Thermidor as a 'hoax' or even a 'mishap'. Joseph de Maistre summed it up in these words: 'A few scoundrels had a few other scoundrels killed.' Others have seen it as the come-back of the bourgeoisie, a phase in the class struggle. In my view, the major problem of 9 Thermidor lies in the indifference of the population or its failure to comprehend. The constraints imposed by the economic dictatorship and the Terror, which cowed the population into apparent submission, had unforeseen repercussions on collective attitudes. Authority was confused with legality. People grew accustomed to obeying orders presented –

whatever their provenance – as the Convention's writ. A rising against the Convention was tantamount to a break with the Republic it embodied. Insurrection, the driving force of the Revolution, became pointless. Automatically, the insurgent became a rebel. These arguments, which were the object of heated discussion among the *robespierristes*, influenced the *sectionnaires*.

Furthermore, there has been no consideration of what the attitude of the *sections* might have been had the two camps fought one another. Asserting the people's will against unworthy deputies by surrounding the Assembly with one's cannon – as on 31 May – or defending oneself against a monarch's treason – as on 10 August – were regarded by patriots as a 'sacred' right and duty. But there was no justification for shooting one's brothers in the name of a deposed Commune merely because those brothers preferred to obey the sovereign assembly. Such bloodshed constituted a gratuitous crime. This argument had a certain impact and seems to have played a part in the hesitations of the Paris authorities. When the events of 9 Thermidor are viewed in their human context, it can be seen that they were engraved on a collective mentality that did not imagine how a modicum of leisure and well-being could pose a threat to the Republic.

Conclusion

The First Republic claimed to follow no model. It developed its own institutions, tried out its own policies, and forged its own spirit according to the circumstances. This originality gave it a prestige that it had not sought. The entire country experienced an uncontrollable crisis for which there was no miracle cure. The exceptional character of the measures proposed was a response to a sense of panic. The situation had to be faced and the nation had to be willing to pay the price.

The first constraint was the emergency itself, which affected the people and its deputies, the rich and the poor: all were patriots but did not agree on policy. The masses, who had nothing – or so little – to lose, threatened to lead their notables beyond the limits of the notables' own interests, which were those of the propertied groups, not of the nation. The office-holding, landed and mercantile bourgeoisie, which tried to govern and administer, succeeded in channelling popular action, but only for a time. The revolutionary movement thus reveals its dual aspect. Seen 'from above', through the government's intentions, attitudes and accomplishments, it proudly wears its label and follows its signposted course. Seen 'from below', the movement represents the Revolution in its raw state – a sort of eruption that buried everything beneath it and propelled history forward. Well before Daniel Guérin, Michelet proclaimed his confidence in the people's genius: 'Left to their own devices, in decisive moments...they realized what had to be done and did it.'

The 10 August 1792 rising was the people's spontaneous answer to the foreign invader and the royalist danger. The people were not asking to be led but to be followed. They exercised power through intimidation, repression and violence, leaving legislation and organization to others. The people's fundamental contradiction resided in this latent force and this signal weakness. It was a dichotomy that

228

proceeded from a more unqualifiable betrayal than that of the people's natural enemy, the aristocracy: one section of the people, and a sizeable one at that, abandoned the other. The thrust towards democracy came up against conservatism and social inertia. This acted both as an accelerator and as a brake on the course of the Revolution. The interplay of conflicting forces has been overlooked: they split the Republic asunder before it had the chance to establish itself.

Revolutionary power encompassed all powers, because it was revolutionary. For the same reason, it created its own legality, which justified its excesses. It made a single cause out of the defence of the homeland and the defence of the Republic. The *Gironde* sealed its fate when it failed to accept the *sans-culottes* as partners in the common undertaking. The Jacobins and the Convention's *montagnards* seized the opportunity: they brought popular forces together. Once again, in September 1793, the *sans-culottes* saved the Republic as it was being harassed by the reaction. Patriotic drive, intensified by danger, consolidated national unity. Revolutionary government was rooted in this impulse.

Dictatorship was established 'from above': it was bourgeois – indeed, it emanated from the petty bourgeoisie that was also called *sans-culotte*; it was inflexible and at times inhuman. The authorities used it as an expedient justified by military and economic imperatives.

The government, which had been declared provisional, had only a limited time in which to prove itself. It was condemned to win. Every deviation became treason. The State, which had been provided with the Terror by the people, used the Terror against the people when they strayed from the narrow path laid down by the Jacobin rulers. Dissent developed at every level – although it can be explained without resorting to the concept of class. Traditional relationships between groups were disrupted by the State-controlled economy. The counter-revolution inherited anti-terrorists, 'fanatics', the weak-minded and the indifferent, all of whom had been excluded from the nation.

Social grievances took second place. As the dictatorship intensified, it called with increasing frequency for equality, justice and virtue. The regime's intentions were pure, but it lacked the means to put them into practice. The disadvantaged were embittered by illusory promises that frightened the rich. The Republic suffered from these fears and disappointments. The favours it granted to property-owners by promoting agrarian individualism, combined with the heavy bourgeois participation in the purchase of *émigré* estates, gave rise to highly

9

precarious political commitments. By moving to the right, the government could not make good the loss of its support on the left. As a result, revolutionary ardour waned. Confusion and suspicion became rife among patriots. The unfinished edifice of the Republic was destroyed from within.

Providing for national defence and assuring the country's supplies required sacrifices from every citizen. The nation as a whole accepted these sacrifices; individuals feared them.

The success of the operation depended on the methods used to persuade or coerce. Repression hit not only nobles and priests, but also a variety of groups, and reached out indiscriminately to all hostile forces. The bourgeois revolution did not spare the bourgeoisie. In the provinces, the Revolution was in the hands of local authorities over whom central government emissaries exercised only intermittent control. The revolutionary government was thus not always present, nor always listened to. Actually, it suffered far more from slow communications than from negligence.

The revolutionary edifice was founded on unity of policy – the key to efficiency. To attain that efficiency, the State interfered everywhere and claimed to exert its sway over individuals and institutions. It came up against established structures and attitudes, which it tried to exploit instead of innovating. While profitable in the short term, such a realistic approach created an ambiguity: the coexistence of two economic systems. The regime concealed its powerlessness behind a fastidious zeal that became intolerable.

Artificial constructions were layered over the old society. Because it was ephemeral, the regime of the Year II could hardly lay claim to more than provisional or imperfect achievements. Its only permanent accomplishment was its army, which anticipated modern military priorities by its appropriation of nearly half the active male population. Just like civilian society, the army had its share of ambition, idealism, ingenuousness and profiteering. But discipline, hierarchy and danger preserved the civic spirit of the soldiers who defended the homeland and Jacobinism. Thus the army was the regime's success and outlived its maker.

Around the army there gravitated a contingent of parasites who belonged to the great mass of the Republic's wage-earners. The State employed an excessive personnel both to staff its numerous services and to win over zealous patriots. Clerks, civil servants and other paid agents demonstrated their loyalty. Nevertheless, to be worthy of and to keep their jobs, they overplayed their hand. Their obedience and smug conformism concealed the people's true feelings from the government. Workers in arms factories and shipyards, who were proven *sans-culottes*, regarded working conditions and wage controls as reasons to unite against the State's demands. The relative concentration of workers contributed to the emergence of a class consciousness of sorts.

But Jacobin propaganda hardly affected peasant attitudes. The unchanging rhythm of the seasons regulated agriculture and the lives of country-dwellers. The countryside reaped the benefits of the Revolution 'without going through its storms', and even dechristian-ization had only a superficial impact on it. Country-dwellers reacted more strongly to price and wage controls than to requisitioning of foodstuffs and even to conscription, which reduced unemployment and poverty among the young. Smallholders and labourers gave their children: one destitute widow had eleven of her twelve boys in the army. Patriotic feeling held out against disappointments and worries. In Messidor, rural areas reacted with no less enthusiasm than the capital to the news of victories that freed the borders. 'Gaiety and joy are visible everywhere. It is one immense family that is celebrating together the happy events about which everyone is pleased, and in which everyone feels involved.'[1] Rural France maintained its ties with a Terror-free Republic. Most countrymen were convinced that the period of sacrifices was drawing to a close. After the final act of the drama, life began anew.

However, life was no longer quite the same. Despite inertia or because of it, and because of the war, human behaviour had changed. The first proof is provided by demographic trends. Population growth slowed despite an astonishing boom in the marriage rate. Bachelors, who were regarded as bad citizens, contracted marriages, as did young men threatened with conscription and priests who had resigned office. The birth rate did not follow suit, while hardship, epidemics and battles increased the death rate. In all probability, the equality of inheritance rights, which fragmented estates, incited parents of caution. It is also probable that 20 per cent of adult lives were disrupted by military service.

The family unit was no less disrupted. It came under attack from several quarters. The observance of commitments, marital fidelity and domestic attachments suffered from the absence of men and from a

---

[1] Quoted in M. Bouloiseau, *Bourgeoisie et Révolution: les Du Pont de Nemours, 1788–1799*.

social mobility that developed even in the countryside. Debauchery spread in the provinces. Many abandoned children were rescued in the towns and an even greater number of children died of poverty. On the other hand, the introduction of divorce led to fewer genuine separations than is imagined. Old couples dissolved a union consented to for material motives; wives of *émigrés* used the procedure to safeguard their assets. The rehabilitation of illegitimate children, which sometimes prompted touching reconciliations, posed insoluble inheritance problems. Disputes over the sharing of estates led to lasting hatreds in certain families.

Society, whose structures remained intact, thus underwent a quiet change. People on the whole became aware of the precariousness of the most time-honoured practices. Notarized deeds lost something of their value. Religious scruples carried less weight. Jacobinism encouraged society to shake off old taboos and to free the mind in order to put it at the nation's service. A wealth of projects issued from popular thinking, and solutions were suggested for topical problems – solutions that have not been implemented to this day – ranging from the democratization of education to the status of farm rents, the nationalization of mines, and the taxation of capital. In this neglected heritage and in the principles that inspired it still resides the miracle of the Year II. When restored to its concrete perspective and divorced from its emotional connotations, this past remains our present, for never, in their social projects, have men set their hopes so high.

Foreign assessments were accurate on this score. The Jacobin Republic was less a model than a symbol – that of an all-out struggle against all forms of oppression. The conservatives protected themselves from the 'French epidemic', to which patriots appealed for help. Not only in France, 'Jacobin' became synonymous with 'democrat' and 'republican'. Jacobinism found its first sympathizers among intellectuals and the liberal bourgeoisie before reaching the popular level. Partitioned Poland and the subject nationalities of the Habsburg Empire welcomed these 'subversive principles' as promises of liberation. The abolition of slavery led to uprisings among the colonialized black populations. Clubs were founded clandestinely or in broad daylight, as far away as Turkey and the United States. Several of them sought affiliation with the Paris club. In Britain, it was thought the Levellers had returned.

A genuine White Terror was organized at the instigation of foreign sovereigns. Masonic lodges and student associations were disbanded; suspect books, including the works of Kant, were banned. Police repression extended from the Volga to the Rhine. The Inquisition also intervened in the 'most Catholic' kingdoms of Spain and Naples. The Alien Bill was voted in Britain, where the gentry had become concerned.

Despite the desertion of those who feared the Terror, the movement defied every prohibition and its support spread deeper. Its popular following influenced its objectives and it went beyond the phase of political liberalism. Demands were voiced for the emancipation of serfs. In southern Italy, there were peasant uprisings; in Switzerland and Piedmont, the peasants refused to pay seigneurial dues. A revolutionary tribunal was set up in Geneva. 'In those days, the name of the insurrection was Jacobinism',[2] whatever the motives, in the risings in Poland and elsewhere. The Jacobin singled himself out by his desire for change. Whether separatist, reformist or outright democrat, he always chose, from among the French solutions, those that fit in with his national problems. Even Kosciusko, who resorted to mass conscription, refused to copy the French model slavishly. Thus, ideology was distinguished from revolutionary action.

In the film of the Revolution, Thermidor ends a sequence: the Republic of the Jacobins lost its soul. It was never to recover it. Nevertheless, the Year II fascinated the generations that followed, and Jacobinism permeated the political consciousness of the nineteenth century; abroad, it rallied patriots. Was it prophetic by virtue of being unfinished? Does it deserve the passions it unleashed? Has it so aged that one must cast off its relics? Such unscientific and wilfully obscured debates will lead us nowhere. In my view, all that counts is the way in which problems were perceived by contemporaries.

It was their adventure, a human adventure that was variously experienced. It is our memory, that of an exceptional moment of our history and of the Revolution, in which everyone can, as he pleases, discover a message.

[2] Quoted in B. Lesnodorski, *Les Jacobins polonais*, Paris, 1965, p. 3.

Bibliography

All books about the French Revolution – and they are legion – devote several chapters to the Jacobin Republic; some of these works have been cited in the previous volume; others will be listed in the following one. In the present study, I have in fact borrowed little from general histories of the Revolution, and have instead drawn extensively on unpublished or hitherto unutilized French and foreign archives. The sparing use of footnote references gives only a limited idea of the abundance of these mostly new primary sources. [Place of publication for items in French is Paris unless otherwise stated. Trans.]

The major collections of documents are well known. I have myself revised and continued the publication of several of them, including:

1 A. Aulard, *La Société des Jacobins*, 1889–97, 6 vols., with supplement
2 A. Aulard, *Recueil des Actes du Comité de salut public, avec la correspondance officielle des représentants en mission et le registre du Conseil exécutif provisoire*, Comité des Travaux Historiques et Scientifiques (CTHS), 1889–1951, 28 vols., 3 vols. of indexes and 4 vols. of the *Supplément*
3 *Archives parlementaires: recueil complet des débats législatifs et politiques des Chambres françaises*, 1st series (1789–99), CNRS. This publication, which has reached vol. 90 (6 Prairial Year II), covers our period from vol. 52 on.
4 *Oeuvres complètes de Maximilien Robespierre, Journaux* (vols. 4–5) and *Discours* (vols. 6–10), critical edn, 1960–7

Scholarly dissertations also provide rich source material, and are valuable for both their text and their notes. Our period has inspired theses by:

5 A. Soboul, *Les Sans-culottes parisiens en l'an II: mouvement populaire et gouvernement révolutionnaire, 2 juin 1793–9 thermidor an II*, 1958
6 R. Cobb, *Les Armées révolutionnaires, instrument de la Terreur dans les départements*, 1961–3, 2 vols.
7 G. Rudé, *The Crowd in the French Revolution*, Oxford, 1959

But some theses covering a broader time-span also contain chapters that are important for the study of the collective mentality:

8 G. Lefebvre, *Les Paysans du Nord pendant la Révolution française*, new edn, 1959

9 P. Bois, *Paysans de l'Ouest*, Le Mans, 1966

10 E. Le Roy Ladurie, *Les Paysans du Languedoc*, 1966

On another level, a few distinguished works have put forward new interpretations and have thus stimulated research. Despite his far-fetched conclusions, it is well worth examining the point of view of:

11 D. Guérin, *La Lutte des classes sous la Première République*, new edn, 1968, 2 vols.

Guérin's social approach, which was so heavily criticized, made it necessary to revise certain traditional assumptions, as did Furet and Richet:

12 F. Furet and D. Richet, *La Révolution française*, vol. 1, 1965, trans. S. Hardman, London, 1970

Meanwhile, other labourers have opened up new areas. I have relied on their findings, which have appeared in conference proceedings, *Annales Historiques de la Révolution Française (AHRF)*, and local journals. Books and articles consulted have been grouped here under chapter and section headings. Although all these studies have contributed to the book as a whole, I have classified them according to their specific subject matter and to the sequence of paragraphs in each section.

CHAPTER I: FORCES AND ATTITUDES

On the democratic Revolution, see:

13 P. Caron, *Les Massacres de septembre*, 1935

14 P. Nicolle, 'Les Meurtres politiques d'août–septembre 1792 dans le département de l'Orne', *AHRF*, 1954

15 R. M. Andrews, 'L'Assassinat de J. L. Gérard, négociant lorientais', *AHRF*, 1967

16 P. Caron, 'Conseil exécutif provisoire et pouvoir ministériel', *AHRF*, 1937

17 E. Bernardin, *Jean-Marie Roland et le ministère de l'Intérieur, 1792–1793*, 1964

18 P. Caron, *La Première Terreur. I. Les Missions du Conseil exécutif provisoire et de la Commune de Paris*, 1950

19 P. Caron, *Les Missions dans l'Est et dans le Nord (août–novembre 1792)*, 1953

20 J. Godechot, *Fragments des mémoires de Charles Alexis Alexandre sur sa mission aux armées du Nord et de Sambre-et-Meuse*, 1937

On food supplies, see:

21 G. Lefebvre, *Etudes orléanaises*, vol. 2, *Subsistances et maximum*, 1963

22 M. Vovelle, 'Les Taxations populaires de février–mars et novembre–décembre 1792 dans la Beauce et sur ses confins', Commission d'Histoire

Economique et Sociale de la Révolution Française, *Mémoires et documents*, vol. 13

23 P. Caron, 'Une enquête sur la récolte de 1792' *Bulletin d'Histoire Economique de la Révolution*, 1913

On reactionary forces, see:

24 J. Godechot, *La Contre-Révolution: doctrine et action, 1789–1804*, 1961, trans. S. Attanasio, *The Counter-Revolution: Doctrine and Action, 1789–1804*, London, 1972

25 D. Greer, *The Incidence of Emigration during the French Revolution*, Cambridge, Mass., Harvard University Press, 1951

26 M. Bouloiseau, *Etude de l'émigration et de la vente des biens des émigrés (1792–1830)*, 1963

27 J. Chaumié, *Le Réseau d'Antraigues et la contre-révolution, 1791–1793*, 1965

There is no recent analysis of Jacobinism on the national level. The following studies do not fill the gap:

28 Crane Brinton, *The Jacobins: An Essay in the New History*, New York, 1930

29 Gaston-Martin, *Les Jacobins*, 1945, 'Que sais-je?' series

30 L. de Cardenal, *La Province pendant la Révolution: histoire des clubs jacobins*, 1929

31 G. Lefebvre, 'Foules révolutionnaires', *Etudes sur la Révolution française*

32 R. Cobb, *Terreur et subsistances*, 1965

33 M. Dommanget, 'Le Symbolisme et le prosélytisme révolutionnaires à Beauvais et dans l'Oise', *AHRF*, 1925; 1926; 1927; 1928

34 G. Lemarchand, 'Jacobinisme et violence révolutionnaire au Havre de 1791 à septembre 1793', *Cahiers Léopold Delisle*, 1966, special issue

On war and diplomacy in 1792, see the work by:

35 A. Sorel, *L'Europe et la Révolution française*, 1904–11, 8 vols. This is still useful. It should be supplemented by:

36 R. Fugier, *Histoire des relations internationales*, vol. 4, 1954

37 J. Chaumié, *Les Relations diplomatiques entre l'Espagne et la France, de Varennes à la mort de Louis XVI*, Bordeaux, 1957

There are also a number of local studies on the volunteers, such as:

38 J. Vidalenc, 'Les Volontaires nationaux dans le département de l'Eure', *AHRF*, 1949

See especially:

39 M. Reinhard, *L'Armée et la Révolution*, Sorbonne course, 1957

40 J. P. Bertaud, *Valmy, la démocratie en armes*, 1970

CHAPTER 2: THE DIVORCE OF THE BOURGEOISIES

On the *Gironde–Montagne* rivalry, compare the points of view of:

41 A. Aulard, *Histoire politique de la Révolution*, part 2, chapters 3 and 6–8

42 A. Mathiez, *Girondins et Montagnards*, 1930 (collection of articles)

43 A. Mathiez, 'De la vraie nature de l'opposition entre les Girondins et les Montagnards', *Annales Révolutionnaires*, 1923

44 A. Soboul, *La Première République*, 1969
On the elections to the Convention and on the membership of the Assembly, see:

45 E. Auvray, 'Les Elections à la Convention nationale dans le département de Seine-et-Oise', *Actes du Congrès des Sociétés Savantes*, 1953

46 G. Laurent, 'Un conventionnel ouvrier: J. B. Armonville', *AHRF*, 1924
There are many readily available biographies of revolutionary leaders. It seems preferable to mention here a few studies on particular biographical topics:

47 L. M. Gidney, *L'Influence des Etats-Unis d'Amérique sur Brissot, Condorcet et Madame Roland*, 1930

48 E. Bernardin, *Les Idées religieuses de Madame Roland*, 1933

49 M. Bouloiseau, 'Robespierre d'après les journaux girondins, 1792–93', *Actes du Colloque Robespierre*, 1967
On French expansion, see:

50 A. Chuquet, *Jemappes et la conquête de la Belgique*, 1890

51 J. Godechot, *La Grande Nation: l'expansion révolutionnaire de la France dans le monde, 1789–1799*, 1956, 2 vols.
On 'confrontations', see:

52 A. Soboul, *Le Procès de Louis XVI*, 1966

53 Cl. Mazauric, 'A propos de la manifestation de la Rougemare', *Cahiers Léopold Delisle*, vol. 15, special issue

54 H. A. Goetz-Bernstein, *La Diplomatie de la Gironde: Jacques Pierre Brissot*, 1912

55 R. H. Rose, 'Documents Relating to the Rupture with France', *English Historical Review*, 1912, pp. 117, 324

56 J. Richard, 'La Levée des 300,000 hommes et les troubles de mars 1793 en Bourgogne', *Annales de Bourgogne*, 1961, no. 132

57 Ch. Poisson, *Les Fournisseurs aux armées sous la Révolution: le directoire des achats, 1792–1793*, 1933

58 A. Mathiez, 'Servan et les premiers marchés d'Espagnac', *Annales Révolutionnaires*, 1918

59 L. Dubreuil, *Histoire des insurrections de l'Ouest*, 1929–30, 2 vols.

60 E. Gabory, *La Révolution et la Vendée*, Paris, 1925–8, 3 vols.

61 Ch. Tilly, *The Vendée*, Cambridge, Mass., Harvard University Press, 1964

62 A. Mathiez, *La Vie chère et le mouvement social sous la Terreur*, 1927

63 *Assemblée générale de la Commission d'histoire économique de la Révolution*, 1939, vol. 2. Papers by E. Sol, E. Auvray, M. Bouloiseau, R. Laurent, M. Lhéritier and A. Richard, P. de Saint-Jacob, F. Vermale

64 A. Michalet, 'Economie et politique chez Saint-Just: l'exemple de l'inflation', *Actes du Colloque Saint-Just*, 1966

It would be worth revising the old book by:

65 H. Wallon, *La Révolution du 31 mai et le fédéralisme en 1793*, 1886, 2 vols.
    In the meantime, one can refer to:

66 L. Dubreuil, 'L'Idée régionaliste sous la Révolution', *Annales Révolution-naires*, 1919

67 J. Grall, 'L'Insurrection girondine en Normandie', *Cahiers Léopold Delisle*, 1966, special issue

68 E. Coulet, 'La Situation économique de Toulon pendant la rébellion de 1793', *Actes du Congrès des Sociétés Savantes*, Poitiers, 1962

69 E. Herriot, *Lyon n'est plus*, 1937–40, 4 vols.

70 P. Nicolle, 'Le Mouvement fédéraliste dans l'Orne en 1793', *AHRF*, 1936
    On the Constitution, see:

71 A. Mathiez, 'La Constitution de 1793', *AHRF*, 1938

72 Fr. Galy, *La Notion de Constitution dans les projets de 1793*, 1932

73 M. Friedieff, *Les Origines du referendum dans la Constitution de 1793*, 1931
    A. Soboul's thesis (5) and the studies by J. M. Zacker and W. Markov have totally transformed the subject. See especially:

74 A. Mathiez, 'Un enragé inconnu: Taboureau de Montigny', *AHRF*, 1930

75 H. Chobaut, 'Un révolutionnaire avignonnais: André Pacifique Peyre', *AHRF*, 1931

76 M. Dommanget, *Jacques Roux, curé rouge: les enragés contre la vie chère...*, n.d. [1948]

77 A. Soboul and W. Markov, *Die Sans-culotten von Paris: Dokumente zur Geschichte der Volksbewegung 1793–94*, Berlin, 1957

78 P. Leutrat, *François-Joseph L'Ange: Oeuvres...*, 1968

79 Jacques Roux: *Scripta et acta*, introduced by W. Markov, 1969 (in French)

80 W. Markov, *Exhurse zu Jacques Roux*, Berlin, 1970, with extensive bibliography

81 E. Soreau, 'Les Ouvriers aux journées des 4 et 5 septembre 1793', *AHRF*, 1937
    On the 'revolutionary army' and the *bataillons départementaux*, R. Cobb's thesis (6) makes it unnecessary to consult other works.

CHAPTER 3: REVOLUTIONARY GOVERNMENT

The revolutionary government's institutions and their functioning are well-charted areas.

82 J. Godechot, *Les Institutions de la France sous la Révolution et l'Empire*, new edn, 1969, book 3; a convenient reference and one that offers an account of recent research

On the 'great' Committee, see:

83 M. Bouloiseau, *Le Comité de salut public*, new edn, 1968, 'Que sais-je?' series

84 R. R. Palmer, *Twelve Who Ruled: The Committee of Public Safety during the Terror*, Princeton, N.J., 1941

85 P. Caron, 'De l'étude du gouvernement révolutionnaire', *Revue de Synthèse*, 1910

There are many biographies of each Committee member. I shall only mention here, because of the unpublished documents it reproduces:

86 G. Bouchard, *Un organisateur de la victoire: Prieur de la Côte d'Or...*, 1946; see below, bibliography for Chapter 5

On the terrorist apparatus, see the book by H. Wallon (**65**) and:

87 H. Wallon, *Les Représentants du peuple en mission et la justice révolutionnaire dans les départements en l'an II*, 1889–90, 5 vols.

This needs to be supplemented, as does:

88 E. Seligmann, *La Justice en France pendant la Révolution*, 1913

One should consult:

89 Savine, *Les Geôles de province sous la Terreur*, 1911

90 H. Calvet, *Un instrument de la Terreur à Paris: le Comité de salut public ou de surveillance du département de Paris*, 1941

91 Cl. Hohl, *Contribution à l'histoire de la Terreur: un agent du Comité de sûreté générale, Nicolas Guénot*, 1968

92 R. Cobb, 'La Commission temporaire de Commune-Affranchie', *Terreur et subsistances* (**32**)

On the economic dictatorship, see the papers listed in **63**.

93 P. Caron, *La Commission des subsistances de l'an II*, 1924–5, 2 vols.

94 H. Calvet, *L'Accaparement à Paris sous la Terreur: essai sur l'application de la loi du 26 juillet 1793*, 1933

95 H. Calvet, 'Le Commissaire aux accaparements de la section des Champs-Elysées', *AHRF*, 1936

96 H. Calvet, 'L'Application de la loi du 12 germinal sur les accaparements', *AHRF*, 1935

97 G. Lefebvre, 'Le Commerce extérieur en l'an II', *Etudes sur la Révolution française*

98 A. Mathiez, 'L'Argenterie des églises en l'an II', *AHRF*, 1925

99 A. Mathiez, 'Un fournisseur, C. Choiseau: comment le tribunal révolutionnaire traitait les mercantis', *AHRF*, 1924

On Paris, see:

100 E. Mellié, *Les Sections de Paris pendant la Révolution française*, 1898

And especially A. Soboul (**5**); see also:

101 A. Soboul, 'Robespierre et les sociétés populaires', *AHRF*, 1958, no. 1

102 M. Reinhard, *Paris pendant la Révolution*, Sorbonne course, Centre de Documentation Universitaire, 1962, 3 fascicles (for the Jacobin period, see fascicle 3)

103 M. Reinhard, ed., *Contributions à l'histoire démographique de la Révolution française*, 3rd series, 1970
104 P. Sainte-Claire Deville, *La Commune de l'an II: vie et mort d'une assemblée révolutionnaire*, 1946
    On the Ventôse and Germinal trials, see:
105 A. de Lestapis, *La 'Conspiration de Batz'*, 1793–94, 1969
106 A. Mathiez, *L'Affaire de la Compagnie des Indes*, 1920
107 L. Jacob, *Hébert, le 'Père Duchesne', chef des sans-culottes*, 1969
108 M. Dommanget, 'Mazuel et l'hébertisme', *Annales Révolutionnaires*, 1922 and 1923
109 R. Cobb, 'Le Complot militaire de ventôse an II: note sur les rapports entre Versailles et Paris au temps de la Terreur', *Terreur et subsistances* (32)
    Finally, the following article by G. Lefebvre draws on the studies published up to that date:
110 G. Lefebvre, 'Sur Danton', *AHRF*, 1932

CHAPTER 4: THE NATIONAL ARMY AND MILITARY SOCIETY

    Even the oldest studies by military historians are still worth consulting, in particular:
111 A. Chuquet, *Les Guerres de la Révolution*, 1886–99, 12 vols.
    And also the publications of the Section Historique de l'Etat-Major de l'Armée, such as:
112 Colonel Coutanceau, *La Campagne de 1794 à l'armée du Nord*, 1903–8, 4 vols.
113 Commandant V. Dupuis, *Les Opérations militaires sur la Sambre en 1794: bataille de Fleurus*, 1907
114 L. Hennequin, *La Justice militaire et la discipline à l'armée du Rhin-et-Moselle: notes historiques du chef de bataillon du génie Legrand*, 1909
    Similar studies have been published abroad:
115 J. W. Fortescue, *History of the British Army*, vol. 4, 1906
    See also the publications of the Austrian Army's Historical Division. Finally, the Institut d'Histoire de la Révolution Française holds a microfilm copy of Count Rasumovsky's papers, which concern the 1793 and 1794 campaigns against France.
    A number of general surveys are worth comparing:
116 J. Jaurès, *L'Armée nouvelle*, 1910; new edn, 1970, with an introduction by M. Rebérioux
117 P. Caron, *La Défense nationale de 1792 à 1795*, 1912
118 A. Mathiez, *La Victoire en l'an II*, 1916
119 A. Soboul, *Les Soldats de l'an II*, 1956
    But they do not deal with the full range of complex issues.

Biographers of government figures have closely combined a study of their character with that of their actions. Such is the case with:

120 L. Levy-Schneider, *Jeanbon Saint-André*, 1901, 2 vols.

121 Général Herlaut, *Le Colonel Bouchotte, ministre de la Guerre en l'an II*, 1946, 2 vols.

122 M. Reinhard, *Le Grand Carnot*, 1951–4, 2 vols.

Supplemented by the still reliable:

123 O. Havard, *La Révolution dans les ports de guerre*, 1912–13, 2 vols.

And by:

124 N. Hampson, *La Marine de l'an II: mobilisation de la flotte de l'Océan*, 1959

125 C. Richard, *Le Comité de salut public et les fabrications de guerre sous la Terreur*, 1922

A number of articles in *AHRF*, most of them published after 1930, deal with particular aspects and contain valuable information. I have used the following, listed in order of publication:

126 G. Michon, 'La Justice militaire sous la Convention à l'armée des Pyrénées-Orientales', 1926

127 G. Michon, 'L'Armée et la politique intérieure sous la Convention', 1927

128 F. Vermale, 'Lettres inédites d'un sous-lieutenant de l'armée des Alpes, 1792–93', 1929

129 Lionel D. Woodward, 'Les Projets de descente en Irlande et les réfugiés irlandais et anglais en France sous la Convention', 1931

130 S. Tassier, 'Les Sociétés des Amis de la Liberté et de l'Egalité en Belgique en 1792–93', 1933

131 A. Richard, 'L'Armée des Pyrénées-Orientales et les représentants en Espagne', 1934

132 J. Godechot, 'Les Aventures d'un fournisseur aux armées: Hanet-Cléry', 1936

133 Général Herlaut, 'La Républicanisation des états-majors et des cadres de l'armée pendant la Révolution', 1937

134 M. Reinhard, 'La Guerre et la paix à la fin de 1793', 1953

135 M. Reinhard, 'Nostalgie et service militaire pendant la Révolution', 1958, no. 1

136 M. Reinhard, 'Observations sur le rôle révolutionnaire de l'armée dans la Révolution française', 1962

137 J. P. Gross, 'Saint-Just en mission', 1968

Godechot's *La Grande Nation*... (51) and:

138 R. Devleeshouwer, *L'Arrondissement du Brabant sous l'occupation française*, 1964

inspired an international symposium in 1968 on *Occupants-occupés 1792–1815* (summary in *Revue Historique*, June-September 1968; proceedings published by the Université Libre de Bruxelles, 1969).

Current research has been concentrating on a few specific points, and

the first findings have been presented in national and international conferences. The topics are:
  (a) the social origins of the armies of the Revolution:

139 J. Vidalenc, 'Le Premier Bataillon des volontaires de la Manche', *Cahiers Léopold Delisle*, 1966, vol. 15

140 J. P. Bertaud, 'Les Papiers d'administration des demi-brigades', *Revue Internationale d'Histoire Militaire*, 1970

141 R. Dupuy, *Recherches sur la garde nationale en Ille-et-Vilaine*, 'thèse de 3ᵉ cycle', Rennes, 1971
  (b) *insoumission* and desertion:

142 J. P. Bertaud, 'Aperçus sur l'insoumission et la désertion à l'époque révolutionnaire', *Bulletin d'Histoire Économique et Sociale de la Révolution Française*, 1969
  (c) non-combatant services:

143 R. Werner, *L'Approvisionnement en pain de la population du Bas-Rhin et de l'armée du Rhin pendant la Révolution*, Strasburg, 1951

144 P. Wagret, *Les Services auxiliaires à l'armée de Sambre-et-Meuse en l'an III*, 'diplôme d'études supérieures', Sorbonne, 1945

145 M. Bouloiseau, 'L'Approvisionnement de l'armée de l'Ouest d'après les registres du commissaire-ordonnateur Lenoble', *Actes du Congrès des Sociétés Savantes*, Tours, 1968
  (d) the soldier mentality:

146 J. P. Charnay, *Société militaire et suffrage politique en France depuis 1789*, 1964

147 A. Merglen, *La Naissance des mercenaires*, 1969

148 Général Gambiez, 'La Peur et la panique dans l'histoire', *Report of the 13th Congrès International des Sciences Historiques*, Moscow, 1970

149 M. Bouloiseau, 'Malades et tire-au-flanc à l'armée de l'Ouest, an II – an III', *Actes du Congrès des Sociétés Savantes*, Toulouse, 1971

CHAPTER 5: THE TERROR IN THE PROVINCES

A general history of the provinces during the Terror would be over-ambitious and premature. Most studies cover the revolutionary period as a whole in a single *département* or locality. Among the most useful are:

150 L. Jacob, *Joseph Lebon: la Terreur à la frontière Nord et Pas-de-Calais*, 1933, 2 vols.

151 F. Clérembray, *La Terreur à Rouen*, Rouen, 1901

152 E. Dubois, *Histoire de la Révolution dans l'Ain*, vol. 4, Bourg, 1931–4, 6 vols.

153 Ch. Jolivet, *La Révolution dans l'Ardèche*, 1930

154 G. Aubert, 'La Révolution à Douai', *AHRF*, 1936

155 A. Troux, *La Vie politique dans le département de la Meurthe d'août 1792 à octobre 1795*, Nancy, 1936, 2 vols.

156 J. Kaplow, *Elbeuf during the Revolutionary Period: History and Social Structure*, Baltimore, Md., 1964

I have made frequent use of Cobb's massive work (6) and of his *Terreur et subsistances* (32) which includes reprints of some of his numerous articles. He has published many others, not only on the membership of the 'revolutionary armies', but on their action and the places where they operated. For example:

157 R. Cobb, 'L'Armée révolutionnaire dans le district de Pontoise', *AHRF*, 1950

158 R. Cobb, 'Les Débuts de la déchristianisation à Dieppe', *AHRF*, 1956

Town and country — on this see in addition to G. Lefebvre (8), P. Bois (9) and E. Le Roy Ladurie (10):

159 M. Faucheux, *L'Insurrection vendéenne de 1793: aspects économiques et sociaux*, 1964

160 A. Soboul, 'La Communauté rurale: problèmes de base', *Revue de Synthèse*, 1957

161 M. Vovelle, 'Formes de dépendance d'un milieu urbain: Chartres, à l'égard du monde rural', *Actes du Congrès des Sociétés Savantes*, 1958

162 Y. G. Paillard, 'Fanatiques et patriotes dans le Puy-de-Dôme', *AHRF*, 1970

163 F. Arsac, 'Une émeute contre-révolutionnaire à Meymac', *AHRF*, 1936

On institutions and men: local studies provide scattered information on provincial authorities. In addition to R. Cobb's above-mentioned studies, I have used:

164 L. de Cardenal, 'Les Sociétés populaires de Monpazier', Comité des Travaux Historiques..., *Etudes et documents divers*, vol. 10, 1924

165 H. Destainville, 'Les Sociétés populaires du district d'Ervy', *AHRF*, 1924

166 A. Richard, *Le Gouvernement révolutionnaire dans les Basses-Pyrénées*, 1926

167 M. Henriot, *Le Club des Jacobins de Semur*, Dijon, 1933

168 P. Gérard, 'L'Armée révolutionnaire de la Haute-Garonne', *AHRF*, 1959

Finally, there is an extremely useful but incomplete overview in:

169 J. B. Sirich, *The Revolutionary Committees in the Departments of France*, Cambridge, Mass., 1941

On revolutionary action: again, I have confined myself primarily to listing monographs. On provisioning, see G. Lefebvre (21), vol. 2.

170 A. Sée, 'Clémence et Marchand: trois mois sous la Terreur en Seine-et-Oise', *Assemblée générale de la Commission...*(63), vol. 2, 1939

171 R. Cobb, 'Le Ravitaillement des villes sous la Terreur: la question des arrivages', *Terreur et subsistances* (32)

Dechristianization and the cult of Reason have been studied in a number of works of varying interest. Among them:

172 B. Plongeron, *Conscience religieuse en Révolution*, 1969, offers a general assessment and a new approach to the issues.
On the local level, see:

173 Ed. Campagnac, *Les Débuts de la déchristianisation dans le Cher*, 1912

174 M. Dommanget, 'La Déchristianisation à Beauvais et dans l'Oise en l'an II', *Annales Révolutionnaires*, 1916 and 1917
The survey conducted under the supervision of M. Reinhard on the occasion of the Congrès des Sociétés Savantes held in Lyons in 1964 provides the first results of coordinated investigations:

175 M. Reinhard, ed., *Les Prêtres abdicataires pendant la Révolution française*, 1965
Finally, on the topic of civic festivals, the following studies are still useful:

176 P. Mautouchet, 'Les Fêtes des victoires à Paris sous la Révolution', *Revue de Paris*, 15 July 1919

177 B. Bois, *Les Fêtes révolutionnaires à Angers de l'an II à l'an VIII*, 1929

178 E. Chardon, *Dix ans de fêtes nationales et de cérémonies publiques à Rouen, 1790–1799*, 1911
The problem has been examined from a new angle in:

179 A. Soboul, 'Sentiment religieux et cultes populaires pendant la Révolution: saintes patriotes et martyrs de la Liberté', *AHRF*, 1957
On agrarian issues, see:

180 G. Lefebvre, *Questions agraires au temps de la Terreur*, La Roche-sur-Yon, 1932; 2nd ed, 1954; which serves as a research guide and a collection of documents, irreplaceable
One can also consult the survey by:

181 M. Garaud, *La Révolution et la propriété foncière*, 1969
Early studies of the sale of nationalized land were very unsophisticated. The latest ones rely on more scientific methods:

182 R. Caisso, *La Vente des biens nationaux de première origine dans le district de Tours (1790–1822)*, 1967; *La Vente des biens nationaux de seconde origine et les mutations foncières dans le district de Tours (1790–1830)*, 1977.

183 J. Sentou, *La Fortune immobilière des Toulousains et la Révolution française*, 1970

184 R. Marx, *La Révolution et les classes sociales en Basse-Alsace: structures agraires et vente des biens nationaux*, 1974
On the Ventôse decrees, one ought to compare the points of view of G. Lefebvre (**180**), A. Soboul (**5**) and:

185 A. Mathiez, 'La Terreur, instrument de politique sociale des Robespierristes', *AHRF*, 1928
For the local impact of the decrees, see:

186 R. Schnerb, 'L'Application des décrets de ventôse dans le district de Thiers', *AHRF*, 1929

187 R. Schnerb, 'Les Lois de ventôse et leur application dans le département du Puy-de-Dôme', *AHRF*, 1934

Scattered information may be found in several studies, including:

188 M. Eude, 'La Politique sociale de la Commune robespierriste le Neuf-Thermidor', *AHRF*, 1936

But how those measures were greeted is still not well known.

CHAPTER 6: THE END OF THE JACOBIN DICTATORSHIP

Political and institutional developments have been analysed several times by:

189 A. Mathiez, 'La Division des Comités gouvernementaux à la veille du 9 thermidor', *Revue Historique*, vol. 118, 1915

190 A. Mathiez, 'La Réorganisation du gouvernement révolutionnaire, germinal–floréal an II', *AHRF*, 1927

191 A. Mathiez, 'Les Séances des 4 et 5 thermidor aux deux Comités de salut public et de sûreté générale', *AHRF*, 1927

192 G. Lefebvre, 'La Rivalité du Comité de salut public et du Comité de sûreté générale', *Revue Historique*, vol. 157, 1931

193 A. Ording, *Le Bureau de police du Comité de salut public*, Oslo, 1930, makes it necessary to revise exaggerated assessments of the repressive role of the Committee of Public Safety

The regime's excesses: for each of the aspects discussed, one should refer to:

194 G. Thuillier, 'Saint-Just et la cité usurpée par les fonctionnaires', *Revue Administrative*, no. 47, 1955

195 F. Theuriot, 'La Conception robespierriste du bonheur', *AHRF*, 1968

196 A. Z. Manfred, 'La Nature du pouvoir jacobin', *La Pensée*, no. 150, 1970

197 Gaston-Martin, *La Mission de Carrier à Nantes*, Nantes, 1935

On the 'great' Terror, see:

198 D. Greer, *The Incidence of the Terror: A Statistical Interpretation*, Cambridge, Mass., 1935; provides a rough but useful aggregate estimate

See also:

199 J. L. Godfrey, *Revolutionary Justice: A Study of the Organization, Personnel, and Procedure of the Paris Tribunal, 1793–1795*, Chapel Hill, N.C., 1951

On plots:

200 A. Mathiez, *Etudes robespierristes*, 1st series, *La Corruption parlementaire sous la Terreur*; 2nd series, *La Conspiration de l'étranger*, Paris, 1917–18, 2 vols.

201 R. Schnerb, 'A propos d'Admirat et de Batz', *AHRF*, 1952

202 A. de Lestapis, 'Autour de l'attentat d'Admiral [Admirat] *AHRF*, 1957

203 A. de Lestapis, 'Admiral [Admirat] et l'attentat manqué', *AHRF*, 1959

204 M. Eude, 'Points de vue sur l'affaire Catherine Théot', *AHRF*, 1969

A. Mathiez's interpretation of the law of 22 Prairial has been discussed by:

205 A. Calvet, 'Une interprétation nouvelle de la loi de prairial', *AHRF*, 1950

206 G. Lefebvre, 'Sur la loi de prairial', *AHRF*, 1951

All works on the Terror devote a few pages to the general unease on the eve of Thermidor. On Paris, see A. Soboul (5) and:

207 A. Mathiez, 'L'Agitation ouvrière à la veille du 9 Thermidor', *AHRF*, 1928

208 G. Rudé and A. Soboul, 'Le Maximum des salaires parisiens et le Neuf Thermidor', *AHRF*, 1954

On the provinces, see:

209 E. Soreau, 'La Révolution française et le prolétariat rural', *AHRF*, 1933

210 D. Ligou, 'L'Epuration des autorités montalbanaises par Baudot', *AHRF*, 1954

211 O. Festy, *Les Délits ruraux et leur répression sous la Révolution et le Consulat*, 1958

212 R. Cobb, 'Quelques conséquences sociales de la Révolution dans un milieu urbain: Lille, floréal–messidor an II', *Terreur et subsistances* (32)

213 A. Soboul, 'Survivances féodales dans la société rurale au XIXᵉ siècle', *Annales ESC*, 1968

The ninth of Thermidor has been treated with scant objectivity by:

214 E. Hamel, *Thermidor*, 1891

215 L. Barthou, *Le 9 thermidor*, 1926

Despite some bias, P. Sainte-Claire Deville's book (104) is still valuable for the unpublished documents on which it is based. One should add A. Soboul's thesis (5) and:

216 A. Mathiez, 'Robespierre à la Commune le 9 thermidor', *AHRF*, 1924

217 A. Mathiez, 'La Campagne contre le gouvernement révolutionnaire à la veille de thermidor: l'affaire Legray', *AHRF*, 1927

218 A. Mathiez, 'Rapport du commandant du bataillon de l'Arsenal sur les événements du 9 thermidor', *AHRF*, 1930

CONCLUSION

Demographic trends are well known thanks to the studies published by M. Reinhard (103).

219 J. Godechot and S. Moncassin, *Démographie et subsistances en Languedoc*, 1964

See also:

220 M. Reinhard, 'La Révolution française et le problème de la population', *Population*, 1946

221 A. Fage, 'La Révolution française et la population', *Population*, 1953

On Jacobin influence abroad, the key work remains J. Godechot (51). See also:

222 G. Michon, 'Le Jacobinisme dans les débats du Parlement anglais en 1793 et 1794', *AHRF*, 1925

223 E. L. Burnet, *Le Premier Tribunal révolutionnaire genevois, juillet–août 1794*, Geneva, 1925

SUPPLEMENTARY BIBLIOGRAPHY

J.–P. Bertaud, *La Révolution armée: les soldats-citoyens et la Révolution française*, 1979

R. Bienvenu, *The Ninth of Thermidor: The Fall of Robespierre*, Oxford, 1968

A. Boursier, 'L'Emeute parisienne du 10 mars 1793', *AHRF*, 1972

R. Cobb, *The Police and the People*, Oxford, 1970
Reactions to the French Revolution, Oxford, 1972

A. Forrest, *Society and Politics in Revolutionary Bordeaux*, Oxford, 1975

A. Groppi, 'Sur les sections parisiennes', *AHRF*, 1978

N. Hampson, *The Life and Opinions of Maximilien Robespierre*, London, 1976
Danton, London, 1978

P. Higonnet, *Class, Ideology, and the Rights of Nobles during the French Revolution*, Oxford, 1981

D. P. Jordan, *The King's Trial: Louis XVI vs the French Revolution*, Berkeley, Calif., 1979

M. Kennedy, *The Jacobin Clubs in the French Revolution: The First Years*, Princeton, N.J., 1981

G. Lewis, *The Second Vendée: The Continuity of Counter-Revolution in the Department of the Gard, 1789–1815*, Oxford, 1978

C. Lucas, *The Structure of the Terror*, Oxford, 1973

M. Lyons, *Revolution in Toulouse: An Essay on Provincial Terrorism*, University of Durham Publications, Berne, 1978

M. Ozouf, *La Fête révolutionnaire, 1789–1799*, 1976

A. Patrick, *The Men of the First French Republic: Political Alignments in the National Convention of 1792*, Baltimore, Md, 1972

R. B. Rose, *The Enragés: Socialists of the French Revolution?*, Melbourne, 1965

S. F. Scott, *The Response of the Royal Army to the French Revolution, 1787–1793*, Oxford, 1978

W. Scott, *Terror and Repression in Revolutionary Marseille*, London, 1973

A. Soboul, 'Robespierre ou les contradictions du jacobinisme', *AHRF*, 1978

D. Sutherland, *The Chouans: The Social Origins of Popular Counter-Revolution in Upper Brittany, 1770–1796*, Oxford, 1982

M. Sydenham, *The First French Republic, 1792–1804*, Berkeley, Calif., 1974

M. Vovelle, *Religion et Révolution: la déchristianisation en l'an II*, 1976

Index of names

(In keeping with eighteenth-century practice, given names have been listed only for women and namesakes.)